HANDGUNS '89

BY
WILEY M. CLAPP

DBI BOOKS, INC.

HANDGUNS 89

OUR COVERS

Impressive is just about the best term to describe the massive Desert Eagle pistols, and we're delighted to be able to show them in full color on our front and back covers.

The big pistol was designed in the United States but is made in Israel by Israel Military Industries. It's imported by Magnum Research Industries of Minneapolis, Minnesota.

Desert Eagle pistols are chambered for the three popular magnum revolver cartridges — the .357, .41 and .44 magnums, which is a big advantage in that the ammunition is available nearly anywhere ammunition is sold, and in a variety of styles.

These pistols are available with either alloy, steel or stainless steel frame (weight ranging from 52 ounces to 66.9 ounces) and with interchangeable barrels in 6-inch, 10-inch or 14-inch lengths. There's also a choice of finish — satin, bright nickel, hard chrome and polished blue. In addition, you can have either fixed or adjustable sights and an adjustable trigger, if you wish. Want to add a pistol scope? The Desert Eagle has a dovetail milled into the top of the barrel for a Weaver-type rail mount.

On our front cover is the newest Desert Eagle chambered for .41 magnum in satin nickel finish with bright gold hammer, sights, safety lever, trigger, take-down lever and magazine base plate. This chambering is sure to breathe new life into the .41 magnum cartridge!

The back cover shows the .357 Magnum Desert Eagle with two barrel lengths and two sighting arrangements. Mounted on the gun is the 14-inch polished blue barrel with an Aimpoint 2000 optical sight and below it is the interchangeable 6-inch barrel with a Simmons 2x pistol scope.

You can read all about how these intriguing guns perform beginning on page 12.

Photos by John Hanusin.

PUBLISHER
Sheldon Factor

EDITORIAL DIRECTOR
Jack Lewis

PRODUCTION DIRECTOR
Sonya Kaiser

ART DIRECTOR
Denise Comiskey

ARTISTS
Paul Graff
Gary Duck

PRODUCTION COORDINATOR
Pepper Federici

COPY EDITORS
Shelby Harbison
Burt Carey

PHOTO SERVICES
C'est DAGuerre Labs
Sylvie Sanner

Produced by

GALLANT CHARGER

OUTDOOR GROUP

ISBN: 0-87349-028-2   Library of Congress Catalog Card Number: 88-72115

Contents

Acknowledgements

LOTS OF PEOPLE HELP IN HUNDREDS OF SMALL WAYS WHEN YOU TIE INTO ONE OF THESE BOOK PROJECTS, SO HANDGUNS '89 HAS ITS SHARE OF HELPFUL PEOPLE WHO'LL HAVE TO GO UNIDENTIFIED IN THE INTERESTS OF SPACE. THANKS BE TO ALL OF THEM. I CAN'T GO WITHOUT OFFERING MY DEEP APPRECIATION TO:

JACK LEWIS, FOR PATIENCE UNDER INSANE CIRCUMSTANCES
DEAN GRENNELL, FOR SO MANY SUPERB PHOTOGRAPHS
DENISE COMISKEY, FOR UNFAILING GOOD-HUMORED ARTISTIC SKILL
GEORGE DILEO, FOR HIS WISE COUNSEL AND GUNSMITHING CRAFT
STAN WAUGH, FOR MANY DAYS OF HELP WITH THE HARD STUFF
IRV STONE, FOR MAKING AUTOMATICS ACCURATE
CHUCK RANSOM, FOR GIVING ME CERTAINTY ABOUT WHAT I WAS SAYING
...AND SOMEONE SPECIAL, FOR KEEPING ME GOING

THANK YOU

HANDGUNS 89

Section One

TODAY'S HANDGUNS

COVERAGE OF TODAY'S HANDGUNS SHOULD PROPERLY BEGIN WITH AN OVERVIEW OF THE WORLD OF HANDGUNS. YOU'LL FIND IT IN CHAPTER ONE, THE HANDGUN SCENE, A COMMENTARY ON THE TRENDS THAT INFLUENCE HANDGUN DESIGN, IMPORTATION AND PRODUCTION IN 1989.

FROM THERE ON, IT'S PURE GUN. THIS SECTION OF THE BOOK DETAILS THE NEW AND SIGNIFICANT HANDGUNS OF THIS YEAR. WE BEGIN WITH THE GUN ON THE COVER, THE MASSIVE DESERT EAGLE. IT IS AN AUTOMATIC FOR THE MAGNUM REVOLVER CARTRIDGES AND A FISTFUL OF POWER.

THERE WERE PLENTY OF NEW GUNS TO SHOOT AND EVALUATE THIS YEAR: S&W CLASSIC HUNTER, COLT DELTA, RUGER P85 AND SUPER REDHAWK, WALTHER P88 AND THE SPRINGFIELD OMEGA. WE FIRED THEM ALL, BOTH BY HAND AND BY THE MACHINE REST. YOU'LL FIND TABULATED TEST RESULTS ON EACH AND EVERY ONE. THERE ARE OTHER GUNS THAT HAVE COME ALONG IN THE PAST FEW YEARS THAT MERIT SIMILAR ATTENTION: RUGER'S GP-100, BROWNING'S COMPETITION MODEL, THE SMITH & WESSON .45s, AMT'S AUTOMAG II AND THE L.A.R. GRIZZLY. ALL OF THESE HANDGUNS GET THEIR DESERVED SHARE OF TEST AND EVALUATION.

HANDGUNS 89

CHAPTER 1

THE HANDGUN SCENE

Handguns Americana — Coming Up On The Last Decade Of The Twentieth Century

---

IT'S A CLICHE of sorts, but nonetheless appropriate to say we're in a Golden Age where handguns are concerned. Never before have there been so many people using so many different kinds of handguns for so many different purposes. Sure, lots of the handguns are in use for the grim business of personal defense and law enforcement, but there are increasing numbers used for pure sporting purposes. And the choices available to today's handgun buyer are staggering. In the few short decades since the end of World War II, handgun variety has increased significantly. In the past fifteen years, it has exploded.

Cruising the catalogs of the major makers is a buyer's delight. It also gives credence to the Golden Age argu-

ment. Consider the Colt catalog, where I counted no less than eighteen variations on the grand old .45. You can have a Government Model in four different centerfire calibers, three barrel lengths and a whole bunch of finishes. Colt even has a Custom Shop to turn out a GM plushed up to your own personal specifications.

Smith & Wesson started this magnum business in 1935 with the .357. Today, you can buy a S&W .357 magnum built on three different frame sizes and with barrels ranging from a bunty 2½ inches all the way out to a grandiose 8⅜ inches. Counting the S&W finish options and other calibers, not to mention their wide variety of automatic pistols, is a job for a fleet-fingered Chinese storekeeper with an abacus.

When World War II was over and the makers got back to civilian production, no one had ever heard of William B. Ruger. In 1989, he pays a bevy of fine craftsman to put his name on a wide variety of sporting firearms, including some of the best handguns in the world. They're good enough to make a lot of other people in the busines damned nervous.

Imports. Stoeger used to bring in a handful of Lugers every year and that was about it. The choices in imported handguns stagger the mind; they come from Austria, Spain, Germany, France, Yugoslavia, Belgium, Hungary, Czechoslovakia, China, and probably a half dozen more I couldn't think of. Perhaps most significantly, one of them comes from Italy.

After a series of tests which may or may not have been flawed in their execution and conclusion, the Army decided to go with the Beretta Model 92 pistols as the new service sidearm. The current guns are being made in the U.S., but it is a purely Italian design. Apparently, it is a pretty good one. I have had nothing but good luck with my own personal pistol. Also, it seems that every cop on gun-wise

LAPD that I see on my way to work is wearing one of them.

The Beretta 92 (M9 in uniform) is a gun that falls into a class that some nameless gunwriter dubbed "wondernine." Never in history have so many different makers attempted to build the same thing for the same market. The wondernines are almost monotonously alike, with double-column magazines and double-action triggers. Some of them play with extra features like ambidextrous controls and special operating drills. There's an obvious effort to idiot-proof the pistols with all kinds of passive safeties. This is what the gunmakers perceive to be the gun of the future.

In the United States, there are only the Ruger P85 and several variations of the basic Smith & Wesson. The imports are a different story with frontrunning guns from Germany (Walther, H&K, Sig-Sauer), Austria (Glock) and Italy (Beretta). Some well-made pistols are in the marginal category as far as sales popularity is concerned: three good ones from Spain (Llama, Star and Astra), another Italian (Bernardelli) and a big Austrian (Steyr GB). The Belgian Browning P35, atrociously outmoded with a single-action trigger, sells atrociously well despite it.

In the wake of all of this wondernine frenzy, it might be fitting to note that Smith & Wesson makes — *and sells* — a couple of trainloads of revolvers every year and Colt stays afloat with a pistol that first slid into a GI holster about 1911 or 1912. A fellow has to keep his perspective about him, now doesn't he?

Perspective be damned, more and more firepower seems to be a profound preoccupation with the nation's handgunners. After-market pistol magazines with a round or two

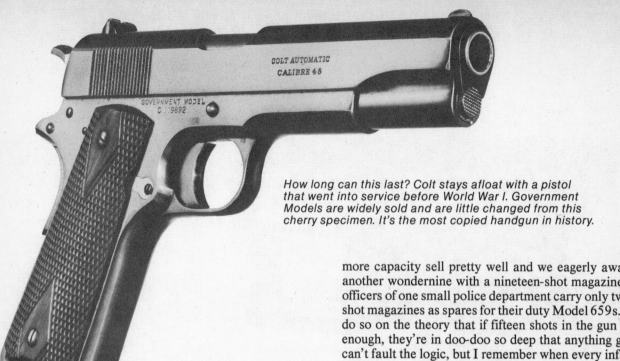

How long can this last? Colt stays afloat with a pistol that went into service before World War I. Government Models are widely sold and are little changed from this cherry specimen. It's the most copied handgun in history.

The Beretta is THE wondernine, since it was adopted by the U.S. military as the M9. It has all of the essentials, including the double-action trigger. How come Browning still sells so many Hi-Powers when they don't have it?

more capacity sell pretty well and we eagerly await yet another wondernine with a nineteen-shot magazine. The officers of one small police department carry only twenty-shot magazines as spares for their duty Model 659s. They do so on the theory that if fifteen shots in the gun aren't enough, they're in doo-doo so deep that anything goes. I can't fault the logic, but I remember when every infantryman all of a sudden needed a thirty-shot magazine. It was Vietnam, and we lost that one.

There's probably a greater logic to more *whumpf* per shot than there is to more shots, but we are clearly expecting more from the handgun as a sporting instrument. Numerous smaller makers are marketing handguns that will shoot harder, heavier and farther. A lot of this is traceable to the antics of the silhouette shooters, who have redefined

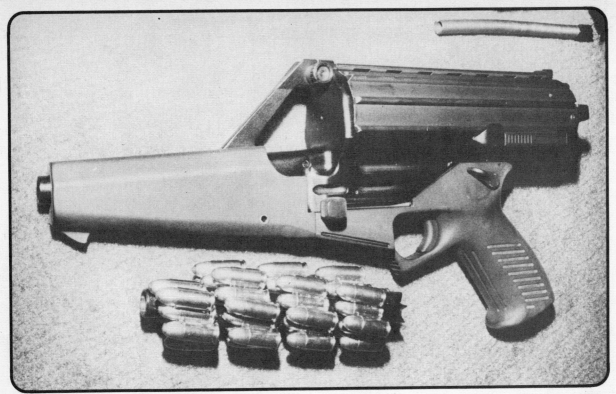

Firepower: One. This is a fifty-shot 9mmP handgun and emblematic of the "more shots" school of firepower. It is also an amazing piece of firearms engineering which must be taken seriously. It also works exactly as billed.

handgun accuracy in their own relatively quiet way. Their most recent coup is conning Dan Wesson into producing a superb stretched-cylinder revolver which handles an extra-long version of the .44 magnum. More is due to the growing sport of handgun hunting, where lots of capable sportsmen are going afield with big handguns — and the blessing of the fish and game departments.

Firepower in this sense has greater credence. A handgun which stretches the envelope, as my flight engineer son puts it, should be taken seriously. Some of them are marvelous innovations, like the fine Grizzly pistol in the new wildcat .357/.45 Grizzly cartridge. Some are magnificent

examples of American manufacturing skill. If you don't think so, look closely at a .454 Casull revolver. This is the finest factory-made American revolver since 1915, when Smith & Wesson took the Triple-Lock out of production.

We have a lot of fine handguns in these United States and more and more people every year take them up for a variety of shooting purposes. In addition to plain old bullseye, the NRA outdoor pistol game, we have folks shooting at steel animals way out yonder and others tackling bowling pins up close. Cardboard silhouettes die by the thousands each year, some of them with PPC scoring rings. Plates, big and little, round and square, all attract the firm gaze of the nation's marksmen over the slide and

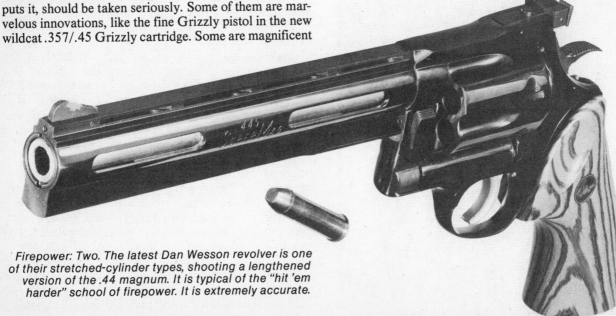

Firepower: Two. The latest Dan Wesson revolver is one of their stretched-cylinder types, shooting a lengthened version of the .44 magnum. It is typical of the "hit 'em harder" school of firepower. It is extremely accurate.

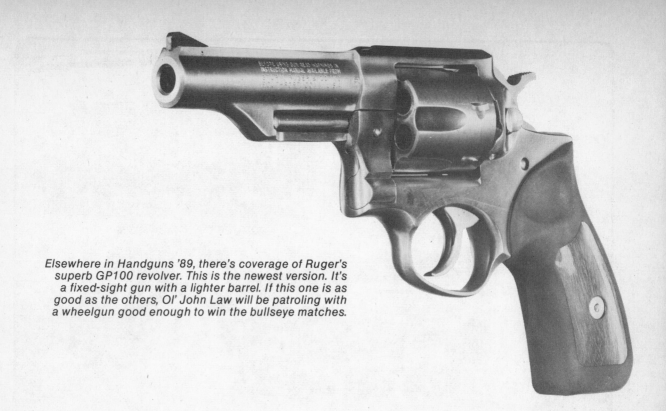

Elsewhere in Handguns '89, there's coverage of Ruger's superb GP100 revolver. This is the newest version. It's a fixed-sight gun with a lighter barrel. If this one is as good as the others, Ol' John Law will be patroling with a wheelgun good enough to win the bullseye matches.

Gunmakers are beginning to recognize women as a market in their own right. It's not surprising that one of S&W's marketing staff is Sherry Collins, who's been to the armorer's school, where she built her very own Model 65..."The times, the times, they're a'changing."

cylinders of highly customized handguns that warrant their own section of a book like the one you hold.

It's people who are doing all of this shooting and people who are demanding better guns and accessories for them. Someone finally woke up and realized that more than half of the population is of the feminine gender, so we are beginning to see handgun ads obviously directed to at least the family and sometimes to women. One of the major makers up there in Connecticut's Gun Valley flirts with the idea of a special 9mmP pistol made just for the women's market. I have handled prototypes and, despite bone-deep masculinity, I'd love to have one. Women are beginning to rise in the corporate structure of the gun companies. It's time, I guess.

There are still some holes in the market, though. Despite all of the fancy stuff we do have, there are some things we don't. For one thing, whatever happened to the plinker? We need more choices in moderately-priced .22 handguns of small size and with respectable accuracy, the sort of gun that was so much Saturday-morning fun with your dad when you were a kid. Only the Ruger .22 and the new S&W 422 are available and they are both pretty adult-sized.

On the serious side of things, we need a truly compact, concealed-carry automatic pistol in a caliber larger than 9mmP. At the SHOT Show in 1987, Evan Whildin of Action Arms showed me a compact version of the CZ-75 he intended to market. I handle lots of guns in the course of my work, but few of them leave an impression as did the AT-84P. It had an excellent balance of features: DA first-shot trigger combined with a cocked-and-locked option, double-column magazine, good sights and balance. The chunky little powerhouse has that intangible feel that experience tells me would really be easy to point and shoot. Best of all, it was chambered for a new cartridge called the .41 Action Express.

I haven't seen the UPS man pull up with a carton holding

There is an unfulfilled market out there. It's a market for a medium- to small-sized automatic pistol chambered for something heavier than 9mmP. This AT-84P may be out in the new .41 Action Express caliber. Author Clapp waits for one patiently, as do other big-bore afficionados.

the pistol yet, but I am waiting and hoping. This gun promises to have a market all its own — unless someone finds a way to tame the Ten and get it into a package the size of a Star PD — or S&W performs a butt-'n-slide-*ectomy* on the 645.

Little guns have an appeal all their own, and probably just as many legitimate uses. You won't find coverage of the newest little revolver in this book, because it came along after the content was pretty well cut in stone. The revolver is the SP101, a five-shot stainless steel .38 Special from Ruger. There will be a choice of three barrel lengths and eventually caliber options: .22 Long Rifle and .32 H&R magnum. I have fired one of them extensively and I am impressed with both handling and accuracy.

Ruger also has a fixed-sight variation of the GP-100. It sports a trimmer butt than the adjustable-sighted guns. And if it shoots like them, well...(see Chapter Four).

Americans, their handguns, and their handgun sports are a fascinating subject that we'll consider in this book. The volume is divided into sections dealing with the new and recent guns, their ammunition, their use and their custom variations. Finally, we'll take a look back at a few of the better handguns of yesterday.

As much affection as we all have for particular handguns, they are, in the final analysis, lumps of contoured metal. It takes a handgunner to give them life.

We've lost one of the best handgunners of all time. Skeeter Skelton died this year and I am only one of thousands who'll miss him. Skeeter gave life to lots of handguns by his uncanny way of rolling a gun over in words the way you'd roll it over in your hands. His writing was far better than anyone gave him credit for — and he had a big following. The best of Skeeter's writing wasn't that far from Mark Twain, particularly when he got going on the human frailties of handgunners, desperadoes — and small boys.

So long, friend.

The sad fact of life in our troubled times is that cops are facing more and more protracted gunfight situations. Some policemen are carrying 20-shot magazines as their spares. A gun that hits harder might be a better choice.

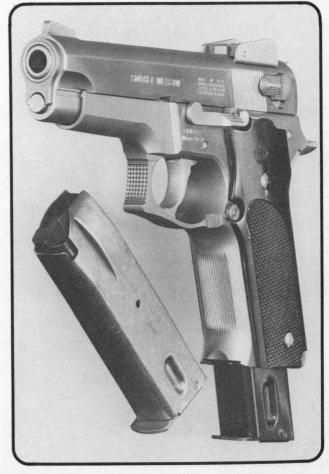

CHAPTER 2

*A Massive Magnum
For Autoloading
Afficionados*

THE MAGNUM EAGLE

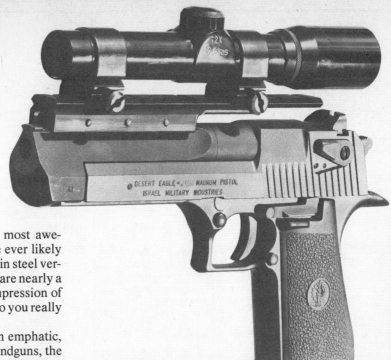

DESERT EAGLES are among the most awesomely impressive handguns you're ever likely to handle. At sixty-two-plus ounces in steel versions, the shorter Desert Eagles still are nearly a foot long. They are simply so huge that the impression of most shooters who pick one up is the same: "Do you really *shoot this thing?*"

The answer to that rhetorical question is an emphatic, "You betcha!" While they certainly are big handguns, the size should not be allowed to detract from the fact that they are accurate, powerful and thoroughly shootable guns. Further, they have some distinct characteristics which set them apart from anything else on the production handgun scene.

Desert Eagles are automatic pistols chambered for the three popular magnum revolver cartridges — the .357, .41 and .44 magnum. That, in itself, is different; the only other really successful revolver-cartridge auto is the Coonan and it only handles the .357. The other big autos of recent years, the Auto Mag and Wildey, both required special rimless ammunition. The Wildey's rimless .45 Winchester magnum round works well in the contemporary Grizzly pistol.

The Desert Eagle has a mechanism which handles typical wide-rimmed revolver cartridges. That's a big advantage in that ammunition for the guns is available nearly anywhere ammunition is sold. It's an additional advantage in the sense that a wide variety of ammunition is on dealers' shelves in each of the three calibers.

With its gas-type operation, the Desert Eagle has a rotating bolt with heavy locking lugs engaged in matching locking lug recesses. While this is an unusual place to find such a locking system, there's no reason why it won't work.

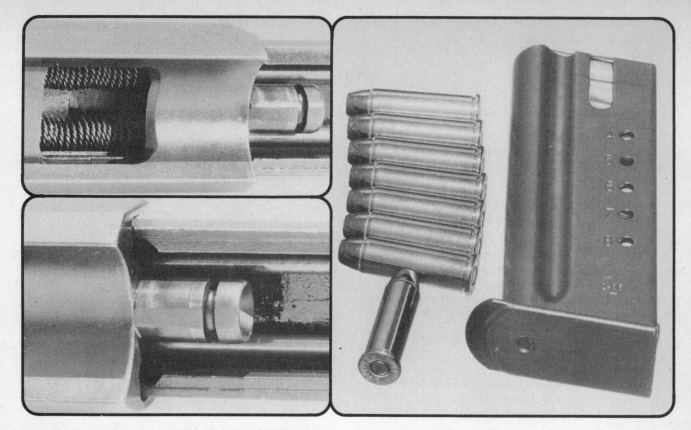

Above photos show the critical gas piston, which rides in the frontmost portion of the slide. The end of the piston goes into a recess in the underside of the barrel. When the pistol fires, expanding gases are routed to the face of the piston, which carries the slide to the rear.

The Desert Eagle magazine holds eight .41s or .44s and nine .357s. It is a hefty sheet steel box with a clever follower and spring arrangement. The Israeli-made pistol effectively solves the problem of feeding troublesome rimmed revolver cartridges from a vertical magazine.

The system does demand a certain amount of heavier parts and springs, but in the course of shooting examples in all three calibers, I had absolutely no problem with any sort of malfunction.

From a strict design standpoint, the feed system is about as ingenious as the operating system. The heart of the feed system is the magazine; capacity is eight in the .44s and nine in the .357s. A magazine that will stack this many magnum revolver cartridges is fairly tall and has a pretty hefty fore-and-aft dimension. The Desert Eagle's is certainly that, but the real ingenuity lies in the way that the magazine stacks the rims.

That, after all, is the real problem. Rimmed cases don't stack worth a hoot. The outsized rims tend to get tangled up together and always curve the stack. In the Desert Eagle, the magazine is a whopping big sheet metal box with magazine lips at the top contoured to position the particular round for which the magazine is made.

The individual rounds go into the magazine in conventional fashion, but once in, they position themselves to alternating sides of the magazine. It isn't even close to the double-column magazine of the wondernine, but it has enough slack to allow the individual rounds to locate themselves. The combination of positive forward movement of the operating parts, plus a well shaped feed ramp in front of the magazine's feed lips combine to make it work.

The magazine is clever, but so is the basic operating system of the pistol. This gun is fully operated by the action of expanding powder gases. It works in fashion much like the one used in a long series of gas-operated military firearms — M1 Garand, M14, M1 carbine and others.

The Desert Eagle's operating system is built around the slide, an open-topped affair containing a short, rotating bolt with three lugs on its top surface. The slide rides on more-or-less conventional rails on the receiver of the pistol. Between the two, there's a recoil-spring assembly which has a pair of recoil springs riding on long rod guides. The entire upper front portion of the pistol is the barrel.

The barrel fits onto the lower portion of the pistol by means of fittings at both ends. The front end fits over an extension of the frame and the rear locks down by means of a cross-shaft through the receiver of the pistol. At the rear end of the barrel are recesses that mate with the locking lugs in the slide-mounted bolt. Also, riding in the forward end of the slide, there's a piston. When the slide is in battery in the forward position, the piston nestles into a recess in the underside of the barrel.

With a cartridge in the chamber and the safety off, the shooter fires by pulling the trigger and dropping the hammer on a live round in the chamber. Gas pressure forces the bullet down the barrel which is locked tightly to the slide by means of the bolt head engaged in the barrel locking recesses.

As the bullet passes down the bore, the pistol begins to act like a conventional gas-operated weapon.

Part of the gas is bled off through a gas port in the bottom of the barrel just forward of the chamber. The gases pass into an expansion chamber running the full length of the barrel's underside. At the forward end of the barrel, the gas makes a ninety-degree turn into a continuation of the chamber in the forward barrel projection. At this point, the gas encounters the face of the gas piston. While the bullet has exited the bore by now, there's plenty of gas to fetch that piston a hefty lick.

The piston, in turn, smacks the slide, which moves smartly to the rear against the force of the recoil springs. The springs compress as the slide comes to the rear and the bolt head turns, unlocking the bolt from the barrel. As the slide is freed completely, it moves all the way to the rear and the conventional autoloader functions occur — extraction, ejection and cocking of the external hammer. The forward motion of the parts occurs when the springs expand, forcing the slide and bolt forward to scoop a round from the magazine, feed it into the chamber and lock the bolt closed behind it. One more pull of the trigger and the whole cycle happens again.

This solidly built system uses established principles of

Dean Grennell's superb photos show the Desert Eagle barrel from both front and rear. The top picture views the barrel from the rear, showing the recesses for a trio of locking lugs on the bolt. It also shows the hole in the front underside of the barrel in which the gas piston rides. It's a clever, workable operating system.

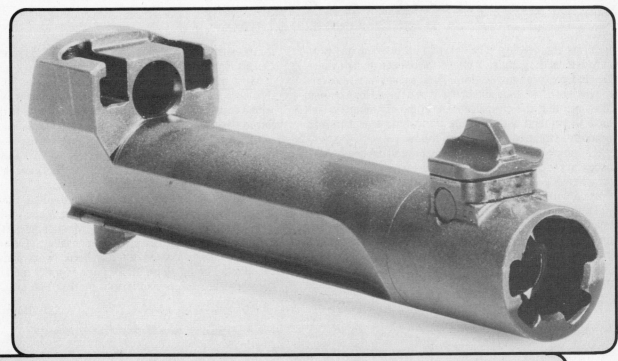

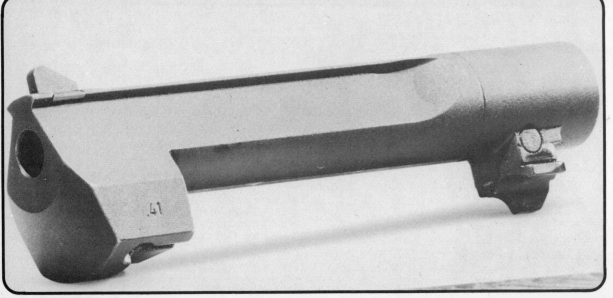

While the Desert Eagle is made in Israel, it was designed in the United States. The pistol's markings tell us that it was made in a factory of Israeli Military Industries. The fitting of parts is excellent and the finish is functional, a dull matte effect.

firearms engineering. The delay in introducing gas pressure against the gas piston allows the bullet to exit the muzzle and gas pressure to drop. That means the rearward movement of the slide and bolt will be delayed long enough to insure that the cartridge case in the chamber doesn't have to contend with pressure that would tear it in half. Smooth extraction and ejection follow.

The combination of a long magazine and the heavy parts necessary to do all of the things in the foregoing cycle make for a heavy gun. It is nevertheless a thoroughly functional firearm with some desirable characteristics.

There is a bit more firepower in a Desert Eagle. The .44 magnum version holds eight rounds in the magazine and presumably another in the chamber. That's a fifty percent increase in the on-tap power over a conventional revolver. Also, the shots can be delivered more rapidly, a function of the gun's greater weight and autoloading action. The need

for this sort of firepower is arguable, but if it's essential, the Desert Eagle will deliver it.

Most other characteristics of the guns are quite like those of a host of smaller pistols. The hammer is external, with a serrated spur, and the magazine catch is in the preferred position adjacent to the trigger guard on the left side of the pistol. When the catch is pushed in, the magazine drops free of the gun. The safety has levers on both sides of the slide for use with either hand. On this gun, the lever goes down to the safe position.

Desert Eagles, imported into the United States by Magnum Research of Minneapolis, are made in the factories of Israeli Military Industries. Most of the parts seem to be precisely machined investment castings. On all three of the pistols evaluated for this book, workmanship is excellent. The finish on major parts is a flat matte black and there are some visible tool marks. The grips are a

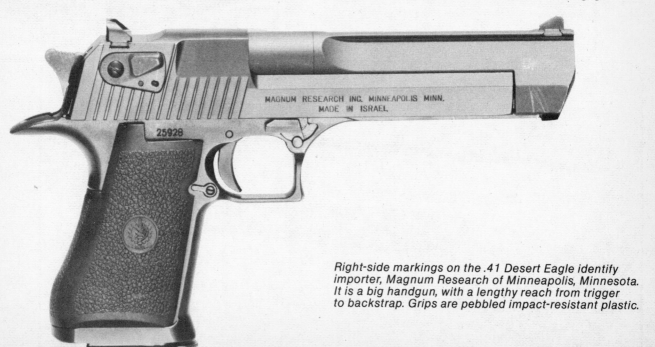

Right-side markings on the .41 Desert Eagle identify importer, Magnum Research of Minneapolis, Minnesota. It is a big handgun, with a lengthy reach from trigger to backstrap. Grips are pebbled impact-resistant plastic.

The rear sight is rudimentary, apparently in recognition of the fact that a lot of the shooters who buy the pistol will want to use a scope. The importer does offer a rear sight that may be adjusted for both windage and elevation. If costs extra.

pebbled plastic, molded from an impact resistant material.

Some shooters may wish to take advantage of the option available from the in-country custom shop. Desert Eagles may be had with two-tone finishes, alloy frames and a choice of longer barrel lengths. Presumably, longer-barreled versions would up the velocity figures reported here by a considerable amount.

Another available option is a virtual necessity, unless the pistol is to be scoped. You can order a Desert Eagle with an adjustable rear sight, and if you plan to stay with iron sights, you should equip your pistol in that way. The stock rear sight is a fixed square-notch type, dovetailed into the slide and drift adjustable for windage. Elevation then becomes adjustable with interchangeable front sights in differing heights. It is a pain in the butt to have a pistol of this quality that doesn't mount standard adjustable sights.

But the manufacturer may be wiser than you'd think.

Recognizing that many — probably most — shooters will use the pistol for hunting and will want a scope, he offers the pistol with rudimentary iron sights. With or without adjustable iron sights, the Desert Eagle has a built-in base for a Weaver-type rail.

The top edge of the barrel is milled to a dovetail shape and it is the work of only a moment to bolt an appropriately contoured rail in place. Weaver rings clamp to the rail and hold a scope. For our test, we used a scope on the newest Desert Eagle, a .41 magnum, and fired the others with the fixed rear sight.

In the course of firing all of the guns, we had little in the way of functioning problems. Ammo for the guns was a variety, chosen from the available stock, with four different kinds used for each gun. Since Chuck Ransom doesn't offer machine rest inserts for the Desert Eagle, I fired five-shot groups off the bench and you'll have to distill

The slide travels a considerable distance on the Desert Eagle. This profile view shows the pistol with the slide locked to the rear, as if the shooter had just emptied the eight-shot magazine. Magazine catch is on the left.

the performance of the pistols through my murky marksmanship skills.

There is another point about the pistol that demands attention before going into a discussion of performance — and there is no nice way to say it. The trigger action of the Desert Eagle varies from poor to horrible. Not one of the three guns we tried had even a marginal trigger. They were all quite heavy, with lots of start-and-stop creep. Shooting a pistol so equipped challenges the patience and skill of any marksman.

At the range, shooting buddy, Stan Waugh, and I settled into solid positions and took turns over sandbags with the three different pistols. Shooting in this way, we were able to minimize the effect of the poor trigger pulls and some of the groups we shot are downright respectable. We also chronographed the various loads as they were fired in the three pistols.

There has been some erroneous information printed recently about the six-inch Desert Eagle pistol fired in comparison to a revolver with an equivalent length barrel. It's also been alleged that the gas-operated action of the Desert Eagle uses gas to the detriment of the pistol's velocity performance. If you look closely at the cycle of the pistol, it should be obvious that the bullet is long gone before enough gas escapes to cause velocity to deteriorate.

Also, comparing a six-inch revolver to a six-inch Desert Eagle is to compare apples to oranges. They're both nice, but not the same. The real *de facto* barrel length of a six-inch S&W revolver is more like about 7⅝ inches, as measured from breech face to muzzle. Gas loss in a revolver? There's not enough to be statistically significant.

The .357 Desert Eagle was first in order. With Black Hills Shooter's Supply 125-grain JHPs, five shots clustered into a tight 1.587 inches, a best effort from that pistol. In a gun that heavy, a light bullet load like this one causes more shooter annoyance from blast than recoil; it was a true pussycat.

The .44 was a different story. There was a bit more recoil, but still far less than you might expect. The best group was just under two inches with the Remington 180-grain JHP. The best performance came from the .41 magnum, a variation just recently available in the United States.

As a fan of the .41, I'd like to be able to say it was the most accurate of the Desert Eagles. I can't, because this

Groups! The Desert Eagles all shot quite well, but the 'scoped .41 was easier to aim. Top group is from the .357 and measures 1.760 inches. The lower left photo is a 1.927-inch group from the .44. The Burris scope...

...gave the edge to the .41. The lower right group came from that gun and measures under an inch. Even better accuracy might be possible after greater practice with the Desert Eagles. A better trigger system might help.

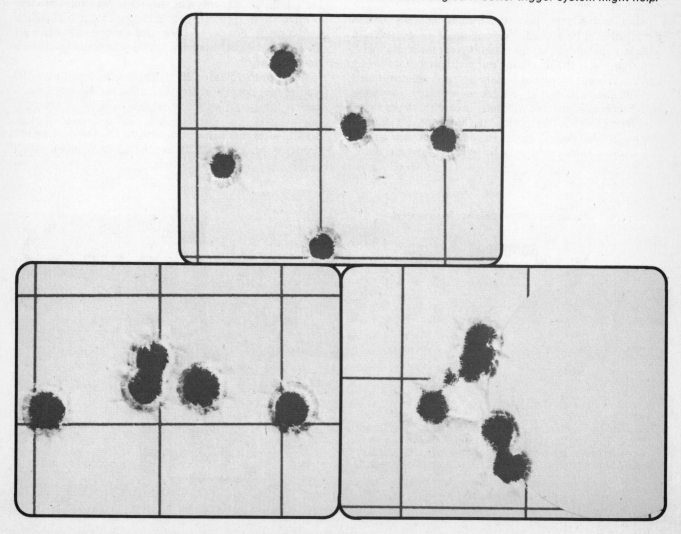

was the only gun fitted with a scope and that gave it a decided advantage. The glass used was the excellent Burris 2x and that made aiming a breeze, particularly from the braced position I was using on a concrete shooting bench. The performance could be measured; it was a tight five shots into .973-inch at twenty-five yards.

There are lots of places in this book where I report groups of ten, twelve or even twenty shots. Invariably, they are fired in the Ransom Rest, which has an infinite attention span. I was working hard to shoot these groups hand-held and I stopped at five shots, lest I screw up a good group. The accompanying table charts the performance of the three Desert Eagles and I believe the group sizes are fully representative of the accuracy you can expect from the guns.

The Desert Eagles are fine handguns, combining accuracy and power in a hefty pistol. Flawed only by a poor trigger which will no doubt respond to gunsmithing, the pistols are fine choices for the shooter who prefers an autoloader and demands a magnum.

DESERT EAGLE FIRING TABLE

.357 MAGNUM	ES	AVG	SD	G.S.(")
Black Hills 125 JHP	36	1359	16	1.760
Hornady 125 JHP	39	1502	18	1.766
Remington 125 JHP	117	1523	49	2.462
Federal 180 JHP	21	1135	8	2.503

.44 MAGNUM	ES	AVG	SD	G.S.(")
Hornady 180 JHP	72	1401	30	2.595
Remington 180 JHP	102	1554	41	1.927
Federal 240 JHP	24	1268	11	2.514
Black Hills 240 JHP	24	1253	10	2.241

.41 MAGNUM	ES	AVG	SD	G.S.(")
Winchester Silvertip 175 JHP	34	1299	14	2.808
Winchester 210 JHP	63	1380	23	2.556
Winchester 210 JHP	86	1379	36	.973
PMC 210 JHP	60	1362	23	1.504

Five Shot Groups Fired From Benched Sandbags At 25 Yards
ES=Extreme Spread
AVG=Average Velocities
SD=Standard Deviation
G.S.=Group Size In Inches

Equipped with a telescopic sight, the .41 magnum Desert Eagle stands pretty tall. It is a big handgun, to be sure, but the trend is towards bigger guns. Despite the aura of raw intimidation, the pistol is rather easy to shoot. The mass trims tigerish recoil to pussycat proportions.

THE SMITH & WESSON CLASSIC HUNTER:

The Classic Hunter isn't quite as big as some of today's magnum revolvers, but it is big enough. Most important, perhaps, is the fact that the Classic Hunter will shoot with the best of the guns S&W has ever put together.

CLASSIC HUNTER is a name that sort of catches your attention. It's intended to do just that and a lot of thought went into choosing it. Smith & Wesson allowed the thousands of satisfied customers who use the big magnums to choose a title for their newest creation. When the dust cleared and the pundits who make the decisions in Springfield had mulled over many thousands of suggestion letters, Classic Hunter emerged the winner.

Smith & Wesson has indulged a periodic fondness for catchy names for their products. In 1907, when the Twentieth Century was new and innocent, a beautifully made revolver called the .44 Hand Ejector was dubbed the New Century model. Collectors called it the Triple Lock. At one point, the Massachusetts firm called a light, easy-to-carry little .38 the Terrier. At the same time, they produced a massive, rough-service .38 called the Outdoorsman. We've all seen Masterpieces — light, heavy and combat — as well as Chiefs Specials, Bodyguards and Centennials. L-frame just doesn't sing, so it became the Distinguished Combat Magnum.

Classic Hunters come with a Hogue Monogrip installed. Normally, this is an extra-cost, after-market item. The grip makes the big .44 easier to shoot. The soft rubber cushions recoil to some degree; the surface is non-skid.

Throughout, Smith & Wesson's names were logically descriptive. The latest name, Classic Hunter, is no exception. It touches two major elements in the nature of the gun it describes. One is old and the other quite new.

The Classic Hunter is a .44 magnum and, like all other S&W .44s, it's built on the big N-frame which dates to the Triple Lock. If you took a new Classic Hunter, unscrewed the barrel and removed the cylinder from its crane, you'd have the same starting point as the other Smith .44s — the famous N-frame. The Classic Hunter differs from the other Model 29s only in the sense of a heavier barrel and non-fluted cylinder. But those two parts make the new revolver a lot better for its intended purpose. The older, or classic, design is thus updated for a new purpose.

And the purpose is, of course, hunting. Never before

HANDGUN TESTS

A Functional Facelift
For The Famous Forty-Four

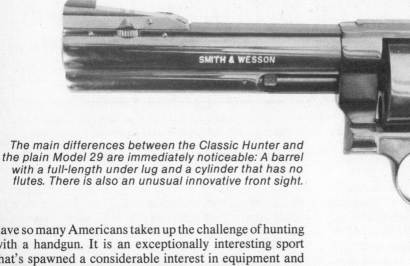

The main differences between the Classic Hunter and the plain Model 29 are immediately noticeable: A barrel with a full-length under lug and a cylinder that has no flutes. There is also an unusual innovative front sight.

have so many Americans taken up the challenge of hunting with a handgun. It is an exceptionally interesting sport that's spawned a considerable interest in equipment and guns. The Classic Hunter is Smith & Wesson's answer to the demands of shooters who want one of their handguns for pure hunting use. It's a pleasure to report the new handgun seems up to the job.

The Model 29 Classic Hunter is a six-shot, blued steel .44 magnum with a heavy six-inch barrel. Smith & Wesson has made such a revolver since the mid-Fifties, but the Classic Hunter is a bit different. It has a barrel made from the same blank forgings as the Model 586 L-frame. That includes a rounded underrib which extends clear to the muzzle. The rib adds several ounces to the weight of the revolver. There's also additional weight in the cylinder,

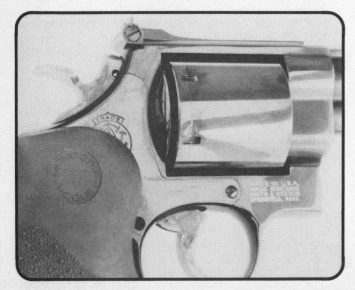

which has no flutes cut into its circumference.

The total effect is a heavier Model 29, with the balance of the piece shifted subtly forward. In the two-handed grip used by hunters, the revolver points and handles quite well, more so than a standard M29 with six-inch barrel. For the intended purpose of the gun — hunting at moderate handgun ranges — the new revolver is a delight to use. It's easier to carry than the longer-barreled Model 29. The shorter barrel is easier to draw in a fast-paced hunting situation, where some form of two-hand stance is the rule.

There is another reason for the extra weight on the gun, a reason that evolved from the shooting done by the avid pistoleros of the International Handgun Metallic Silhouette Association. These devoted shooters put thousands of rounds through their revolvers every year. It didn't take long for them to discover the fact that a standard Model 29 will quickly develop timing problems on a steady diet of stiff handloads. The cylinder, suspended on a rather fragile crane mechanism, takes a hefty jolt when the gun is fired. A few thousand rounds and timing often, but not always, suffers.

Reaction to the heavy, unfluted cylinder is mixed. Some of our more tradition-minded shooters think it's ugly; others find it functional and attractive. The amount of weight added to gun when flutes are omitted is minimal.

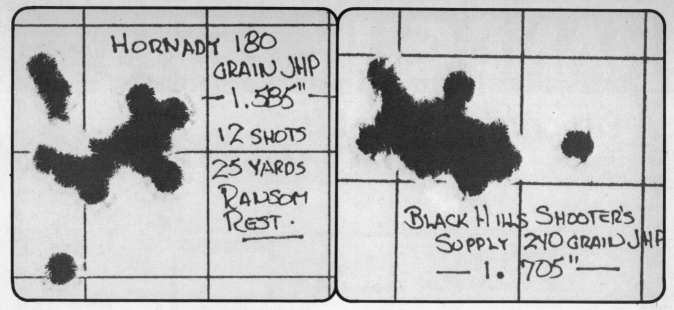

Above: This is more than you can usually expect from a .44 magnum. Our best group was produced with Hornady 180-grain JHP ammunition. That's twelve shots, twice around the cylinder. The target is on a one-inch grid.

Above: The one flyer out to the right raised hell with this group, which still ranked second best. Black Hills Shooter's Supply is a small ammo maker in South Dakota. Their ammunition is often as good as anyone's: 1.705-in.

The Classic Hunter cylinder is heavier than the standard Model 29 version, by virtue of having no flutes cut into the circumference. Without the cuts made to remove stock, the cylinder is a few ounces heavier. It would seem that the designers hope the somewhat heavier cylinder will resist the violent back-and-forth motion that results from firing a stiff load. It also is possible that the heavier cylinder will, in fact, increase the possibility of violent battering of the cylinder and crane. Time will tell.

While the heavier cylinder adds weight to the revolver, the greater amount of mass is in the heavy, underlugged barrel. It's made from the same barrel forging as used for the L-frame series of guns. The barrel produced from this forging has a heavy rib of approximately cylindrical shape running from the front of the frame to the muzzle. Thus contoured, the barrel adds weight forward and shifts the balance towards the muzzle.

There is an immediately noticeable difference in the handling of a Classic Hunter over the conventional Model 29 with the same length barrel. The Classic Hunter absorbs recoil well, but better yet, it hangs on the target a little better as the shooter lines up his shot. Competition shooters will appreciate this feature. In fact, most competitors who use revolvers in bowling pin, PPC or action-type shooting contests modify stock revolvers for their matches and usually add this type of rib. It is a shooter's feature.

There are other features of this new Model 29 that are there to make the revolver appealing to the man who will really shoot the gun a lot. The grip is different and overwhelmingly superior to the typical S&W grips. On the typical N-frame Smith, the shooter gets a set of so-called target stocks, usually made from the South American wood called goncalo alves. The wood is handsome and, at times, can be downright beautiful. The checkering on the factory grips is neatly executed, but far too sharp for comfortable shooting. Further, the basic grip is not completely compatible with the shape of the human hand.

Flared outwards at the bottom, the S&W grip is hard to hold consistently from shot to shot. The .44 magnum recoil tends to twist the gun downwards in the hand. The shooter therefore must re-establish his grip after each shot. This is not a good idea when fast repeat shots may be required by hunting circumstances. Classic Hunters come with a one-piece grip by Guy Hogue made of a resilient rubber to absorb recoil and shaped to make fast repeat shots possible. The grips have finger grooves moulded into them, as well as a functional and attractive pebbled surface. They help make a hard-kicking handgun easier to shoot.

The sights on the Classic Hunter also are an improvement. The rear sight is the conventional Smith & Wesson adjustable type, without the distracting and unnecessary white-outlined rear sight notch. The front sight is completely different and intended to solve the hangunner's dilemma of zeroing a handgun for a variety of ranges.

That's no small chore. Even the high-velocity magnum handgun cartridges have a trajectory that's akin to a rainbow in shape. Zeroing for one range means you'll have to hold off for any range. In handgun hunting, where the targets are small and the ranges varied, this means a fair likelihood of a miss. What is needed is a sight that can be changed quickly for different ranges. The Classic Hunter front sight solves the problem nicely.

This sight has a narrow front post which may be set quickly to any one of four pre-determined ranges. There's a horizontal wheel in the base of the sight and it turns through a full circle when manipulated by the shooter. There are also four positive click stops in the course of a full turn. Each stop corresponds to a point in the cycle where an internal cam has been adjusted to a particular depth via an Allen screw in the top of the front sight base.

The shooter adjusts the cams for a series of ranges that he anticipates he might shoot. It might be an even 25, 50, 75 and 100 yards, but the capability is there to set the sight for odd ranges just as easily — perhaps 35, 60, 85 and

110. Once the cams are adjusted, the hunter just rotates the wheel to the correct setting for the range he needs, aligns the sights on his target and shoots. The position of the front sight changes up and down by virtue of the spring-loaded cam arrangement inside the sight. It's made easier with a tiny window in the left side of the front-sight base. The wheel is marked with numerals 1 through 4 for the four front sight settings. All things considered, it is a clever little sight.

All the clever touches in the world don't mean the gun will be sufficiently accurate for field use and hunting. We have pretty well established the credentials of the revolver as a well designed and functional hunting handgun. It remains to be seen if the Classic Hunter can measure up in shooting.

I took the Classic Hunter to the range on several occasions, one of which involved machine-rest testing at ranges as far as a hundred yards. Most groups at that range were on the order of seven inches, with the best just over five. In that evaluation, several types of ammunition produced groups proportionate to the range at which the group was fired. I am satisfied that the general trend is for the tightest-grouping ammo at twenty-five yards to be at least one of the best at one hundred.

The table below displays the results of a shooting test conducted at twenty-five yards. Each of five types of am-

munition was fired, twelve shots in the Ransom Rest. The twelve shots were fired, using all of the revolver's six chambers, two shots from each. This procedure gives a little better picture of the performance potential of a single specimen than the customary method of determining the best five chambers and excluding the one that throws the flyers.

This particular Classic Hunter is a performer. The five types of ammunition used in the test came from my available supply on hand, but the Classic Hunter delivered accuracy better than I expected, with all of them. The average for twelve-shot groups was just over two inches (2.038 inches) and the worst didn't break the 2½-inch mark (2.447 inches). The excellent ammunition produced by Black Hills Shooter's Supply, a 240-grain JHP design, plopped twelve into a beautiful 1.705-inch group. Still, the best performance was with Hornady 180-grain JHPs, which clustered a dozen shots into 1.585 inches.

This is excellent downrange performance. An out-of-the-box revolver that shoots an honest twelve rounds, twice around the cylinder, into groups this tight is a performer. I also have tried some carefully crafted handloads and produced some groups that are a bit better. If Smith & Wesson holds quality control to this level in all Classic Hunters, the gun will be one of the best hunting revolvers available

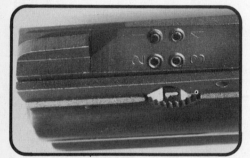

Left: Looking down on the tricky front sight. In use, a shooter uses the Allen screws to pre-set internal cams for different ranges. The wheel on the left side turns the sights to the selected ranges. It is a versatile rig.

Below: The Handguns '89 test gun was unquestionably accurate. The test table shows the results of firing a twelve-shot group with each of five different kinds of ammunition. As is our custom, we used the Ransom Rest.

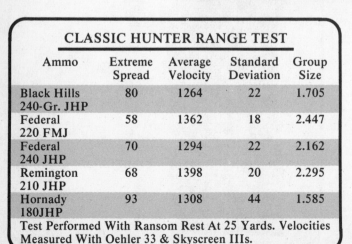

CLASSIC HUNTER RANGE TEST

Ammo	Extreme Spread	Average Velocity	Standard Deviation	Group Size
Black Hills 240-Gr. JHP	80	1264	22	1.705
Federal 220 FMJ	58	1362	18	2.447
Federal 240 JHP	70	1294	22	2.162
Remington 210 JHP	68	1398	20	2.295
Hornady 180 JHP	93	1308	44	1.585

Test Performed With Ransom Rest At 25 Yards. Velocities Measured With Oehler 33 & Skyscreen IIIs.

COLT'S DELTA ELITE:

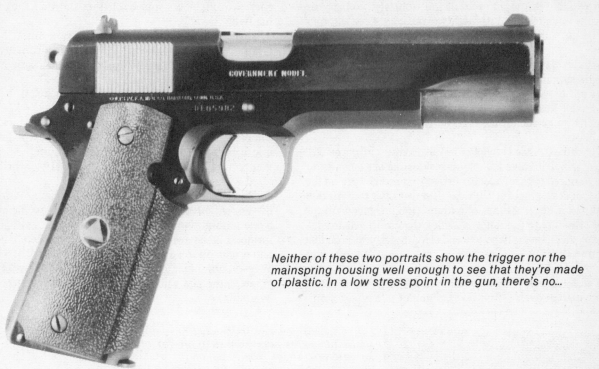

Neither of these two portraits show the trigger nor the mainspring housing well enough to see that they're made of plastic. In a low stress point in the gun, there's no...

Below: This is an early Delta with the Pachmayr grips. All versions of the gun have the three-dot sight system.

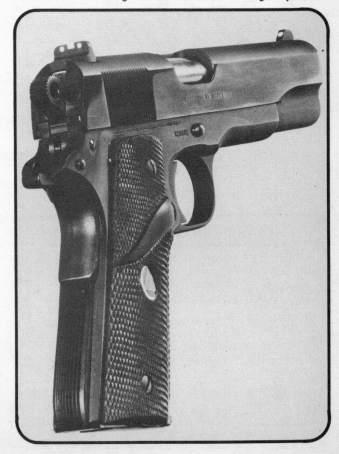

COLT'S SAA, or Single Action Army revolver, was in production for a record-breaking sixty-eight consecutive years (1873-1941). There was a wartime break until the mid-1950s, but the old thumb-buster had a comeback career that lasted until recent years. That is an enviable record, made surprising in view of the fact the Peacemaker was essentially out-moded in the first thirty years of its life. It lasted more for reasons of nostalgia than practicality.

That is not the case with the Colt ranking Number Two in terms of longevity. In an amazingly short period of gestation, John Browning came up with the Colt .45 pistol. It has been used all over the world since 1911. The pistol still comes out of the Hartford plant and has done so without interruption for something like seventy-eight years. The Government Model is almost exactly the same gun that John Browning developed.

A series of modifications to the cosmetics of the gun following WWI resulted in a nomenclature change, from M1911 to M1911A1. In the 1970s, the factory fitted the pistol with a collet-type barrel bushing and it became the Series '70. In the early 1980s, they added the firing pin safety and the pistol changed to a Series '80. At the heart of the matter, there remains the same basic trouble-free and durable old pistol.

The pistol under consideration here is a version of the old one; the same gun. It has a fancy name roll-marked on the slide and an unfamiliar designation on the barrel. This is Colt's Delta Elite, the first 10mm pistol to see general distribution. Nobody could argue that it is the most powerful version of the Government Model that Colt ever produced.

A Troubled Home For The Ten Millimeter Round

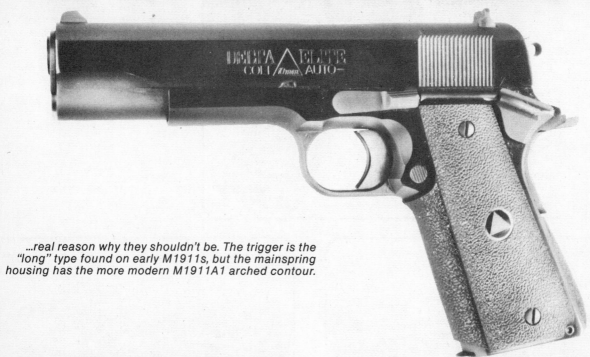

...real reason why they shouldn't be. The trigger is the "long" type found on early M1911s, but the mainspring housing has the more modern M1911A1 arched contour.

The other side of the same pistol, showing Pachmayr's thumb rest grips and the flashy new slide markings.

COLT DELTA ELITE FIRING TEST				
Ammo Used	Extreme Spread	Average Velocity	Standard Deviation	Group Size
Pro-Load 180-gr JHP	70	1221	17	2.581
PMC 200-gr FMJ	92	1080	46	3.462
PMC 170-gr JHP	33	1187	8	2.991
Norma 200-gr FMJ	48	1182	12	4.181

The original ammunition for the 10mm was made by Norma for the ill-fated Bren Ten pistol. Brens are no longer in production, but the ammo is. It is ammunition that claims to have velocities in the range of 1250 fps with a 200-grain bullet. Our chronograph results are a bit more modest at around 1180.

There is an enormous appeal to a pistol that handles such a potent package. The other caliber options in the Colt pistol feature lighter bullets at the same or higher velocities or heavier ones at substantially slower speeds. The 10mm concept is a slightly lighter than .45 bullet traveling at 9mmP velocities. The ammunition is becoming refined, also discussed in Chapter Nine. The question is whether or not the Delta Elite is up to the task.

We have to look at the pistol itself before we can go much farther. As received from the Colt factory in the current maroon and gold box, the Delta weighs the usual thirty-eight ounces and has an overall length of 8½ inches. In spite of the fact that the 10mm cartridge is smaller in body diameter than the .45, there is no increase in magazine capacity. The special Delta magazines hold seven rounds.

The Delta is a handsome pistol. The slide flats are polished and blued, while the remainder of the pistol is an even and functional matte black. The right side of the slide is marked simply "Government Model," but the left side has the triangular Delta symbol and the Delta Elite legend.

As a pistol intended for combat shooting, the Delta needs some special features and the Colt factory supplies most of them. The combat shooters usually prefer the Commander hammer with its knurled ring: It's standard on

Left: The early Delta, as field-stripped for inspection. On the newer pistols, Colt has cut the slide rail on the receiver away at the indicated point. It's an apparent attempt to forestall the possibility of rails cracking.

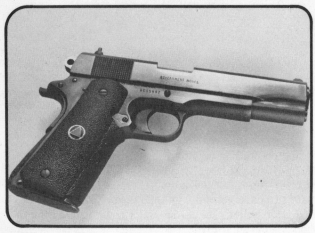

The right side of the Delta is like so many other Colts except for the new prefix on the serial number. Newer Delta 10s have the pebbled grip surface as shown here.

It's a flashy slide marking and an eye-catching Delta symbol in the grip of the newest Colt. Colt offers the Delta only as a blued full-sized pistol, no variations.

the Delta. The sights show the influence of the combat shooters, also. The rear sight is the large fixed unit, once called the National Match type. It's matched up with a semi-ramped front sight. Both of them are highlighted with big white dots, two on the rear and one on the front, which offers the popular three-dot sighting arrangement. The rear sight notch and front sight blade are large and easy to pick up even in dim light.

There are a few more shooter amenities worthy of com-ment. The tang of the grip safety is contoured to match the shape of the underside of the Commander hammer. It would be hard to find a shooter with hands so fleshy that he's going to suffer hammer bite. On early examples of the Delta, the grips were a special run of rubber Pachmayr wrap-arounds bearing the special Delta red-and-black medallions. Those were typical Pachmayrs, with moulded checkering and vestigial thumb rests on both sides. The current pistols are shipped with another type of rubber

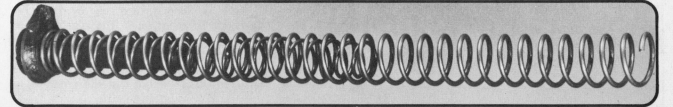

The Delta Elite recoil spring is actually two springs, with the shorter, stiffer one wound inside the longer one. The recoil spring guide is a compressible synthetic material. It doesn't hold up well in extended firing.

Despite the smaller body diameter of the 10mm round, the Delta magazine has the same capacity as the .45's. The eight-shot column on the right represents the full magazine of seven, plus one more up the spout. Power potential of eight 10mms is probably a bit higher than eight .45s. We'll find out when the 10mm is really used.

picks up the pistol and fires a magazine for the first time almost invariably has the same reaction and that is why the buffer is there.

The Delta kicks. It is by no means unbearable or as severe as, say, a four-inch Model 29 S&W with firewall handloads, but it does kick. The recoil impulse is not just a harder one, it is also somewhat quicker. It's a sharp, stabbing punch to the hand accompanied by a fast, upward flip of the muzzle. Most pronounced when the gun is shooting the heavy 200-grain bullets, the recoil is a bit of a problem.

The recoil comes from the movement of a heavy bullet down the barrel at a considerable velocity. Since the basic system was designed to shoot a heavy bullet at low velocity, it isn't particularly surprising to find the pistol stressed to handle it. Shooters can learn to handle it and would be well advised to do so. The terminal ballistics performance of the gun justifies it. This pistol hits like a sledgehammer.

There is about thirty percent more theoretical energy in the 10mm 200-grain load than in a typical .45 230-grain round. Since the 10mm bullet is more efficiently contoured for flight, it will tend to shoot flatter and farther than the .45. All of these are worthwhile characteristics of serious combat ammunition. Sadly, there is a fly in the ointment and it isn't recoil so severe as to constitute a training problem.

The pistol that I fired to compile this report is my own, purchased locally in Southern California. Several boxes of ammo went through the gun in order to break it in and form a general shooter's impression. Then it was used in a machine rest test to produce the groups and data reported in the nearby table. I also sent the pistol out to Irv Stone at Bar-Sto Precision to have one of his match barrels installed, after which the 10mm ammo test reported in Chapter 9 was performed. Most recently, I used the pistol in a major handloading project. This adds up to a total of between eight hundred and a thousand rounds.

There are signs of severe battering inside the pistol. The recoil spring guide, made of the compressible synthetic material, is cracked and shattered to the point I would not care to fire the pistol without replacing it. No, it wasn't the handloads, because none of them was as hot as factory ammunition. I believe this system is not well-suited to the recoil of 10mm ammunition.

So what to do? The problem might be solved partially with a heavier slide, stronger spring, a heftier buffer or a combination of all three. Nevertheless, you can only do so much strengthening of a sound mechanism in order to get it to perform above and beyond. The differently engineered lockup of the Omega pistol or one similar to that of the Bren 10 would seem to be a better way to go about it.

In the meantime, Delta shooters need to be aware of the stress that is at work inside the spring system of their pistols. I know of at least one other pistol that has suffered the same fate and with far fewer rounds. Inspect your pistol with regularity and make sure that buffer and spring are in good shape.

I plan to change to a better buffer and a stronger spring, just in the interest of keeping a fine pistol shooting. It is a matter that Colt needs to address *post haste*. The 10mm cartridge is a fine one, offering power and accuracy in a combat pistol.

grips and these have neither checkering nor thumb rests.

The Delta comes with an arched, M1911A1 mainspring housing most combat shooters don't like and a long trigger which they do. Both of them appear to be made of one of today's miracle synthetics. As much as I might like to be the surly old curmudgeon who condemns plastic in guns, I can't see a reason in the world why it won't do just fine, particularly in non-stress-bearing points like these.

It is when the shooter who is familiar with the Government Models pulls the pistol down that he sees the profound differences in the gun. On this pistol, Colt does not use a typical Series '70 or '80 collet barrel bushing. Instead, we have the short rigid type found on the Commander pistol. The most noticeable difference is in two other parts of the disassembled pistol.

The Delta has a double recoil spring. There's what seems to be a standard recoil spring, but it has a second, smaller diameter, shorter and somewhat stiffer spring wound inside it. It looks like the second spring is not compressed much, if at all, when the pistol is in the ready-to-fire position with the slide forward. There has to be some other purpose for the second spring.

Another part of the system which is different is the recoil spring guide. On the Delta, it is made of a compressible synthetic material with a sheet metal plate on its rearward side. The shaft of the guide fits into two springs, forming what amounts to a three-stage buffer. The .45 shooter who

RUGER P85:

Above: One of the Ruger design engineers test-firing the new auto. The P85 is the first centerfire automatic from the Ruger company. It could be the start of something big. Left: Disassembled view of the P85 shows some strong design influence from other makers. The barrel link is quite similar to those found on Colt autos. Why not? It works. Below: There are lots of consumer's hands that would like to wrap around the butt of this much-awaited new auto. The main selling point of the Ruger is a modest price.

AMERICAN SHOOTERS are a prejudiced lot. They are reluctant to accept guns made of materials other than walnut and steel. They're slow to accept sight innovations like the Aimpoint. In an age of ballistic sophistication, lots of unsophisticated .30-30s go across the gun store counter. American shooters are still just a tad suspicious of change. They remain rather fond of American products and mistrust the results of an Army board that chose an Italian pistol to ride in GI holsters. Smart enough to understand that it was a pretty good gun, they still would prefer to see an American design. They like the idea of a winner rising from the ranks of the good ol' boys. They like Bill Ruger.

De-bugging The Design Of A Domestic Wondernine

It might be better to say they like what Bill Ruger represents. In a time when the other gunmaking firms are big corporations, American sportsmen can identify with a man who has come from humble origins and given them so many fine guns in the space of a few years. When Sturm, Ruger and Company announces a new design, shooters want it.

One of the most recent designs to be announced by Ruger was the P85 pistol. I routinely engage in a form of reader research called "Saturday Afternoon Gun Store Browsing." This means forcing myself out to several gun stores in my local area to talk to shooters about what interests them. In the last year or so, what interests them is the Ruger P85.

It's somewhat of a boxy, square automatic in the hands but it handles well. Later versions of the pistol have better triggers than those found on the first-issue guns.

Ruger marks all their guns with product warnings. On the P85, the marking is found on the right side of the receiver. Also note the cast grip panel and the tricky magazine catch. The catch is completely ambidextrous.

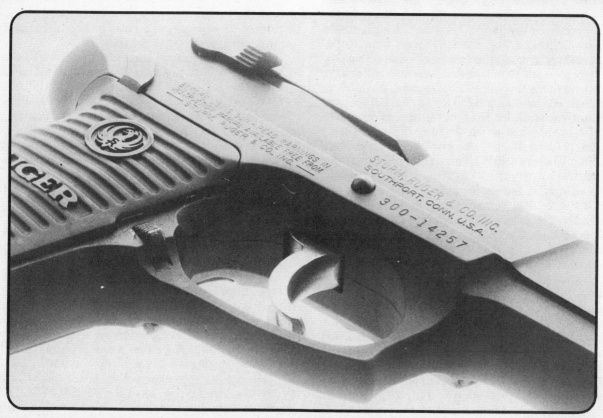

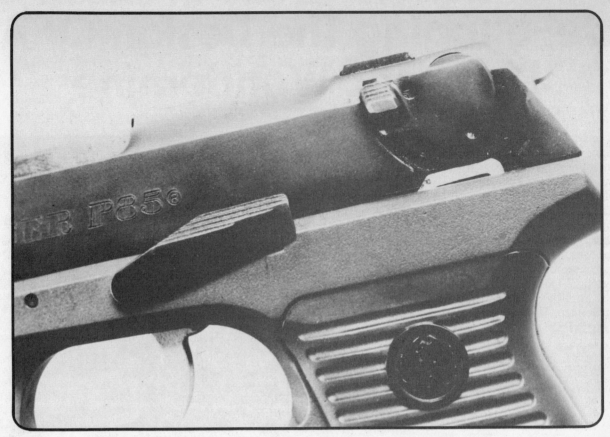

The Ruger P85 slide stop, as found on the latest guns, has been re-designed. It's a lot easier to manipulate. The safety/de-cocking lever works like many others.

I can't recall any firearm in several years that has attracted shooter attention like the new 9mmP from Ruger. There are several reasons for this. One is simply that they like Ruger guns and this is the first Ruger centerfire auto. Another reason is that the P85 represents an American wondernine and an alternative to the S&Ws. But the most significant reason is price. In a time when prices on the best wondernines approach the one-grand mark, way out of the price range of most shooters who would like to get involved in this 9mmP business, the P85 remains priced under three hundred bucks.

Put it all together and you have a pistol with a rosy sales future. It's priced right, comes from an American company of impeccable credentials, and has most of the characteristics of those fancy German and Italian guns. With all of that in its favor, why aren't tens of thousands of shooters happily nine-millimetering themselves into a state of shooter's euphoria with a P85?

The guns have been in markedly short supply, despite an ad campaign that continues unabated. Having never been given a reason why, I can only theorize that there may have been a few problems with the pistol. The first pistol I was able to lay hands on for evaluation had two major problems and the second was on hand for a short period of time before the Ruger plant needed it back. The difficulties on the first pistol were an absolutely horrible trigger pull and mediocre accuracy. I have other reports of similar difficulties with other guns. This may be a contributing factor to the poor availability of the gun.

But as this is written, I am seeing a few P85s in the course of my Saturday afternoon wanderings. Also, the pistol Ruger sent along for evaluation is quite a bit different than the one I fired in mid-1987. It looks like the Prescott, Arizona, plant where the P85 is made is getting their act together.

Ruger's P85 pistol is a recoil-operated, double-action, semi-automatic pistol with a steel slide and an alloy frame. The double-column magazine holds fifteen shots. The sights are a drift-adjustable rear and a fixed front. It weighs a feathery two pounds empty. The barrel is 4.50 inches long and the entire pistol measures 7.84 inches.

That's the basic data describing the pistol, but there is a lot more to it. The P85 is an ingenious combination of tried-and-true features combined with innovations. The magazine catch, for example, is ambidextrous. There are latches on both sides of the pistol at the junction of the trigger guard and the frame. When the shooter presses the latch inward with the thumb, it is shaped to roll forward and presses against a long leaf spring in the magazine well. A bump in that spring clears a recess in the face of the magazine, leaving the magazine to drop free by gravity.

The ambidextrous nature of the pistol continues in the safety/de-cocking lever, which is repeated on either side of the slide. When the lever is in the down position, the firing

Ruger's P85 has the features of most of today's leading wondernines: DA trigger system, fifteen-shot magazine, combat sights, ambidextrous safety/de-cocking lever.

pin is internally blocked from movement. In fact, the entire firing mechanism is disengaged from contact with the trigger. The safety goes up to the firing position. In that position, a red dot is visible through a hole in the safety lever. It is blocked from view when the pistol is on safe.

The grip panels of the P85 are cast from a hard black synthetic called Xenoy. Someone made a neatly shaped mould for those grip panels. It incorporates deep horizontal grooves and the name Ruger as well as the familiar eagle logo. Better yet is the way the panels fit into the frame of the gun; a trifle reminiscent of the Luger.

The locking system is pure Browning, via a swinging link that looks oh-so-familiar. The barrel is different in other ways, though. It's actually made in two pieces, with a cylindrical barrel screwed into a monoblock. When the pistol is in battery, the monoblock indexes into the ejection port, *a la* Sig-Sauer 226. The actual point of locking contact is a flat on the front juncture of barrel and monoblock. It contacts a matching flat on the roof of the slide. This is a modern and easy-to-make way of doing it.

The exposed hammer of the P85 is a round Commander type. There's a prominent lanyard ring on the lower rear of the butt. Like so many of today's automatic pistols, the face of the P85 trigger guard is squared for the finger-forward hold preferred by some shooters. The trigger guard itself is huge, with plenty of room for the meatiest of fingers or for those with gloves.

Aesthetically, the P85 seems more the sturdy pickup truck and less the fleet sports car. It sits chunky and businesslike in the hand, a little top-heavy due to the thick slide and barrel. The trigger, which was poor on the first pistol I handled, has been improved to the point that it is acceptable. Few of the modern wondernines have good DA triggers. Routing that trigger pressure around so many corners demands a drawbar and it doesn't contribute to good trigger pulls. The single-action trigger on the new version was heavy and a bit creepy.

There are some distinct differences in the newer pistol as opposed to the older one. For one thing, the slide stop is contoured to ride higher on the left side of the pistol, making it considerably easier to work with the thumb of the right hand. There may also be some other contour changes of a more subtle nature, because the new gun just generally feels better.

It looks better than the 1987 edition. There are far fewer visible casting marks, showing either better quality casting or more attention to detail in the finishing of the pistol over there in Arizona.

Looking better has a limited value in the marketplace, unless it can be mated to improved performance. To accurately determine performance, I took the new P85 to the range with the Ransom Rest where I found it did shoot better than the first edition. Since so much was expected of the newest Ruger, I took a healthy supply of ammunition and

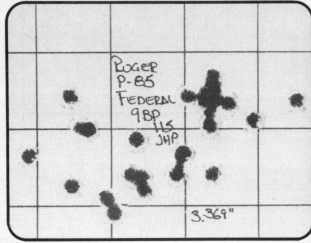

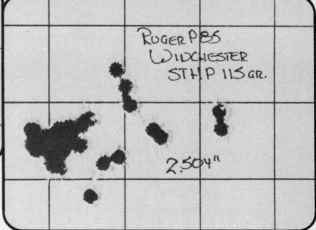

These groups show that the P85 will shoot ammunition that it likes with commendable accuracy. Federal's new 9MP was best, with Silvertips not so very far behind.

RUGER P85 FIRING TEST RESULTS

Ammo Used	ES	VEL	SD	GS (")
Pro-Load 115-gr. JHP	43	1298	10	3.380
Pro-Load 114-gr. FMJ	42	1160	18	4.500
Federal 115-gr. JHP	77	1192	18	3.369
Federal 95-gr. JSP	75	1307	22	4.418
Black Hills 115-gr. JHP	35	1141	8	4.406
Samson 115-gr. FMJ	116	1156	33	6.005
Norma 116-gr. FMJ	102	1169	27	5.102
Hornady 124-gr. FMJ	46	1108	13	3.362
Winchester 115-gr. STHP	39	1201	19	2.504
Federal 115-gr. Match	22	1074	8	2.234

Abbreviations Used Are: ES = Extreme Spread Of Velocities;
VEL = Average Velocity;
SD = Standard Deviation Of Velocities;
GS = Group Size In Inches As Measured W/Dial Caliper, Center Spread
20 Shots Per Group From Ransom Rest, 25 Yds.

planned a thorough test.

There were ten different kinds of ammunition and I fired twenty rounds of each through the new pistol. The Ransom-resting did not begin before the pistol had a couple of boxes of mixed loads run through it hand-held, as a form of breaking in. In this shooting, as well as in later machine-rest testing, I had a number of malfunctions, most commonly failures to chamber. It would appear that the pistol's magazine and feed ramp are quite sensitive to the cartridge's overall length. In the case of the ultra-short Federal 95-grain JSP load, the rounds would sometimes nosedive sharply in the magazine.

The P85 is also somewhat ammo-sensitive. As the accompanying chart shows, this pistol will shoot with the best of them as long as it gets ammunition it likes. There are particularly good results with Silvertips and the new Federal match fodder. Both rounds are accurate to the same general level in a wide variety of guns. But some of the other loads tried were also accurate in other guns and the P85 would not shoot them well.

When the P85 did not like a particular brand and type of ammo, it showed a marked tendency to string shots horizon-

tally, rather than in a generally large group.

On balance, I am perfectly prepared to believe this is not the best example of the P85 ever assembled. Friend Ken Hackathorn who contributed Chapter 15 to this book tells me he has fired a recently-made P85 that delivers groups at the one-inch mark. Massad Ayoob also rates the new Ruger highly and his judgement is to be respected.

It would seem the P85 still has a glitch or two to be resolved. As it presently stands, the gun seems to be a mildly problem-plagued design, whose major difficulty is proper performance with a variety of ammunition. In my own gun, as long as I stick to Silvertips (which ain't that bad an idea), I have a sturdy and reliable wondernine of good accuracy.

RUGER SUPER REDHAWK:
...Another Hawk Goes Super

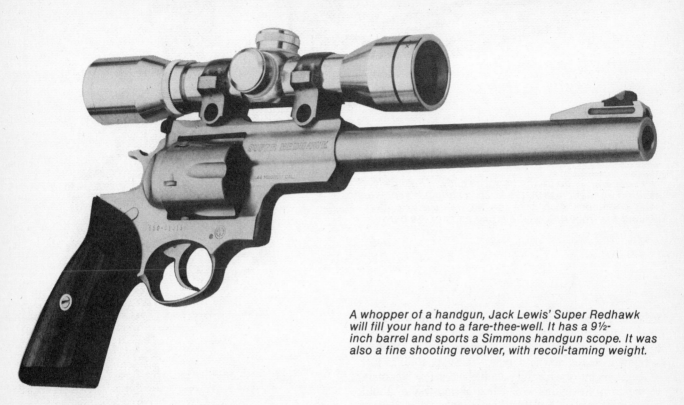

A whopper of a handgun, Jack Lewis' Super Redhawk will fill your hand to a fare-thee-well. It has a 9½-inch barrel and sports a Simmons handgun scope. It was also a fine shooting revolver, with recoil-taming weight.

WAY BACK when Elmer Keith was bedeviling the executives at Remington and Smith & Wesson, trying to get a *real* .44, Bill Ruger was making damned nice little .22s. Elmer eventually convinced the top brass of those companies and they came out with the first .44 magnum; the gun from Smith & Wesson, the ammo from Remington.

By a stroke of good luck, Bill Ruger heard of the new development and lost no time in putting together a fine single-action revolver for the new cartridge. Those original flat-top Ruger Blackhawks now are prized collector's items. At least most of them are; I know of several still riding where they have been for three decades — in the holster of outdoorsmen who appreciate them for what they are.

In time, shooters asked for and received a newer and heavier version of the Blackhawk, called the Super Blackhawk. Elmer wanted to call the gun the Ruger *Dragoon,* because of the distinctive butt shape and the weight and mass of the gun. The Super Blackhawks were, and are, big, heavy revolvers. But they aren't as big or heavy as the revolver under consideration here.

The Super Redhawk is the latest in a succession of brawny magnum handguns from Ruger and if it isn't the best, it may be the most impressive in terms of size, strength, and a general aura of raw power. The Super Redhawk is a

double-action revolver, made of stainless steel and with a swing-out six-shot cylinder. It's a *big* handgun and one with interesting antecedents.

There's an earlier double-action .44 revolver in the Ruger catalog and it likely will remain there for some years

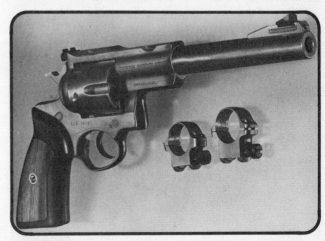

The Redhawk also comes in a 7½-inch barrel version and that size may be a bit more practical. In the box, you'll find a pair of stainless steel scope rings. Butt of the Super Redhawk is just like the one on the GP-100.

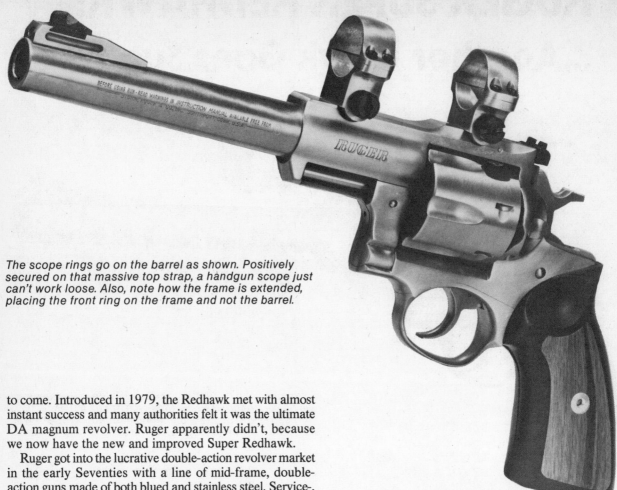

The scope rings go on the barrel as shown. Positively secured on that massive top strap, a handgun scope just can't work loose. Also, note how the frame is extended, placing the front ring on the frame and not the barrel.

to come. Introduced in 1979, the Redhawk met with almost instant success and many authorities felt it was the ultimate DA magnum revolver. Ruger apparently didn't, because we now have the new and improved Super Redhawk.

Ruger got into the lucrative double-action revolver market in the early Seventies with a line of mid-frame, double-action guns made of both blued and stainless steel. Service-, Speed- and Security-Six revolvers came in a number of variations and barrel lengths. They established beyond a doubt the ability of the maker to produce a quality service revolver at a reasonable price. There are hundreds of thousands of them in policemen's holsters around the country.

The original 1979-era Redhawk is a logical design in the succession of things. The Redhawk came in two barrel lengths and the three magnum calibers: .357, .41 and .44

RUGER SUPER REDHAWK FIRING TEST 7½-INCH BARREL				
AMO USED	EXTREME SPREAD	AVERAGE VELOCITY	STANDARD DEVIATION	GROUP SIZE
Black Hills 240JHP	109	1338	26	2.236"
Federal 220FMJ	46	1422	13	2.981"
Federal 240JHP	90	1360	33	2.648"
Remington 210JHP	71	1516	22	2.272"
Hornady 180JHP	66	1422	22	1.982"

Groups are twelve shots each fired at 25 yards to the machine rest. Oehler 33 Chronograph.

magnum. It had a radically different system of lockwork which used a single spring to tension the hammer as well as to return the trigger. When Ruger brought out the GP-100 revolver to eventually replace the Security-Six series, that revolver was different yet.

The Super Redhawk is much like the GP-100 in the shape and function of internal parts. Ruger's press releases in recent years talk about a family of three frame sizes. The GP-100 and the Super Redhawk are the medium and heavy members of the family. The little gun, a five-shot .38, exists in production prototype form. I've handled it and it looks like a miniaturized, fixed-sight GP-100. Not surprisingly, that's exactly what it is.

But the Super Redhawk is a brute. Many shooters, handling the gun for the first time, make comments like: "Gawd, that's a big gun!" or "Does it come with wheels?" It is a massive handgun, but it is entirely reflective of what shooters themselves demanded. The Super Redhawk is a revolver for long-range six-gunning, either on the silhouette range or in the field.

When Bill Ruger built his first .44 magnum in the 1950s, people would have laughed themselves silly had you shown up at the local range with a scope on one of them. After all, everyone *knew* a handgun was only good to twenty-five

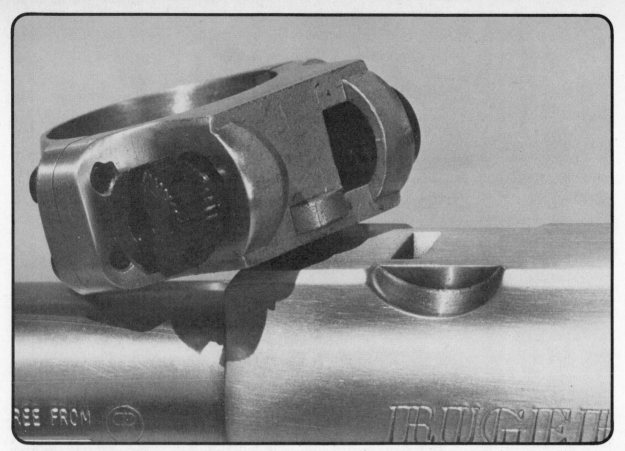

Dean Grennell's camera work caught this excellent photo of the ring and its relationship to the milled recesses in the top of the frame. The crescent-shaped cut on the side mates with a matching lug on the inside of the ring. The cut on the top of the frame matches up with a lug on the ring's underside.

yards; fifty at the most. Why would anybody waste his time trying to make a belt gun perform like a rifle? The very same people didn't regard these super-powerful handguns as anything more than a flash in the pan.

Times have changed and there are both wildcatters and factory ammo makers stretching the magnum handgun envelope well beyond the performance levels of original factory .44 magnum fodder. More importantly, the unsung champions of the metallic silhouette world have established beyond any doubt the accuracy potential of handguns. They shoot at massive steel rams at a far-distant two hundred meters. There is a need for powerful and accurate handguns, as much for the newly popular sport of handgun hunting as for silhouette shooting.

The Super Redhawk is Ruger's best shot at dominance in the magnum revolver market. It is a stainless steel, double-action six-shot .44 magnum revolver, available with two different barrel lengths: 9½ and 7½ inches. The lockwork, as noted earlier, is a scaled-up version of the GP-100's and that's hard to fault.

There are a pair of other features which are like the GP-100. The grip of the Super Redhawk is formed around a cast lug or spike that projects downwards from the frame of the revolver. Ruger provides a pair of firm rubber grips which surround that lug. The resulting shape is far and away the best butt that ever found its way to a production handgun. Ruger dresses them up with panels of grainy gon-

calo alves wood on either side. As noted in our commentary on the GP-100 elsewhere in the book, this is a superb shape from the standpoint of the shooter, even with the hottest loads. The grips are interchangeable with those on the GP-100.

The front sight is similar to both the Redhawk and GP-100. Both of those guns use a front sight base that is integral with the top rib on the barrel. The Super Redhawk uses one that is attached to the revolver's round barrel. On all of them, the front sight blades are interchanged easily when a lug in the front of the sight base is depressed. Ruger offers a number of front sight options on the Redhawk and Super Redhawk, including reinforced plastic blades in several easy-to-see colors. They're innovative sights, matched to a windage and elevation-adjustable rear sight on the top rear of the revolver's frame.

Most Super Redhawk buyers will try a scope. There weren't any suitable pistol scopes when the .44 magnum boomed for the first time, but all of the scope manufacturers offer at least one model. Some of them, like Burris, will even sell you a variable. No pistol scope is worth a damn, unless it's firmly anchored to the handgun. No handgun ever came with a better mounting system than the Super Redhawk.

Some of the earlier Redhawks came with crescent-shaped cuts in the rear of the revolver's top strap and matching cuts in the barrel rib. The cuts would accept and lock securely in

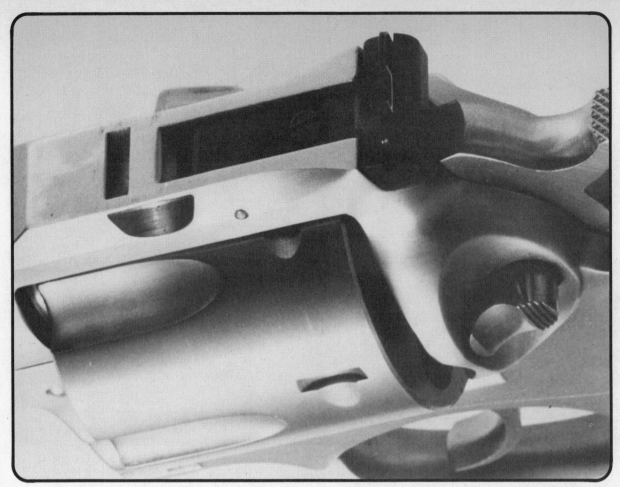

The scope mounting system is excellent, but it isn't the whole story. The Super Redhawk also has a set of fine metallic sights. The rear sight seen here is adjustable for elevation and windage. Like all Ruger DA revolvers, the Super Redhawk has the rock-inward type of cylinder latch, the best there is.

place a pair of stainless steel scope mount rings. It was a pretty good system, but the one on the Super Redhawk is superior.

On the Super Redhawk, the scope goes completely on the frame, rather than front ring on the barrel and rear ring on the frame. Ruger went to a lot of trouble to make the frame extra long for just this purpose. On most revolvers, the frame stops just forward of the cylinder. On the Super Redhawk, that portion of the frame which surrounds the barrel extends forward several inches. This means there is enough fore-and-aft dimension on the frame to allow a scope to be mounted. It also means the tapered round barrel threads into a hefty boss of stainless steel. The whole thing is probably stronger than it needs to be.

Even the rings, which come in the box with every Super Redhawk, are unique and sturdy. Each of them has a crescent-shaped lug which mounts in semi-circular cuts on the side of the rib. As added insurance that the scope mount will not move, the underside of each ring has another lug which mates with a cut in the top of the rib. The glass portion of the scope would have to be torqued completely loose before the scope tube and mounting rings could possibly come unstuck. The Super Redhawk is made for scope mounting.

It's made for shooting, too. The cylinder, which gets battered out of time in other handgun designs, is locked in place at the instant of firing at front and rear. The front lock in particular is positive and strong.

In the course of evaluating the Super Redhawk for *Handguns '89,* we had one of each of the two barrel lengths. Both revolvers came with excellent single-action trigger pulls and double actions that were pretty respectable. Despite the double-action character of the revolver, most shots are likely to be fired with the hammer manually cocked. A fine single-action pull is clearly of greater performance.

All of which brings us around to the true test of the handgun's worth: How does it shoot? The answer is simple. It shoots damned well. After protracted sessions with the revolvers and an assortment of factory and handloaded ammunition, I can tell you that the design is sound and the guns are more than acceptably accurate, at least on the basis of looking at a pair of specimens.

We tried the longer-barreled gun early last year, with friend and fellow writer, Dean Grennell, doing the majority of the initial shooting. At twenty-five yards, Grennell fired the big six-gun from a benched and braced sitting position. The results were such that Dean declared the long Redhawk

Above: The rings in this photo are actually mounted backwards, but it serves to illustrate how they fit. Below: Like the GP-100 and the earlier Redhawk, the Super Redhawk has the excellent snap-in front sight. Red ramp comes on gun, others are available.

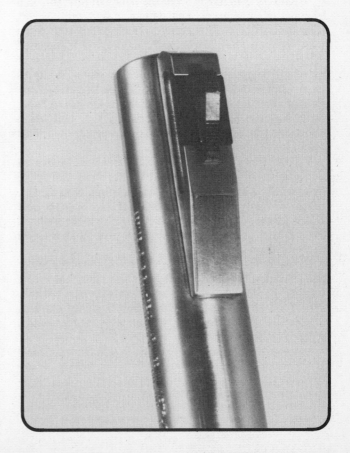

one of the more accurate .44s he had ever fired. With that endorsement, I used the same revolver in the course of compiling load data for another DBI book, called *Gun Digest Book of Handgun Reloading.* The initial reputation was fully justified, as I concocted a number of handloads that plopped six rounds into groups that went between an inch to an inch and a half. The gun was solidly clamped into the Ransom Rest for my testing.

I also got out the Ransom Rest when the 7½-inch Redhawk showed up. For the test-firing that delivered the results tabulated nearby, I used five different kinds of commercial ammunition and fired a group of twelve shots with each of them, using each chamber twice. This gives an accurate picture of the gun's accuracy potential.

It would seem the 7½-inch revolver is only slightly less accurate than its longer cousin. The best group was just under two inches and the average was about 2½. For a bellerin' .44 magnum, this is fine accuracy. It is also remarkably consistent from one kind of ammunition to another.

When the shooting world has a chance to evaluate the Redhawk, I'm betting it will become one of the most popular .44s ever made and I'll even bet it will outsell the venerable Super Blackhawk. It is a massively strong revolver with the best scope-mounting system ever used on a handgun. But I also will wager that the shorter of the two barrels will be the most popular. With at least one kind of ammunition — Federal's 220-grain FMJ — there seems to be a ballistic advantage to the shorter barrel: 1422 feet per second as opposed to 1366. The shorter gun is anything but small, but it is somewhat easier to manage.

And lots of shooters will be managing them in the years to come.

WALTHER P88:

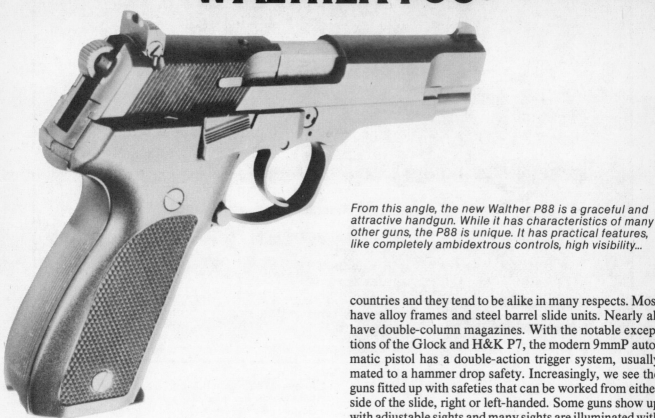

From this angle, the new Walther P88 is a graceful and attractive handgun. While it has characteristics of many other guns, the P88 is unique. It has practical features, like completely ambidextrous controls, high visibility...

SERIOUS STUDENTS of the handgun probably can point to some obscure handgun as a first, but it seems clear the commercially successful double-action auto began with Walther. The gun was the PP model, which appeared in 1929 and which was the first in a long succession of excellent handguns. Throughout the succession, Walthers have used some form of double-action trigger system. Beginning with the PP and continuing to the gun at hand, most Walthers have the characteristic DA trigger which allows the pistol to be carried with the hammer down and a round in the chamber.

Various forms of double-action systems have been used on countless other handguns, but Walther was clearly the first to make it an economic success. As popular as the DA trigger certainly is, Walthers would not have been the best sellers that they are without something else to recommend them. There's a lot more to a Walther pistol than a clever trigger system.

Nowhere is that so true as in the case of the pistol under consideration. The Walther P88 is the latest automatic pistol in the world market and undeniably the best Walther ever. The P88 is an uncommonly usable handgun, one with a bunch of unique features. It competes in a crowded, vigorous marketplace.

Modern 9mmP handguns are made in most free world

The serrated lever in the dead center of this photo is called the operating lever. This is the right side of the pistol and there's another mirror image lever over on the left side. Slide release and de-cocking lever in one.

countries and they tend to be alike in many respects. Most have alloy frames and steel barrel slide units. Nearly all have double-column magazines. With the notable exceptions of the Glock and H&K P7, the modern 9mmP automatic pistol has a double-action trigger system, usually mated to a hammer drop safety. Increasingly, we see the guns fitted up with safeties that can be worked from either side of the slide, right or left-handed. Some guns show up with adjustable sights and many sights are illuminated with bars or dots for quick target aquisition. A lot of them are well-designed for service pistol use; some are quite accurate. All of these are worthwhile characteristics.

The Walther P88 has all of them.

As a matter of fact, the Walther P88 has features that none of the other guns have. There's plenty of logic behind calling the P88 the best of all service 9mmP handguns. In addition to a long list of desirable characteristics, the P88 has a feature associated with few other service handguns of

The Wondernine Approaches Perfection

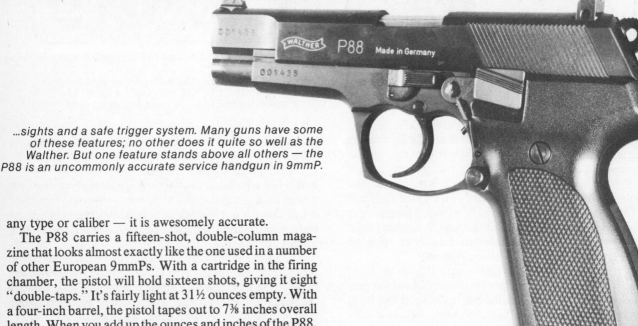

...sights and a safe trigger system. Many guns have some of these features; no other does it quite so well as the Walther. But one feature stands above all others — the P88 is an uncommonly accurate service handgun in 9mmP.

any type or caliber — it is awesomely accurate.

The P88 carries a fifteen-shot, double-column magazine that looks almost exactly like the one used in a number of other European 9mmPs. With a cartridge in the firing chamber, the pistol will hold sixteen shots, giving it eight "double-taps." It's fairly light at 31½ ounces empty. With a four-inch barrel, the pistol tapes out to 7⅜ inches overall length. When you add up the ounces and inches of the P88, you get a compact, lightweight handgun with a steel barrel/slide unit and an alloy frame. The grips are plastic, lightly grained except for checkered side panels.

The P88 sights are just fine for the pistol's intended use as a service handgun. The front sight is dovetailed tightly into the slide and can be adjusted for windage by means of a sight pusher. For most eyes and most loads, that won't be necessary, since the rear sight is windage-adjustable with a screwdriver. Elevation adjustments should be easy to make by replacing the entire front sight with a higher or lower

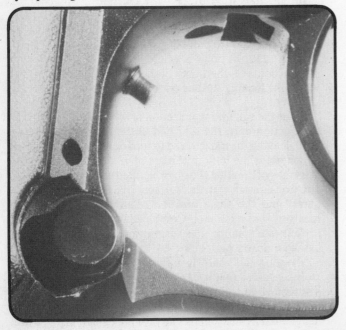

version as needed. The front sight is shaped just right — a slight ramped effect, but still a prominent, easy-to-find blade. There are white dots on the sights, two on the sides of the rear sight and a single one on the rear of front sight. They aren't to my personal liking on any handgun, but they are nonetheless popular.

P88 controls are unique. The hammer and trigger are essentially conventional, but the other controls are not. Begin with the magazine catch. It is mounted where it should be, at the junction of the trigger guard bow and the frame. It's a button that pushes in to release the magazine. Most modern handguns have this feature, but none of them dump the magazine when the *button is pushed in from either side.*

A shooter with the pistol in his right hand can release his expended magazine by pushing in with the tip of the trigger finger from the right or thumb from the left. The functions are just the opposite for a shooter with the piece in his left hand.

This either-hand business goes even farther. While many handguns have ambidextrous safeties and/or hammer drops, almost none have ambidextrous slide release levers. And

Here's the magazine catch on the right side of the gun. There's another one on the left side and they both push in to drop the magazine. The P88 is what we might call tactically ambidextrous. It operates from either hand.

Left: With the grips removed, the stepped frame and moulded grip are visible, along with the draw bar systems of the trigger and operating lever. In the photo above, the P88 rear sight. Adjustable for windage only, the sight uses highlight dots.

there is no other handgun which combines the de-cocking lever and slide release into one ambidextrous unit. On the P88 receiver, there's a lever in the approximate position of the typical slide release. When the slide is to the rear, the shooter has but to thumb the lever down and the slide will run forward, chambering a round, if a loaded magazine is in place. That leaves the hammer cocked. A further stroke of the same lever will drop the hammer safely and pop the trigger forward for a double-action first shot.

It's no surprise that the Walther manual calls the lever the operating lever. It is the primary control used to operate the pistol. Like the magazine catch, the operating lever is repeated on the right side of the pistol, making it fully ambidextrous. That's a positive sales point.

It's true that shooters can be taught to operate most handguns left-handed. Depending on the pistol, there are even some advantages to shooting an essentially right-handed gun with the left-hand. But if the pistol is simply ambidextrous to begin with, there is no special training effort required to get everyone used to handling it. And there is more reason for ambidexterity than appeasing the southpaws. Tactical circumstances often demand that right-handed pistol packers shoot around the left side of a barricade, wall or the like. It's also possible a combat soldier or policeman might suffer wounds that force him into weak-hand shooting. Ambidextrous handguns make sense.

The one remaining control to examine is the takedown latch. It's on the left side, just forward of the operating lever. The P88 comes apart faster than any of its contemporaries. Starting with a clear gun with the slide forward, pivot the takedown latch down ninety degrees and pull the slide forward off the frame. Turn the slide over and remove the recoil spring and guide, then pull the barrel out to the rear. I can do it in about a tenth of the time that it takes me to two-finger type a description of what I'm doing.

The trigger system used on the P88 is like the one on the P5 pistol of the 1970s. It's a first-shot double-action. The trigger is linked to the sear and hammer by a drawbar that runs down the left side of the pistol. That makes for a bulky grip, but something like this is pretty much universal on modern autos. The P88 is a little different in the manner in which it handles the firing pin safety. Unlike a great many other automatic pistols, the Walther uses the action of the rearward-moving trigger to lift the entire firing pin into the path of the falling hammer. It does so against the pressure of a spring. This means that the trigger pull, either double

or single, is a bit mushy. It is one of two criticisms that I have of an otherwise fine handgun.

Might as well deal with the other here and now. The P88 butt is just a little too thick for my medium-sized hands. It makes for a pistol that is a little hard to shoot in fast exercises. There is a possible solution in after-market grips cut wafer-thin from some impact-resistant material — Delrin, Micarta or the like.

The basic shape of the grip is that of a P38, the German service pistol of World War II that survives in service use to the present day. With a single column inside, it's one of the best you'll ever handle. Thickened to accommodate a double-column type, it becomes awkward.

The P38 was an innovative handgun in many ways, not the least of which was the breech-locking system. It works just fine in the P38, so much so that Beretta designers used a similar system in the U.S. service pistol, the M9 (or 92F). The P38 system works around a floating block that pivots into recesses in the pistol slide at the moment of highest pressure. I was astonished to find that the new Walther has gone completely away from this concept and works on the basis of a typical Colt-Browning tilting barrel.

In no small way, this is why the P88 is so accurate. Walther engineers improved the basic idea of a barrel that tilts down at the rear to unlock. They have done so by emphasizing a third point of contact in the lockup system. The first contact point is where the lower barrel lug cam surface contacts the frame of the pistol and the second is where the locking surface on the barrel top mates with the slide roof.

Since the squared rear section of the barrel indexes into the ejection port, the rear end of the barrel is forced up hard, leaving the muzzle end to turn down. The third point of contact is the bottom surface of an eliptical hole in the front face of the slide. The barrel, lifted at the rear, is forced into firm contact with this surface. The total effect puts the barrel into the same position relative to the slide and receiver, shot after shot. Combined with a Walther barrel of first-rate quality, the system makes a well designed handgun nearly perfect.

Shooting the pistol in informal one- and two-handed style suggested that it was going to be accurate. The shots just seemed to cluster into pleasingly small groups. While the P88 is relatively light, it handles as well as many heavier handguns. There's no pronounced muzzle flip and

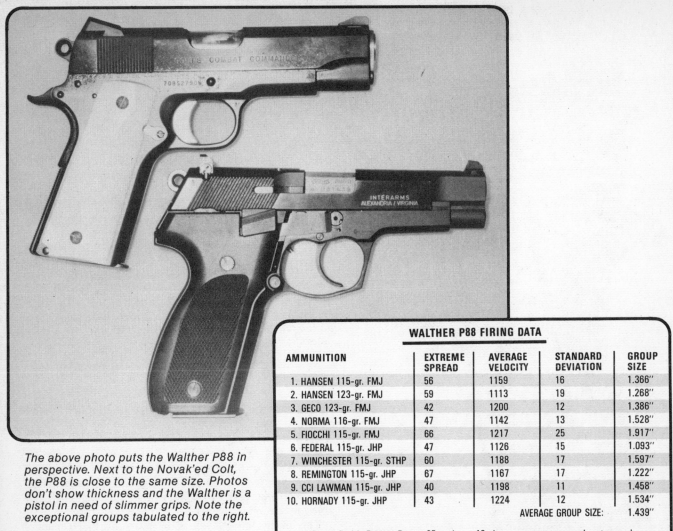

The above photo puts the Walther P88 in perspective. Next to the Novak'ed Colt, the P88 is close to the same size. Photos don't show thickness and the Walther is a pistol in need of slimmer grips. Note the exceptional groups tabulated to the right.

WALTHER P88 FIRING DATA

AMMUNITION	EXTREME SPREAD	AVERAGE VELOCITY	STANDARD DEVIATION	GROUP SIZE
1. HANSEN 115-gr. FMJ	56	1159	16	1.366"
2. HANSEN 123-gr. FMJ	59	1113	19	1.268"
3. GECO 123-gr. FMJ	42	1200	12	1.386"
4. NORMA 116-gr. FMJ	47	1142	13	1.528"
5. FIOCCHI 115-gr. FMJ	66	1217	25	1.917"
6. FEDERAL 115-gr. JHP	47	1126	15	1.093"
7. WINCHESTER 115-gr. STHP	60	1188	17	1.597"
8. REMINGTON 115-gr. JHP	67	1167	17	1.222"
9. CCI LAWMAN 115-gr. JHP	40	1198	11	1.458"
10. HORNADY 115-gr. JHP	43	1224	12	1.534"
			AVERAGE GROUP SIZE:	1.439"

Groups fired in Ransom Rest at 25 yards — 10-shot groups were measured centerspread with dial caliper. Velocity and statistical summary via Oehler 33 chronograph.

the big, easy-to-see sights pick up quickly. The mushy trigger is bit hard to deal with, but I have hopes the custom gunsmiths might be able to improve it.

Approaching serious accuracy testing of the P88, I was pretty well convinced the pistol was a winner. It had all of the right stuff: first-shot double-action trigger system, high-capacity magazine, utterly unique controls, good sights — all in a light, compact package. All in all, a really likeable pistol.

Then I put it in Chuck Ransom's machine rest — and found that the P88 is an *exceptionally* accurate handgun. Since the level of accuracy with most kinds of ammunition used is so high and the means of achieving that accuracy are so practical, the P88 is a pistol that will serve well in hard police or military service. There's no reason at all to believe the gun is fragile or so tightly fitted that it's ill-suited for hard use.

We do not normally associate match accuracy with service guns. That's partially due to the fact that we seldom see a service pistol that will shoot one-inch groups at twenty-five yards. In my first go-round with the P88 in the machine rest, the pistol delivered a number of twenty-shot groups that averaged under two. Using seventeen different kinds of ammunition, the average group size was just under two inches. That's just normal service ammunition, not selected lots. The best groups were close to the one-inch mark.

On a more recent occasion, I traveled to a local test facility and tried the best of the ammunition that had done well in the first effort. Declining supplies of ammo forced me to shoot ten-shot groups. The machine rest groups are tabulated nearby, averaging 1.439 inches. The best group was with Federal's excellent 115-grain JHP. That particular load is in the winner's circle so often when I test 9mmP handguns that I have come to regard it as the standard.

The value of such accuracy is both subtle and direct. Directly, there's always the possibility that a police officer or soldier may have to place a shot with great precision in crisis circumstances, particularly if he's assigned to a SWAT or hostage rescue unit. The more subtle implication is that any man or woman trained in marksmanship appreciates a good shooting gun and will use it with confidence. Untrained persons have no business with guns.

Walther has but to keep up the quality control on the P88 and hope the international currency changes in such a way the U.S. price of the pistol comes down ($1175 retail — ouch!) and they'll sell a bunch of them. As it now stands, the P88 approaches perfection.

SPRINGFIELD'S OMEGA:

On the other end of the big pistol shown here, there's a ported barrel. The Omega is heavier than the Colt and the weight makes it easier to shoot. Still, the port helps.

results on target were certainly graphic — groups an inch wide and seven inches high.

As it turned out, there were other reasons for the peculiar way the test Omega performed. This handgun is a re-designed version of the gun that John Browning put together so many years ago. It has the same general characteristics, but offers what I believe might be the first genuinely valuable improvement over the .45 in half a century.

The salient characteristic of the new gun is that it changes calibers with little more than a barrel and magazine substitution.

The Omega's maker is Springfield Armory, a family-owned operation located in a rural farm country of south-

"DERE, DERE — look at dat!" Joe Peters exclaimed vehemently. His Germanic accent was strong, but his meaning was coming through with abiding clarity. Joe was a little perturbed with me, because he felt that I had unjustly criticized his handgun. From my point of view, the first review I had done on the Omega was accurate. As the amiable German designer continued the discussion of the pistol, I got a sinking feeling in the pit of my stomach. Joe Peters was right about that first story — and I was wrong.

The conversation occurred at the SHOT show in Las Vegas in January 1988. It concerned a story I had written about the Omega pistol, in which I had asserted that the design on the 10mm barrel might be faulty in the way that the cam angles were cut on the barrel locking lugs, causing an inconsistent locking and unlocking of the breech. The

This view of the muzzle shows the front sight and the porting system. Also note the massive contour of the slide and Germanic proof marks near the beveled face.

It May Be The First-Ever REAL Improvement On The M1911A1

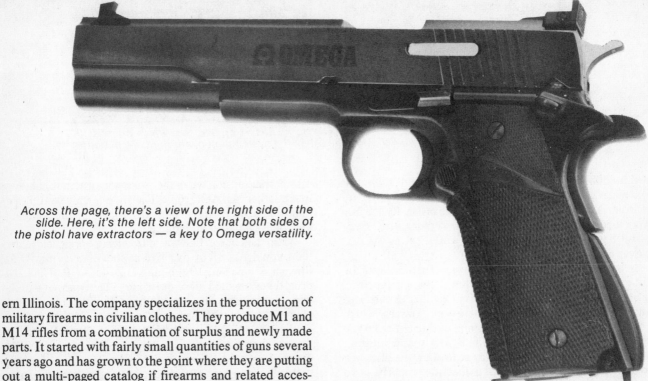

Across the page, there's a view of the right side of the slide. Here, it's the left side. Note that both sides of the pistol have extractors — a key to Omega versatility.

ern Illinois. The company specializes in the production of military firearms in civilian clothes. They produce M1 and M14 rifles from a combination of surplus and newly made parts. It started with fairly small quantities of guns several years ago and has grown to the point where they are putting out a multi-paged catalog if firearms and related accessories. Some of their products, like match quality service rifles, are unobtainable elsewhere.

In the few years they've offered them, Springfield Armory .45 pistols have earned an enviable reputation for quality at a relatively low price. The pistol is essentially the World War II-era GI .45 and Springfield offers them set up in different styles. When the Springfield people got together with Peters-Stahl of West Germany, the result was the Omega pistol.

Peters-Stahl makes conversion units for automatic pistols. For a time, they were marketed in the United States by Pachmayr, the rubber grip maker in Los Angeles. While the units once were made for a number of pistols, they are offered presently only for the Colt and its clones. Springfield imports the Peters-Stahl units and assembles them onto receivers of their own manufacture, thereby creating the Omega pistol.

There is one big advantage to the Omega over all other convertible caliber pistols. The Omega will shoot a variety of handgun calibers by simply switching barrels and magazines, and in a few cases, the recoil spring. Most other attempts to build a handgun that will do for all reasons require a different slide. This is because the slide is manufactured to handle a particular-sized case head. There isn't a lot of commonality in the dimensions of the popular auto pistol cartridge case heads.

The heart of the Omega pistol is the convertible slide. It

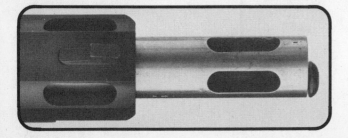

Left and left above: Closeups of a pair of the features that make the Omega sizzle. Extractor above and the clever barrel and slide porting below. It's easy to shoot.

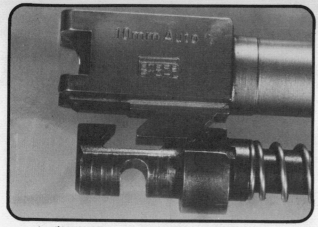
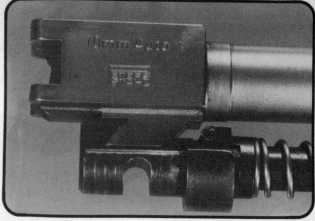

Inside the Omega, the locking system looks like this. The barrel has an angled cam which mates with a matching cam on the recoil spring guide. View to the left is the system unlocked; right, it's in battery.

will function properly with case heads as small as 9mmP and as large as .45. It might even work with some that are both larger and smaller. Just as the massive RCBS Big Max loading press has a Universal shell holder, the Omega pistol has a universal bolt face. It works by means of a clever dual extractor.

In an automatic pistol, the bolt face lies in the rear of the slide. In the very center is the hole through which the firing pin moves to strike the primer of a chambered cartridge and fire the round. To the side, there is an extractor which catches the rim of the cartridge and extracts it from the chamber, when the round is fired. The round must fit against the bolt face in such a way as to allow the firing pin to be centered and the extractor to function properly. It's a question of spacing.

The ingenious Omega has *two* extractors, one to either side of the pistol slide. Each of the two is a thick chunk of milled steel, fitted into the slide in such a way that the extractors are visible from the outside of the slide. Stiff coil springs insure that the extractor has sufficient tension to spring inward enough to grasp small 9mmP rims. There is

also proper tension when the extractor system is handling much larger .45 ACP rims. The slide is universal; it will handle nearly any pistol cartridge for which the company also offers a barrel and magazine.

When the Omega first was introduced, Springfield stated they would make it up as a five-caliber pistol: 9mmP, .38 Special, .38 Super, 10mm auto and .45 ACP. The early prototypes handled all of those cartridges without a problem. Conceivably, they could have handled a number of others with a suitable barrel and magazine. In time, Springfield's marketing research told them the 9mmP and .38 Special barrels would not be popular and they were dropped.

While the universal slide is part of the Omega system, the barrels are also worthy of interest. They are more like Browning barrels than Colt GMs. There is no pivoting link on the bottom of the barrel. Instead, the barrel has a solid lug that mates with a matching surface on an extension of the recoil spring guide. The sliding fit of one angled cam against the other is what causes the action to lock and unlock as required.

The clever dual extractor at work holding a .45 ACP round. Omega's slide is much thicker and heavier. The top of the slide is milled flat with deep flutes cut on the edges.

The Omega barrel differs from the Colt in that there are no radiused locking lugs on the top of the barrel to fit matching recesses in the roof of the slide. Omega barrels have a massive squared section which cams into the ejection port to lock. It is a rugged system that stays closed a bit longer than the 1911's. This latter characteristic is important when the 10mm barrel is in place, because that cartridge operates at some pretty hefty pressures.

The Omega pistol is an essentially conventional 1911-type pistol in its operation and functioning. Safety lock, slide stop and magazine catch all are located in the same relative positions and perform the same functions. The slide is markedly different in appearance. It is an inch longer, housing a full six-inch barrel. It is also thicker and heavier, with flat sides and top. There are lengthwise flutes across the top edges of the slide. Also, there are some really decent sights on the Omega slide. The front sight on our test pistol was a sharply undercut Patridge type; the rear a fully adjustable match quality sight with a plain square notch of generous proportions. First-rate sighting equipment.

The first test pistol I handled and fired was a tri-calibered Omega: .38 Super, 10mm Auto and .45 ACP. Accuracy with the .38 Super and .45 ACP barrels was excellent. The 10mm barrel produced the previously mentioned vertically elongated patterns on the target.

Subsequently, I got hold of another Omega and took it to the range with a wider variety of ammunition. This time, I had both 200- and 170-grain Norma ammunition, as well as Pro-Load 180-grain JHPs. The 200-grain Norma shot pretty well, but the 170-grain JHPs in the familiar woodgrain box from Sweden were erratic in their velocities and shot

the same vertical groups as had the first pistol. I have learned since that a large lot of this ammunition was imported and sold, only to find that it was not up to Norma's high standards. The Federal ammo people who import the stuff are understandably concerned, but there is little that they can do.

The second Omega pistol came to me only as a 10mm, no replacement barrels. It was a good bit more accurate as a 10mm than was the first. I believe it's fair to assume that it would have been just as good as the other one in other calibers, if the other barrels were available.

The Omegas have ported slides and barrels and that tends to tame the lusty recoil of the 10mm cartridge down to more manageable proportions. Since the Omega is a longer gun — at least, as we tested it — and has a heavier slide, we found it to be pretty easy to handle. The recoil impulse is sharp, but not so much so as in the Colt Delta pistol. This would be an easy gun for most shooters to handle, although it seems a bit on the heavy side to carry with any degree of comfort.

Remember my description of Joe Peters' vehement defense of his pistol at the beginning of this section? What he was pointing to was an incredible piece of photography that our printing system could not reproduce for your information. It was a series of high-speed X-rays of a Colt and an Omega in the act of firing. The trick camera lets you peer through the sides of the gun and clearly see the relative positions of the major components of the pistol in the various stages of the operating cycle.

It also lets you see the position of the bullet in the barrel as all of this is going on. What Peters was showing me was a picture of a bullet several inches forward of the Omega's muzzle...*and the breech still was locked firmly shut!*

In other words, the picture establishes clearly that the vertical stringing problem could not have been caused by erratic unlocking. It was a function of the erratic velocities of the bad batch of Norma ammo. Look at the accompanying chart and you'll see that the Norma 170-grain ammo has an extreme spread of velocities: well over 300 feet per second.

Now that you explain it, Joe, I *do* see what you are talking about.

SPRINGFIELD OMEGA FIRING TEST

Ammo Used	Extreme Spread	Average Velocity	Standard Deviation	Group Size
Norma 200-gr. FMJ	14	1276	5	2.596
Norma 170-gr. JHP	333	1279	81	3.426
Pro-Load 180-JHP	52	1313	16	2.447

Test performed at 25 yards with Ransom Rest
Groups are ten shots, center spread.
Oehler 33 Chronograph with Sky Screen IIIs used.

CHAPTER 4
RUGER GP-100:

*The GP-100 is a beefy fistful of sixgun.
It is available in blued steel and stainless
with either four- or six-inch barrels. There
are other lengths coming, with fixed sights.*

A S MAGNUM handgun cartridges go, the .357 has seniority by a comfortable margin. The round was introduced in 1935, offered in a superb Smith & Wesson revolver which was developed just to shoot it. Early on, the .357 was called the "world's most powerful handgun" and caught the fancy of the shooting public. In the post-war years, .357 ammo diversified considerably. At the present time, there's ammunition on dealer's shelves with bullets weighing from 110 to 180 grains. The handloader's bullet options run even wider. And damned little .357 magnum ammunition is mild.

While the original .357s were built on Smith & Wesson's massive N frame, many other recent models use lighter frames as starting points. When ammunition with much hotter-burning powders started wearing out the lighter guns, it became obvious the parameters had changed and the new .357 ammunition was a far cry from the original lead bullet load. A new system — a whole new gun, really

— seemed to be the order of the day.

Sturm, Ruger & Company introduced the GP-100 revolver three years ago. In that brief time span, the revolver has earned a reputation for great dependability and durability. It is a handgun conceived, designed and produced to be the best .357 magnum revolver in the world. I believe it is just that.

The GP-100 is a six-shot, double-action revolver chambered for the .357 magnum cartridge and equally capable of using the considerable array of available .38 special ammunition. GP-100s come in both four- and six-inch barrel versions. There are additional options available in a choice of blue or stainless steel and in two different six-inch barrel contours. The rear sight is a white-outlined, fully adjustable type mated to a unique user-replaceable ramp front sight. The sight notch mesures .135-inch rather than the customary eighth-inch (.125-inch) and the front sight blade mikes the same. The four-inch GP-100 weighs a hefty forty-one ounces and has an overall length of 9.375 inches, with a 5.52-inch sight radius.

That's the bare bones "tale of the tape" of the gun, but a long way from being the whole story. That this is a massive and ruggedly built DA revolver can be measured. How it handles — its balance, feel and pointability — are subjectives that can't be pinned down with ruler and scale. That takes the hands and eyes of experienced pistoleros. One of the first experienced handgunners to take up the GP-100 was Hal Swiggett, former Outstanding American Handgunner who described it in the 1987 *Gun Digest*. He was lavish in his praise for the gun. So was the late Skeeter Skelton.

It's easy to understand why. The GP-100 has the intangible feel and balance of a using gun. There aren't many sharp edges to annoy the shooter's hands. The butt of the revolver is a story in itself; it's one of two ergonomic features that make the GP-100 easy to use.

*Looking down on the massive frame of a GP-100, it's
easy to see where the strength and weight of the gun
come from. They weren't stingy with the metal when
they designed this strong and modern six-shot .357 mag.*

The Definitive .357 Magnum

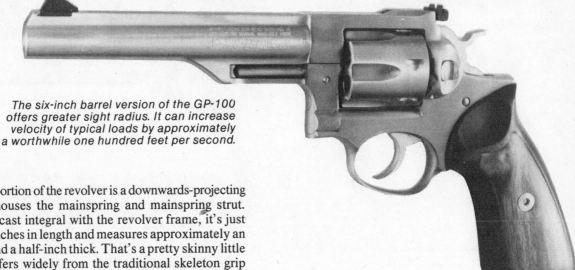

The six-inch barrel version of the GP-100 offers greater sight radius. It can increase velocity of typical loads by approximately a worthwhile one hundred feet per second.

The butt portion of the revolver is a downwards-projecting lug which houses the mainspring and mainspring strut. Investment cast integral with the revolver frame, it's just over three inches in length and measures approximately an inch wide and a half-inch thick. That's a pretty skinny little butt and differs widely from the traditional skeleton grip frame of other handgun models. There's lots of space around the lug and the unique grips use that space to shape a gun handle that's a delight to use. The matching grip panels are made of black rubber, except for the side inserts of fancy hardwood. The basic shape of the handle is rounded subtly like the Herrett's Jordan Trooper model incorporating the wide filler block behind the trigger guard. It differs in that it has a depression for the web of the hand at the top the backstrap. It feels good, invariably eliciting exactly that comment from the shooter who handles it for the first time.

The other handling feature that receives high marks from knowledgeable handgunners is the cylinder latch. This feature is hardly new; it appeared on the first Ruger double-action revolvers in the early 1970s. Unlike the cylinder latches used on other brands of revolvers, the Ruger latch doesn't project outwards from a flat side plate. It's nestled down into the curves of the left-side recoil shield. Instead of a pull or push mode, the Ruger cylinder latch rocks inward. In use, it's the easiest of them all to manage and has the added benefit of being completely out of the way.

So far, the Ruger company has not offered options on the GP-100's clever front sight system, but that probably will change soon. There are a number of front sight options available on the Redhawk and Super Redhawk revolvers and the GP-100's front sight is essentially the same thing.

On the muzzle end of the top barrel rib of the Redhawks and GP-100s, there is a flat-topped sight ramp. There's a crosswise slot milled into the ramp and a spring-loaded plunger fits into the ramp's front surface. The front sight itself fits into the slot, and is retained by the inner tip of the plunger. The involved contour of the sight's underside includes an undercut lug that matches the tip of the plunger. The effect is to have a front sight that snaps in and out in a second, but one that's retained firmly in exactly the same place on the gun. There is no change in the zero sight setting when the front sight is removed and replaced. While the GP-100 revolver offers no options on the unique system, the Redhawks are available with different colored front sights and even a gold bead, all readily changeable.

For a police service or field hunting revolver which will be used in varying light conditions, the implications are considerable. Imagine being able to change the color and shape of the front sights quickly in order to match the light and shooting conditions. Presently, the factory offers the GP-100 front sight in just a plain flat black, but they didn't put the interchangeable feature on the gun for nothing and options should show up soon. It is a *great* system.

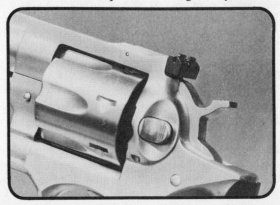

The Ruger cylinder latch won't slice open the inside of your thumb; it's out of the way in the recoil shield. The latch works when the shooter rocks it inward. It also works well with speedloaders; there is good clearance.

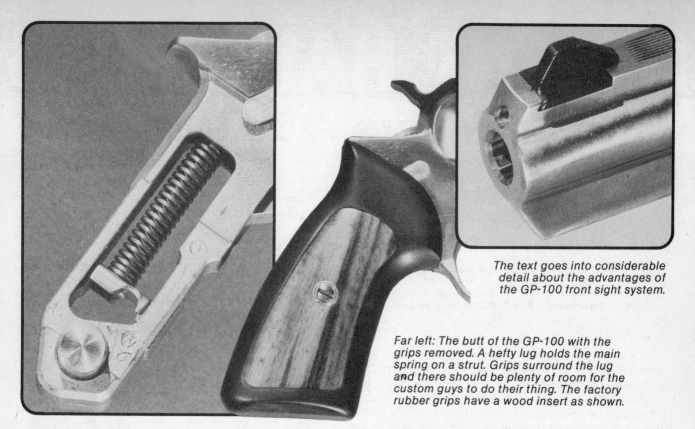

The text goes into considerable detail about the advantages of the GP-100 front sight system.

Far left: The butt of the GP-100 with the grips removed. A hefty lug holds the main spring on a strut. Grips surround the lug and there should be plenty of room for the custom guys to do their thing. The factory rubber grips have a wood insert as shown.

GP-100s are heavy, rugged revolvers. The entire impression is one of sturdy durability. Like all Ruger DA revolvers, the GP-100s have no sideplate. Instead, the lockwork comes completely out of the revolver when the trigger guard is removed. Complete disassembly for care and cleaning is easy and the clear instructions on how to do it come in a well-written manual. The buyer who follows the directions will learn to pull his revolver apart in a matter of seconds.

It's a safe revolver to handle. The GP-100 has a transfer bar system in which the force of the falling hammer is transmitted to the frame-mounted firing pin by way of a transfer bar. The transfer bar is linked to the trigger in such a way that the trigger must be pulled in order to align the transfer bar for firing. It's a positive safety feature. It's also one that promises to be durable.

While GP-100s have been in service for only a short few years, they show signs of turning out to be among the all time champions in the durability race. In a swing-out cylinder revolver, it's critical to have the relatively fragile crane and cylinder locked into place. If they get out of whack, the timing will be affected and both accuracy and safety will suffer. In the GP-100, the cylinder locks positively at both ends. The extractor rod exists for no other purpose than to kick out empty cases. It is not the axle on which the cylinder turns and it isn't even mounted centrally with the cylinder.

The entire revolver is bigger, stronger and tougher than it probably needs to be. In a manner of speaking, the bigger, et cetera, business is a function of the realization that the extra-heavy guns, for which the original .357 ammo was made, might have been better choices. While there is nothing mechanically or metallurgically unsound about lightweight .357 revolvers, the fact remains that heavier ones will last longer, particularly with today's hot loads. And

those loads and how they perform in the GP-100 are what sets the new Ruger off from other models.

On the basis of the first test sample of the GP-100 which I fired, I was impressed with the revolver in general. It was a blued four-incher and I did a fair amount of informal combat shooting with the gun in preparation for another DBI book. A bit later, I acquired a like gun made of stainless steel. That particular revolver turned out to be the most accurate .357 revolver I own. I used it to shoot the smallest group with hand loaded ammunition that I have ever fired with a handgun. The group measured .472-inch for six shots out of a Ransom rest at twenty five yards. No, it's not for sale. Ever.

A gun that phenomenally accurate makes the shooter wonder whether he just lucked out and got the best one they've ever made. To report such a level of accuracy without other test guns being included could be a little misleading, so I put together a test battery of four guns. They were the first two already mentioned, plus Dean Grennell's four-inch stainless steel model and a later six-inch stainless steel gun. With these guns, an assortment of ammunition and the handgunner's lie detector (Ransom rest), I made for the range.

What I found out convinces me that the subtitle of this section "The Definitive .357 Magnum," is completely justified. With four types of ammunition from a pair of makers, *the groups of all four guns averaged 1.572 inches!*

Each group was twelve shots and all six chambers were fired twice. I am fully aware that many revolvers will shoot excellent five-shot groups when the misaligned chamber which occurs in most of them is excluded. I prefer to shoot all six chambers, because that is what the majority of shooters will do. If a particular revolver has a bad chamber, that's a fact and needs to be reported as such.

In recent years, I have done a great deal of shooting with

the Ransom rest and I am thoroughly familiar with the method of using it. It is a marvelous piece of test equipment and one of the subtle advantages of having your gun held by Mr. Ransom's contrivance often goes overlooked. When handgun testing is hand-held, the shooters must look at the gun's sights. When it's machine-rested, the shooter can look at the target. This means he can observe the pattern that the shots make when they form a group on the target.

With a revolver, I am careful to shoot the chambers in the same order for each six shots. It's therefore pretty easy to see whether a particular chamber is throwing its shots away from the rest. To some degree, at least, this occurs with nearly all wheelguns of any make and model. It seems to be a natural fact of life of the revolver manufacturing process. I saw no sign of it whatsoever in the four GP-100s I tested. This suggests to me that the design of the revolver, its barrel dimensions and rifling specifications are right on the money. Further, it would seem the Ruger quality control is first rate.

Where ammunition is concerned, the GP-100 seems to prefer mid-weight bullets at rather high velocities. Having handloaded the gun rather extensively and with bullets from 110 to 180 grains, I am convinced the 125- to 158-grain range will perform better than both heavier and lighter types. It's also true that the middle-of-the-road weight — the 140-grainers from Speer, Sierra and Hornady — will out-perform all others when carefully handloaded.

I didn't handload for the test, but I did take along four different kinds of jacketed hollow-point ammunition from Horandy and Federal. The ammunition was Federal's 125-grain JHP and Hornady's 125-grain JHP, 140-grain JHP and 158-grain JHP. Firing twelve of each load from each of four guns takes a little time, but produces credible results. They are summarized in the included table.

When the superb Hornady 140 JHP load is combined with one of these revolvers, you have a figurative marriage made in heaven. The dial caliper tells me the four guns produced four groups averaging 1.09 inches. I think I'm justified in rounding it off and saying the revolvers will shoot one-inch groups with this ammunition.

If I had a single revolver that shot this well, I would report a damned fine gun. When four of them will do it, I have to say it is a fine model. Since the gun is durable and usable, as well as frighteningly accurate, it is without a doubt the definitive .357 magnum revolver — the standard for the future.

The GP-100 loves handloads, as this spectacular group suggests. In handload testing, a stainless four-incher was doing nearly this well with anyone's 140-grain slug.

Shown on a one-inch grid, this is a group fired with Hornady 140-grain JHPs. It measures .732-inch for twelve at twenty-five yards.

The same gun also liked Hornady 158-grain JHPs. This group was well inside the one-inch mark at .789-inch. All groups from No. 4.

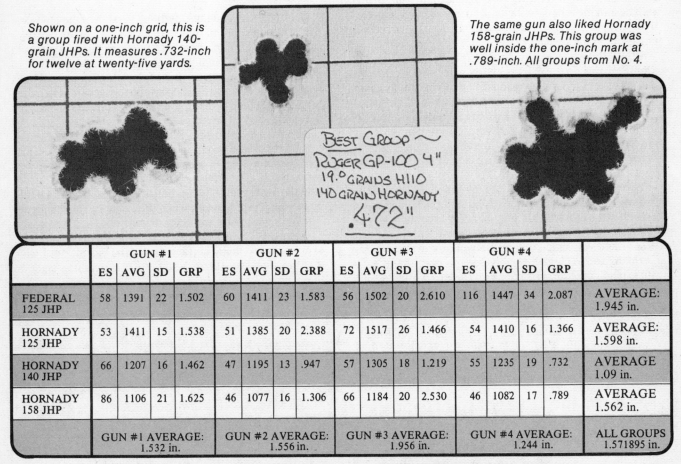

BEST GROUP ~ RUGER GP-100 4" 19.0 GRAINS H110 140 GRAIN HORNADY .472"

	GUN #1				GUN #2				GUN #3				GUN #4				
	ES	AVG	SD	GRP	ES	AVG	SD	GRP	ES	AVG	SD	GRP	ES	AVG	SD	GRP	
FEDERAL 125 JHP	58	1391	22	1.502	60	1411	23	1.583	56	1502	20	2.610	116	1447	34	2.087	AVERAGE: 1.945 in.
HORNADY 125 JHP	53	1411	15	1.538	51	1385	20	2.388	72	1517	26	1.466	54	1410	16	1.366	AVERAGE 1.598 in.
HORNADY 140 JHP	66	1207	16	1.462	47	1195	13	.947	57	1305	18	1.219	55	1235	19	.732	AVERAGE 1.09 in.
HORNADY 158 JHP	86	1106	21	1.625	46	1077	16	1.306	66	1184	20	2.530	46	1082	17	.789	AVERAGE 1.562 in.
	GUN #1 AVERAGE: 1.532 in.				GUN #2 AVERAGE: 1.556 in.				GUN #3 AVERAGE: 1.956 in.				GUN #4 AVERAGE: 1.244 in.				ALL GROUPS 1.571895 in.

ES: Extreme Spread of Velocities. AVG: Average Velocity. SD: Standard Deviation of Velocities.
All groups are twelve shots, machine-rested at twenty-five yards. Velocities measured
with Oehler 33 Chronograph & Skyscreen IIIs. Group size measured with dial caliper.

COMPETITION MODEL HIPOWER:

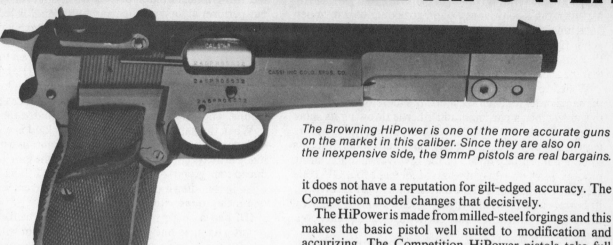

The Browning HiPower is one of the more accurate guns on the market in this caliber. Since they are also on the inexpensive side, the 9mmP pistols are real bargains.

THERE IS increasing interest in the 9mmP cartridge and the guns that shoot it. Part of this is because the new service pistol cartridge is the 9mmP; more is because there are so many fine new auto pistol designs available to American shooters. Inevitably, we will find ourselves shooting the 9mmP cartridge in matches and that means we'll be looking for pistols that are accurate enough to win. Naturally, we'd like to do it without floating a second mortgage on the house.

While there are a number of expensive and accurate 9mmP pistols on the market, there is one which currently can be purchased quite reasonably and which shoots exceptionally well. It's the Competition model of the venerable Browning HiPower. The guns are made by the FN works in Belgium and sold by several different importers in the United States. They are a good buy, typically on sale for as little as half the price of a Heckler & Koch P9s or Sig 210.

The basic HiPower needs little introduction. It was John Browning's last handgun design, built at the behest of the French in the early 1930s, but not adopted as their service handgun. It was used by a number of armies during World War II and was made both in Belgium by the occupying Germans and in Canada by the Commonwealth forces. It still is made in several locations around the world and still serves as the primary handgun of many police and military forces. A rugged, serviceable, easy-to-maintain handgun,

it does not have a reputation for gilt-edged accuracy. The Competition model changes that decisively.

The HiPower is made from milled-steel forgings and this makes the basic pistol well suited to modification and accurizing. The Competition HiPower pistols take full advantage of the solid construction and proven Browning design. Like its predecessor, the M1911 Colt, the Browning is a recoil-operated automatic pistol, using the basic tilting-barrel principle. It is also the first practical pistol using a detachable magazine of double-column design. The girth of that thirteen-shot magazine forced the designer to route trigger pressure around several corners with somewhat disastrous results where trigger pull is concerned.

Whoever designed the modified version of the HiPower that we'll consider in this chapter did his homework. Not only is the pistol accurate, but it is also an easy pistol to shoot accurately. Somehow, the grating trigger pull of so many typical HiPowers — even the late commercial ones — has been rendered down to an entirely acceptable, crisp, target-type pull. It breaks at around 3½ pounds and makes the pistol easy to shoot.

Shootability also prospers by virtue of the Pachmayr rubber grips which come as standard equipment on the pistol. They are the two-piece variety which completely surround the circumference of the pistol's butt. With the usual slightly tacky feel to them, bullseye shooters won't likely be needing the rosin can when they pick up this handgun. The designers also carried the down-to-business approach to the pistol's finish. It is a plain, no-glare matte black on every exposed metal surface except the barrel. But I wish that they had put a better and more practical rear sight on the pistol.

The sights are unique to this particular model. Below: The front sight is a plain triangle of steel mounted on the barrel weight to increase effective sight radius. The rear sight (box) is a sheet metal contraption that needs to be replaced with a Bo-Mar or other high-quality unit.

Accuracy On A Budget

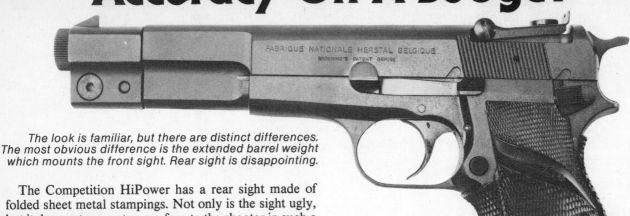

The look is familiar, but there are distinct differences. The most obvious difference is the extended barrel weight which mounts the front sight. Rear sight is disappointing.

The Competition HiPower has a rear sight made of folded sheet metal stampings. Not only is the sight ugly, but it does not present a rear face to the shooter in such a way as to afford him the clean sight picture that's essential to good shooting. Further, the sight adjustments are spongy and don't seem to be repeatable. Of all the features of an otherwise excellent handgun, the rear sight is clearly the worst.

The front sight is a plain Patridge-type blade. It is mounted on a barrel weight that adds weight where the rapid-fire shooter needs it most — out front. I didn't take the pistol completely apart to weigh the barrel weight, but it must add several ounces to the gun. In informal shooting sessions with the pistol, everyone who tried it felt muzzle flip was dampened perceptibly by the extra weight. Since the front sight is on the weight, rather than on the slide, the sight radius is increased effectively by a little more than an inch. Increased sight radius is always a plus where precision shooting is concerned.

Precision shooting is the intended use of this variation of the HiPower and the yardstick of tight groups is how the gun must ultimately be measured. At the range, we used Chuck Ransom's machine rest to evaluate the mechanical accuracy of the Competition model. The on-target results of the accurizing system used by the manufacturers are nothing short of amazing.

Basically, the Competition model is a factory "accuracy job," with the major components fitted precisely together. The slide has a tighter-than-usual fit to the frame, but the most noticeable change is in the positive and consistent lock-up. The special long barrels appear to be manufactured oversize, then fitted to individual guns. This is most noticeable when the pistol is field-stripped. It just doesn't

go back together as rapidly as does the standard HiPower. In addition to the tight fitting, there's a stiff spring in the top of the slide which puts consistent pressure on the barrel towards its muzzle end. In effect, the lock-up is a mixture of both traditional methods of accurizing a conventional auto — spring-loading and hard-fitting.

I had a stroke of good luck when the time came to do the evaluation of the Competition model on the range. A dealer friend wanted to find out exactly how the pistol would perform with a variety of ammunition. Instead of shooting a single specimen, as circumstance usually forces us to do, I had the loan of *four* new and unfired Browning Competition models. With such a sampling, the possibility of a single, exceptional gun is virtually eliminated.

When four guns are fired side by side, particularly under these conditions, the results establish more than which one is best. They also show how consistently the manufacturer is holding his quality control. You also can get an idea how well the ammunition manufacturer is holding *his* quality control.

The test was conducted as follows: Each pistol was fired in a Ransom Rest. In order to speed up the firing, we used a

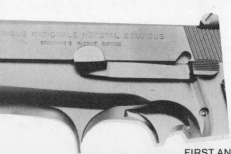

Out of the box, the pistol comes with functional grips made of rubber by Pachmayr. Below: Slide markings are as shown and there's no doubt where the guns were made. The basic HiPower design was John Browning's last. The pistol dates to before World War II, the early 1930s.

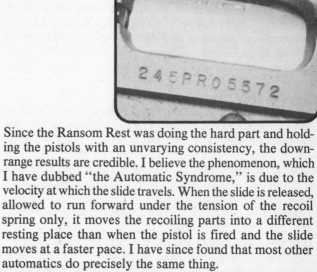

We were lucky enough to have four different examples of the Competition HiPower to work with in this test. One of the four was a bit more accurate than its fellows, but it will take averaging of the figures on the chart to the right to determine the winner. Right: Here are the serial #s of the guns.

pair of Ransoms mounted side by side on a sturdy plank which was, in turn, C-clamped to a solid concrete bench. The rests are spaced sixteen inches apart. A pair of chronographs (Oehler 33s, of course) were also used and their Sky Screens were mounted sixteen inches apart, some twelve feet downrange. The system allowed us to shoot two guns simultaneously.

The procedure used was to settle each pistol into the inserts with a few shots, then shoot a twenty-shot group at a target twenty-five yards distant with each type of ammunition. At the same time, the pistol in the other machine rest was getting exactly the same treatment. Chronograph summaries were recorded, the targets recovered and the next type of ammunition was tried. The twenty rounds of each type of ammunition were fired, using two magazines of ten shots each. When the ten different kinds of ammunition had been fired in the first pair of guns, they were retired and the second pair was mounted in the rests. We fired twenty rounds each of ten different kinds in four different examples of the Competition HiPower; a total of eight hundred rounds. And we developed an enormous amount of information.

Before going into a discussion of results, it might be well to examine a curious phenomenon that surfaced. I had experienced a bit of the same thing in the past, but a test like this really brought it to the fore. Apparently, many automatics shoot the first shot from the magazine to a different spot than the rest. Time after time, I watched the first shot from one of the Brownings land in a particular area of the target, only to be followed by nine more in a tight group in another spot. After reloading with the second magazine, the first shot was fired and impacted close to the first shot from the first magazine. The remaining nine went with the other nine, creating a group of two shots and another group of eighteen.

Sometimes the difference was barely noticeable and other times it was pronounced, but it was always visible to the machine rest operator who was watching the target.

Since the Ransom Rest was doing the hard part and holding the pistols with an unvarying consistency, the downrange results are credible. I believe the phenomenon, which I have dubbed "the Automatic Syndrome," is due to the velocity at which the slide travels. When the slide is released, allowed to run forward under the tension of the recoil spring only, it moves the recoiling parts into a different resting place than when the pistol is fired and the slide moves at a faster pace. I have since found that most other automatics do precisely the same thing.

It can't be avoided, but the automatic syndrome has serious implications. Consider the results of our firing with just one kind of ammunition, Hornady's 124-grain FMJ. The average group size for the four-gun test was 2.349 inches. If you exclude the first shots from each magazine and look at eighteen-shot groups, the average is 1.689 inches. Part of the reason that the syndrome is not widely known is because the pistol has to be quite accurate to start with. If it isn't, the group is so large that a slight divergence in group size on the first shot just doesn't make any difference.

These Brownings were exceptionally accurate handguns. The best group was a twenty-shotter that went into 1.453 inches. More interesting, perhaps, is the fact that the four handguns were *consistently* accurate. There was no clear winner and you would have to pore over the adjacent table in order to determine which of the four was the accuracy champion.

Above view shows a Competition Model with the slide locked back. Barrel weight is fitted as shown. The extra weight dampens muzzle jump to a helpful degree and the increased sight radius is useful.

The test also shows that modern 9mmP ammunition is both accurate and consistent from a statistical viewpoint. There was seldom a great deal of variation in the extreme spread of velocities or standard deviations. Both of these factors are widely regarded as indexes of consistency. Since we only tried ten out of possibly fifty different commercial loadings of the 9mmP round, and produced some excellent groups with them, it stands to reason that others may be just as accurate. Maybe more so.

It's easy to reach a conclusion after this sort of testing. The Competition HiPower is an accurate handgun, one of the best on the market for the 9mmP cartridge. Since it is also an eminently shootable handgun, needing only a match-type rear sight, and is priced hundreds of dollars less than its nearest competitor, the Competition model is one of today's best buys in a handgun.

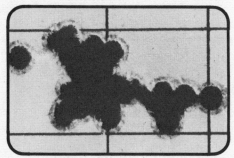

A typical group in the test series saw twenty go into 1.891 inches.

1) Test performed with 4 indentical Browning HiPowers (Competition Model).
2) Test firing at 25 yards in the machine rest (Ransom).
3) All groups are twenty shots, measured with a dial caliper. Centerspread.
4) ES = Extreme Spread; AV = Average Velocity; SD = Standard Deviation; GS = Group Size
5) Four guns, 10 kinds of ammo, 20-shot groups. 800 rounds fired.

	GUN A-572	GUN B-532	GUN C-563	GUN D-533	
ES	88	143	127	153	Rio 115JHP
AV	1213	1199	1219	1193	
SD	25	30	30	42	
GS	2.501"	1.694"	1.707"	1.489"	
ES	86	83	84	83	Federal 9BP
AV	1245	1232	1227	1217	115 JHP
SD	21	23	21	21	
GS	2.400"	1.891"	1.909"	2.454"	
ES	50	72	63	84	Hornady
AV	1168	1177	1170	1141	124 FMJ
SD	1137	1142	1142	1129	
GS	2.548"	3.180"	2.215"	1.453"	
	(18 in 1.894")	(18 in 1.761")	(18 in 1.776")	(18 in 1.324")	
ES	72	71	39	71	Federal Nyclad
AV	1137	1142	1142	1129	123 LHP
SD	20	16	9	18	
GS	2.795"	3.400"	3.698"	4.336"	
ES	49	57	56	99	Federal
AV	1351	1352	1377	1342	95 JSP
SD	13	15	15	26	
GS	3.841"	2.321"	2.327"	1.789"	
	(18 in 1.540")	(18 in 1.550")	(18 in 1.484")	(18 in 1.536")	
ES	93	51	46	57	Black Hills
AV	1162	1165	1170	1140	115 JHP
SD	20	11	10	14	
GS	2.910"	2.596"	2.648"	2.910"	
	(18 in 1.906")	(18 in 2.003")	(18 in 1.938")	(18 in 1.954")	
ES	38	37	42	35	CCI-Blazer
AV	1219	1238	1232	1205	115 FMJ
SD	11	10	12	8	
GS	3.876"	3.709"	3.389"	3.294"	
ES	63	44	101	65	Federal
AV	1137	1130	1127	1133	123 FMJ
SD	16	12	26	17	
GS	2.254"	1.772"	2.465"	1.876"	
	(18 in 1.530")	(18 in 1.640")	(18 in 2.043")	(18 in 1.394")	
ES	64	89	57	56	Remington
AV	1202	1200	1223	1179	115 JHP
SD	19	20	18	14	
GS	4.301"	2.753"	3.280"	2.940"	
	(18 in 2.463")	(18 in 2.019")	(18 in 2.625")	(18 in 2.034")	
ES	67	58	59	61	Hirtenberger
AV	1221	1231	1239	1204	123 FMJ
SD	14	14	15	15	
GS	4.398"	3.237"	3.184"	3.008"	

SMITH & WESSON'S .45s:

The new Smith & Wesson Model 645 is a modern pistol in every sense of the word. Double-action and made of fine quality stainless steel, the pistol will be popular for years to come. Note the ambidextrous safety lever.

WHEN A RUMOR persists as long as this one did, you have to give it at least a little credence. "Smith has a .45 ready to go," went the whispered tale. "They're just waiting for the right time to put it out." Maybe yes, and maybe no, but the fact remains that a lot of shooters were doing a lot of wishful thinking at the same time that S&W was doing lots of careful (and discrete) developmental work. All of this went on for more than two decades, but the result is now a fact of life: Smith & Wesson is currently marketing a pair of fine new autos chambered for the beloved .45 ACP cartridge.

They're damned good guns, as we shall presently see, but their background is also vastly interesting. When competitive shooting got back into full swing after World War II, NRA Outdoor Pistol ruled the roost. There was no IPSC, Steel Challenge, or Handgun Metallic Silhouette. Action shooting was yet to be invented and bowling pins customarily faced no greater threat than misaligned automatic pinsetters.

In the early 1950s, guns for the Outdoor Pistol circuit were monotonously alike: A High Standard or Match Target Woodsman for the .22 events, a K-38 Masterpiece

Smith & Wesson now offers the Model 645 with fully adjustable rear sight. It is essentially the same sight as found on the 9mmP guns. Adjustable sights find favor with most handgunners. These are protected by wings.

or Officer's Model Match for the centerfire and a much-accurized Colt Government Model for the .45 stage. At this time, Smith & Wesson was rebuilding under Carl Hellstrom and wanted a bigger share of the prestigious competition market.

They went after it and eventually secured a big part of two thirds of it, with guns for the .22 and centerfire stages. The guns that turned the trick were the Model 41 in .22 Long Rifle and the Model 52 in .38 Special. Designed from the ground up as competition pieces, both pistols were instant successes. For a while, a shooter had to have friends in high places in order to get one of them. Both the 41 and the 52 are still in the S&W catalog and both had an impact on the fortunes and prestige of the Massachusetts armsmaker.

S&W was primarily a revolver manufacturer and these two automatics, along with the Model 39 in 9mmP, estab-

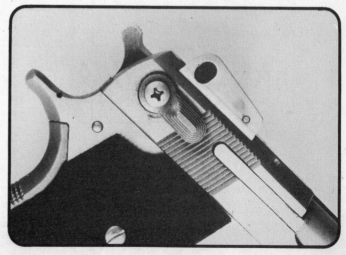

Big-Bore Autos From Springfield

Left side view of the 645 shows the safety and hammer drop lever on that side as well. Grips are made of an impact-resistant plastic material. Sights are the popular white-outlined rear and red ramp front. It handles well.

lished the company as a serious contender in automatic pistol production. When bullseye matches began to lose out to other kinds of shooting sports in the 1960s and 1970s, plans for the other competition pistol in .45 went on the back burner. Rumor has it that a privileged few top-flight shooters were treated to brief glimpses of a prototype gun at Camp Perry.

In the early 1980s, the market for handguns changed and the premium was on the high-capacity 9mmP. S&W answered that one with a series of good pistols based on the 39/59 model. When IPSC shooting demanded "major power" factors and certain police agencies became disenchanted with the marginal stopping power of the various 9mmPs, then it was time for a truly modern, domestic .45. And Smith & Wesson had a doozy.

Everyone must have heard about Tom Campbell's famous Superguns, I and II. The S&W exhibition shooter used hand-built prototype pistols in action-type matches of various sorts for several years. His performance with the guns was more than creditable and the question began to be heard, "When is S&W going to come out with their .45?"

They announced the gun in 1985 and quantity deliveries began in 1986, with the first guns going to police agencies. For the first few months, only fixed sight Model 645s left the plant. After the initial demand cooled a bit, another pistol went into production. It was called the IPSC Tenth Anniversary Model 745. The two pistols share the same basic frame and slide, but there are sufficient differences to make them completely different items.

The Model 645 is essentially a service pistol, intended for uniformed police, civilian security or purely defensive purposes. It is an all stainless steel handgun, except for the aluminum backstrap and high-impact synthetic grips. The 645s weigh 37.5 ounces and are 8.625 inches in overall length. The barrel is five inches long and the sights are a red ramp front and white-outlined blue steel rear.

Like the 9mmP pistols which preceded it in the scheme of things, the 645 has a first-shot double-action trigger system. On both sides of the slide, there is a lever which

The Smith & Wesson 745 is a single-action version of the 645. It has blued slide and was intended for IPSC shooting. The rear sight was designed by Wayne Novak, ace pistolsmith profiled in Chapter 19 of Handguns '89.

The 745 is an interesting pistol. It is the first gun to be offered by a major manufacturer solely for the IPSC game. The pistol comes with features that make it most competitive, right out of the box. The safety lever is larger and easy to use and the sights are much better.

functions as the hammer drop and safety. A passive firing pin safety blocks forward movement of the firing pin until the trigger is deliberately pulled. There's also a magazine disconnect safety which immobilizes the trigger-seat-hammer relationship when the magazine is removed. Carefully used, the 645 is as safe as any modern handgun.

Chambered for the robust .45 ACP cartridge, the 645 is a recoil-operated pistol, using a Browning-type tilting barrel lock system. In this pistol, the barrel locking lugs are much like the Browning HiPower in appearance and identical in function. It is a time-tested and thoroughly workable system.

The 745 is a different pistol, even though it is built on the same frame. The first 745s were the IPSC Commemoratives with special slide markings, but the currently-shipped pistols are just plain 745s. They are intended for competition shooting in action matches, with features that are used for that type of work. The most immediately noticeable difference is the blue steel slide. Since the frame is of the same stainless steel as the 645, the appearance of the 745 is an attractive two-tone. The 745 grips are crafted from walnut and they have a panel of sharp checkering on either side.

The 745s are single-action pistols, best for deliberate target shooting. On our test specimen, the trigger pull broke at about 3½ pounds, with a barely perceptible creep. The locking system is the same as the 645; so is the magazine, which holds eight rounds. To further the match shooting use of the 745, S&W included a few additional features. They are an oversized safety lever on the left of the slide and a well-shaped oversized magazine catch at the rear of the trigger guard.

Finally, the sights on the 745 are designed by custom pistolsmith Wayne Novak. The front sight is dovetailed into the front of the slide and has a sort of semi-ramped shape. The rear sight is the real delight. It's a hefty chunk of machined steel, which rises in a graceful slope from the top of the slide rearwards to the rearmost top edge, where a square notch has been cut. There is no step in the contour of the sight, as viewed from the side, meaning that there's no way the sight can snag a holster edge. Probably of more interest to the match shooter, the sight is not likely to injure the shooter's hand when he sweeps away a stovepipe jam in the course of a clearance drill. The Novak sights are beautifully designed and executed.

Both pistols are made to be used and used hard. They both have checkered panels on the frontstrap of the pistol and on the front of the recurved trigger guard. The controls are well located and the pistol is easy to use after a period of familiarization.

Inevitably, the 645 and 745 have to be contrasted with the Colt Government Model .45, the pistol which Americans have carried to war for most of this century. They are not greatly different from the Colt in size or weight. Both Colt and S&W have advocates, but there are features that commend both. The Colt rests on an incredible record of performance and the features that once sullied the performance potential of the gun are changing as Colt updates the seventy-plus-year-old design. The sights used to be microscopic, but new Colts have pretty decent sights. They even offer a stainless steel version of the old standby.

The main advantages of the S&W are lower cost (as compared to the stainless Colt) and an additional round in the magazine (for a total of eight versus seven). Most of all, the 645 version of the pistol has a modern double-action trigger system. The need for such a system is arguable in some circles, but there is no denying its popularity. The trigger on the 645 is as good as any of the modern DA autos

Left: The rear sight used on the 645 is fully protected by a pair of massive sheet steel wings. This means that the sight itself will be protected from blows, but also offers protection of the shooter's hands while firing.

Below: Tabulated results of the test firing of the three Smith & Wesson autos. They were quite alike in their accuracy potential, with all three averaging under the three-inch mark at twenty-five yards in a Ransom Rest.

and better than the majority. Any automatic chambered for the .45 cartridge has a certain amount of recoil and both Colt and S&W handle it well. Although the 645 sits a little higher in the hand and doesn't point as well as the Colt, I have the impression that felt recoil is a trifle softer in the S&W.

In 1988, Smith & Wesson unveiled a variation of the 645 which a great many shooters will appreciate. It's the same basic pistol with the addition of an adjustable rear sight. Protected by heavy sheet steel wings, the new rear sight is bulky, but does offer adjustments for both windage and elevation.

To evaluate the accuracy potential of the new S&W .45s, we took three of them to the range with a small assortment of ammunition. Firing six different kinds of ammunition in each of three different S&W .45s, we produced the results tabulated nearby. All firing was from the Ransom Rest at twenty-five yards and each of the groups is ten shots, or two magazines of five shots each.

The three autos are quite close to one another in accuracy potential. The 745 has been touted in some circles as a match accurate pistol, but it seems to be better for match shooting only in the sense of shootability, or handling characteristics. The level of accuracy is close to that of the 645s. All three pistols averaged just under three-inch groups, with a random assortment of ammunition. The three guns averaged 2.165 inches, with the only true match quality ammunition used, Federal's excellent 185-grain SWC Match.

The 645s are catching on with police agencies all over the country. It's easy to understand why. While they are large, heavy pistols, the S&W autos are fine, durable guns with unquestioned reliability and excellent accuracy. Good sights, good handling characteristics, stainless steel construction, eight-shot magazines and a wide network of warranty stations are all good reasons why sales of the new big-bore autoloader from Smith & Wesson will surely increase.

S&W 745

EXTREME SPREAD	VELOCITY	STANDARD DEVIATION	GROUP SIZE (in.)	
33	892	9	4.298	Federal 185-gr JHP
33	893	13	3.023	Hornady 200-gr C/T
21	796	8	2.011	Federal 185-gr Match
94	940	30	2.359	Samson 185-gr HV
52	846	15	2.571	Samson 230-gr Match
56	860	18	2.759	Black Hills 200-gr LSWC

Averge Group: 2.836 in.

#1 S&W 645

EXTREME SPREAD	AVERAGE VELOCITY	STANDARD DEVIATION	GROUP SIZE (in.)	
32	889	12	2.902	Federal 185-gr JHP
53	907	16	2.849	Hornady 200-gr C/T
43	821	13	2.567	Federal 185-gr Match
68	964	23	2.568	Samson 185-gr HV
25	880	8	2.478	Samson 230-gr Match
49	883	14	3.814	Black Hills 200-gr LSWC

Average Group: 2.863 in.

#2 S&W 645

EXTREME SPREAD	AVG VELOCITY	STANDARD DEVIATION	GROUP SIZE (in.)	
50	907	16	3.933	Federal 185-gr JHP
28	893	13	2.238	Hornady 200-gr C/T
35	816	8	1.917	Federal 185-gr Match
63	946	11	2.728	Samson 185-gr HV
79	861	17	3.763	Samson 230-gr Match
41	868	15	3.153	Black Hills 200-gr LSWC

Average Group: 2.954-in.

THE AUTOMAG II:

The newest Automag II to be released is this one. It has a four and a half inch barrel and the open-topped slide. Despite the .22 WMR chambering, the Automag II has a style that's much like the best of our combat autos. It is a slim and graceful automatic, a fun gun to shoot.

"AUTOMAG" has a vibrant sort of ring to it — a coined word that combines a pair of concepts near and dear to the hearts of America's shooters. Where is there a shooter whose ears do not perk up at the term "automatic?" Can anyone really resist "magnum?" Putting the two together in a single word caused a furor of sorts back in the early 1970s.

Harry Sanford set up and manufactured an elegant and shootable handgun in a special caliber, giving the gun the Automag moniker. The interest in the pistol was exceptional and the company did everything they could to meet the demand. But when financial problems developed, the .44 Automag disappeared from the shooting scene.

Harry Sanford did not. He owns and operates Arcadia Machine Tool (AMT) corporation, a successful gunmaking enterprise offering several best-selling models and a nifty reloader's scale. His most recently introduced gun borrows a name from yesteryear's handgun. It's called the Automag II.

The Automag II has one aspect of the gun market entirely to itself. It is the only autoloading pistol ever made to handle the potent .22 Winchester Magnum Rimfire (WMR) cartridge. It's even more significant in view of the fact that there are some serious engineering problems to resolve in any self-loading mechanism intended for the powerful rimfire.

The Automag II is the first-ever automatic pistol made for the .22 WMR cartridge. The long, skinny rounds are a bear to make feed, but the Automag designers did it. Crafted from high-quality stainless steel, the magazine holds nine of the high-pressure .22 rimfire cartridges.

Surprising
Stainless Steel Selfloader

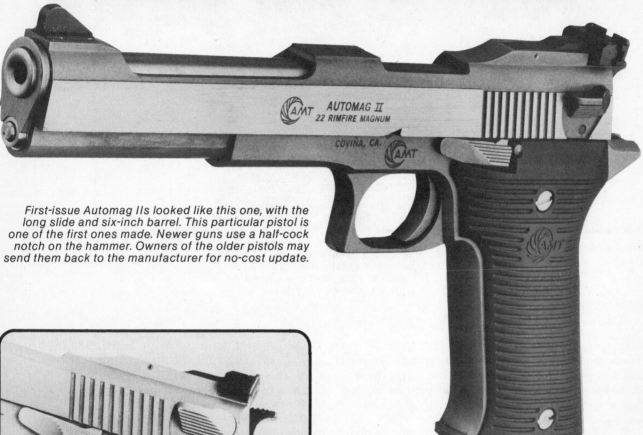

First-issue Automag IIs looked like this one, with the long slide and six-inch barrel. This particular pistol is one of the first ones made. Newer guns use a half-cock notch on the hammer. Owners of the older pistols may send them back to the manufacturer for no-cost update.

The cartridge is an interesting one. It was introduced by Winchester in 1960, intended to be a sort of super rimfire round with small-game hunting implications. As a rimfire, it would not be reloadable and the brass would only have to last for a single shot. While pressures in the new cartridge were pretty substantial, all firearms chambered for it were strong enough. Mostly rifles with locked breech actions, the guns easily stood up to the gaff. In handguns, the round worked equally well, since every one of them was a sturdy modern revolver.

The Automag designers faced a hell of a challenge. Beyond the pressure problem, they had to get around the difficulty inherent in feeding a long, skinny round with an outsized rim through a self-contained, single-column box magazine. I'll bet it took some head-scratching, but the resulting mag works perfectly.

The pressure problems are considerably more complex.

Left: The Automag II comes with grips the maker calls carbon fiber. They are plain flat black in color, with a series of highly functional gripping grooves. There are also custom wood versions available from Dave Wayland. Also note slow-but-sure, heel-mounted magazine catch.

You get good sights on the Automag II. The rear sight is seen above. It is a fully adjustable Millett with the typical winged-"U" rear notch. On the front of the slide is a ramp. The front sight has a panel of red material in the shape of a "T". It is a high-visibility system.

The pistol needed to be relatively inexpensive to make, ruling out some form of complex locking system. A simple blowback pistol would have worked, but only if the slide was heavy enough to slow the action until pressure dropped. That would have resulted in an awkward pistol far too heavy for most shooters.

Instead, the designer used what the company literature calls a gas-assisted action. It borrows somewhat from some earlier designs, but solves the high-pressure difficulty quite handily. Essentially, the Automag II uses the gas generated by firing to hold the action closed until pressure drops, then uses it again to float the cartridge out of the chamber.

The key to all of this is a cleverly designed barrel with some special ports cut into it. The Automag II barrel is cut from rifle stock like all other barrels, but it undergoes several extra steps in the finishing process. First, the barrel's breech end undergoes a special step in which it is lathe-turned to a smaller diameter for the first inch or so. It's deliberately thinned over the chamber.

In the next step, three sets of holes are drilled into the chamber area at a right angle to the bore. Each set has six holes, spaced sixty degrees apart. The set closest to the muzzle is at a point just ahead of where the mouth of a case will be when a round is chambered. The other two sets are farther down toward the base of the cartridge. Next, the maker installs a sleeve over the thinned rear section of the barrel. It fits in such a way as to leave a chamber between the sleeve and the original barrel. The sleeve closes off the chamber at the rear.

The effect of all this is to leave a space — or plenum chamber — surrounding the cartridge chamber, accessible through the series of vents. When a round is chambered and fired, the gas expands the case against the chamber walls and causes it to stick just a little in the lower two sets of holes. As the bullet exits the mount of the case, the gas pressure pushes against the bullet base but also follows into the plenum chamber via the top set of six holes. In that chamber, the gas expands through the lower sets of holes, pressing against the case that was just firmly locked in place. By this time the bullet has left the muzzle and the pressure has dropped. Residual pressure floats the cartridge neatly out of the chamber as the slide recoils to the rear.

The system is so ingenious that one wonders when it will be applied to other and more powerful cartridges.

Aside from the clever action, there are other features to commend the pistol. It has a positive safety lock, fully adjustable Millett sights, grooved carbon-fiber grips and a nine-shot magazine. The most recent innovation in the basic Automag II is the addition of two new versions. The original has a six-inch barrel, but there are new guns with 4½- and 3⅜-inch tubes. The shorter gun has a short receiver with a seven-shot magazine.

We examined a pair of the pistols for this chapter. One was the 4½-inch and the other was an original six-inch. In the time between the introduction of the two models, there has been a distinct improvement in the trigger pull. The newer gun had a downright respectable trigger. The original was pretty sorry.

It was therefore the new gun that went to the range for accuracy testing. Chuck Ransom, the machine rest man, could not help out this time, so I was forced to the bench and my personal marksmanship skill. I tried four different kinds of ammunition in the pistol, a solid and hollow-point each from Federal and Winchester.

This is certainly a consistent pistol. All four kinds of

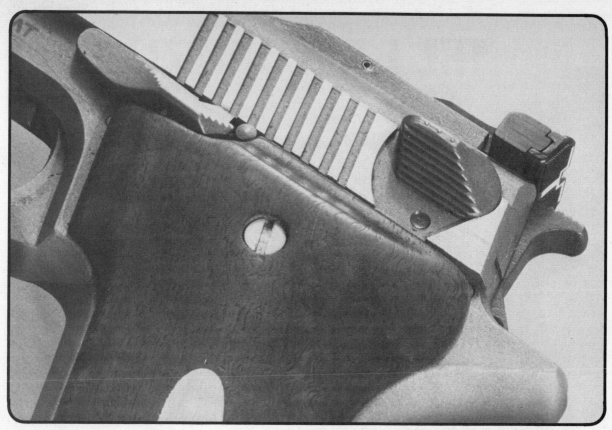

This Automag II has been fitted with fancy walnut grips from Dave Wayland. The safety is located on the slide and pivots up to the fire position. You can also see the conventional slide stop. This is a slim and graceful gun to handle and shoot. There'll be a seven-shot gun soon.

ammunition would put five shots into a group approximately 1.25 inches to 1.50 inches in diameter at twenty-five yards. That's decent accuracy for any handgun. It's interesting to note that, even out of the short Automag II barrel, the velocities are well over 1100 fps. The fastest load, Winchester's FMJ, clocked 1230 fps.

Adding up the inches and ounces of the gun doesn't produce a sum total impression. It is a delightfully slim and graceful piece that sits well in the hand and points naturally. That is the sort of thing that defies measurement. The current retail price is under three hundred bucks and assuredly well worth it.

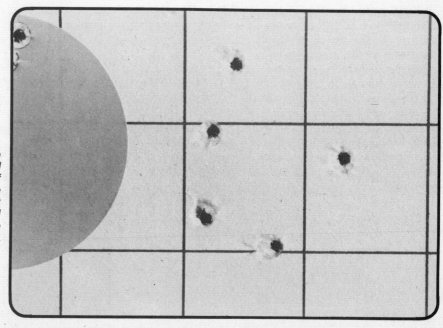

At the range, author settled the little .22 WMR over sandbags and carefully touched off a series of five-shot groups. Group average is about an inch and a half. Not bad at all. First-issue pistols had trigger pulls that did not make precise bench shooting easy to do.

THE L.A.R. GRIZZLY:

The pistol is awesome in its aura of raw power. Here's a big, brawny automatic for off-the-shelf ammunition. The Grizzly is essentially a stretched .45 M1911A1. It shoots the powerful .45 Winchester magnum cartridge.

IT WAS a cartridge without a home. The .45 Winchester magnum was slated to be the primary caliber in the Wildey pistol. Primary caliber, but not the only caliber, since Winchester also intended to market 9mm Winchester magnum ammo for use in the big Wildey gas-operated pistol. For one reason or another, the Wildey hasn't made it and the two cartridges remained without a launching platform. In the case of the .45, Thompson/Center helped somewhat by manufacturing a few Contender barrels.

But the .45 Winchester magnum cartridge held too much alure for shooters to just go away. L.A.R. Mfg., of West Jordan, Utah, introduced a handgun for the cartridge several years ago and it appears that the gun and cartridge are here to stay. The best part of the system is probably the pistol itself. Rather than fiddling with the trials and tribulations of a brand-new handgun design, L.A.R. designers just picked up on an idea that's been around since 1911.

In concept, the massive Grizzly pistol is a stretched M1911 .45 automatic. The stretching process occurs in the receiver area, where the front-to-back dimension of the grip had to be longer. The increase is because the .45 Winchester magnum cartridge is so much longer than the standard .45 ACP. The Winchester magnum is really a magnum, with a case nearly as long as the popular revolver magnums. Obviously, that's a healthy dimension.

Some of the parts in the Grizzly will interchange with their opposite numbers in the 1911, but the major components are different. The resemblance of the Grizzly to the Colt is nonetheless startling: the familiar contours of

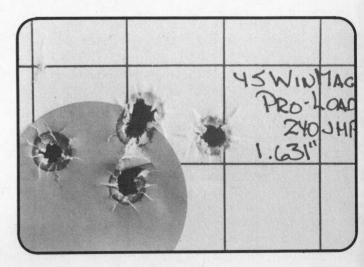

45 WIN MAG PRO-LOAD 240 JHP 1.631"

This group measures slightly more than an inch and a half, center to center, using 240-grain jacketed hollow-point Pro-Load ammunition.

An Oversized .45 And Its Undersized Groups

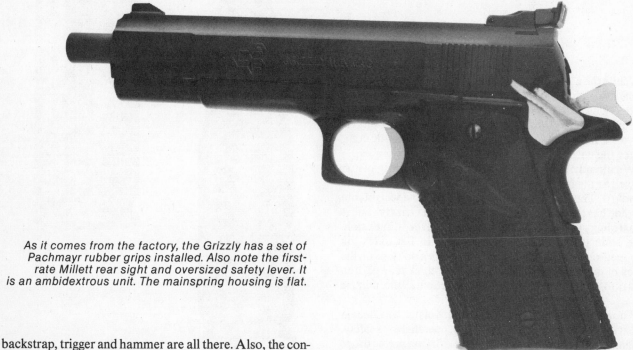

As it comes from the factory, the Grizzly has a set of Pachmayr rubber grips installed. Also note the first-rate Millett rear sight and oversized safety lever. It is an ambidextrous unit. The mainspring housing is flat.

backstrap, trigger and hammer are all there. Also, the controls are in the same place and do the same things — safety, slide stop, magazine catch.

The Grizzly is a big pistol, even in its smallest six-inch-barrel form. That version of the pistol weighs fifty-one ounces and stretches to 10½ inches overall. There are also eight- and ten-inch barrel versions of the basic pistol. Since the trigger reach is quite lengthy, most shooters will probably opt to shoot the pistol in two-handed grasp. Surprisingly, the recoil is relatively mild. It's far easier to shoot than the typical .44 magnum revolver of the same dimensions.

From a technical standpoint, the most interesting aspect of the Grizzly is the manner in which the designers took the basic tilting-barrel, recoil-operated system and adapted it to a heavy-recoiling, high-pressure magnum cartridge. John Browning, who came up with the original idea, likely would be astonished. Not only does the pistol function in satisfactory fashion, but also is quite accurate.

The Grizzly comes from the maker well equipped to head for the hunting field. The grips are Pachmayr rubber wrap-around type. Since the grip reach is so long, the Pachmayrs used are a modified version of the Government Model. The mainspring housing is the flat type, also a Pachmayr rubber unit. A typical Colt-style safety lock, which sweeps down to fire, has a lever on the right side of the pistol as well as on the left. Like the M1911, the slide stop is on the left, but because of the extended receiver this part features a lengthened thumbpiece.

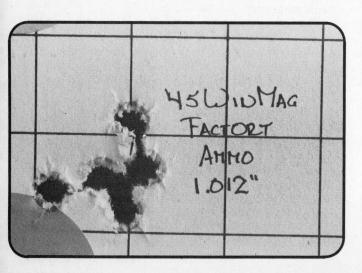

45 WinMag
Factory
Ammo
1.012"

Slightly more than an inch across is the happy result of this group using factory loads. Rounds were fired from braced position on concrete bench.

Left, an interesting variation on the .45 Winchester magnum is the new .357/.45 Grizzly Win. Mag. It is a wildcat, made from 7mm BR brass, necked up to take bullets of .357-inch diameter. Naturally, it shoots fast and flat. Right, only two loadings of .45 Winchester magnum are available on the market. This is Pro-Load's 240-grain JHP version, featuring a Sierra bullet. There's power to spare in this load. The accuracy is also quite high.

While the early prototype pistols had an adjustable rear sight, it wasn't up to the violent recoil of a magnum autoloader. The current production version of the gun mounts one of the sturdy Milletts, nicely integrated into the receiver. A matching front ramp at the front of the slide completes the ensemble.

We already have mentioned the recoil of the big pistol, as well as the fact the gun is deliberately heavy in order to handle it. The receiver carries a good bit of the weight, but the side has a lot more. Investment cast, the Grizzly slide is a real chunk of iron. It is bigger in almost every dimension. The slide is flat on top, transitioning to flat sides via scooped-out flutes on the edges. There are also steps on the sides of the slide taking the excessively thick rear portion down to a slimmer, more graceful section in the muzzle area.

The trigger pull on the borrowed test pistol was heavy, but acceptably clean. All other manual operations — safety, magazine catch, etc. — were positive. The magazine drops clear of the pistol when the catch is depressed.

While the barrel of our test pistol is six inches long, the slide is somewhat shorter and leaves a full inch of barrel beyond the barrel bushing. The company offers a barrel with slots milled into the exposed portion to function as a recoil brake of sorts. The pistol I fired was the shortest and presumably the lightest in the Grizzly litter. It wasn't difficult to manage the recoil and I don't see much point to the brake.

In the several years they've been on the market, Grizzlies have been offered with conversion units for several calibers. The 9mm Winchester magnum chambering died and the primary cartridge is the .45 maggie. Before discussing the performance of that round, we need to take a quick look at a super new innovation in cartridges, presently available in the Grizzly.

It is the bottlenecked .357/.45 Grizzly Win. mag. Original brass was made from .308 Federal stuff, but it would seem that necking up 7mm BR Remington to accept .357 bullets would accomplish the same thing. In either case, the resulting cartridge is a short, stubby, bottlenecked performance round that will take nearly all bullets of .357-inch diameter. The capacity of the case is such that some bullets may be driven perilously close to the two-grand mark (2000 feet per second). Even a .357 140-grain hollow-point at nearly 1700 fps from a carryable automatic pistol makes a lot of sense.

For our test-shooting purposes, the only available gun was the plain .45 Winchester magnum. Testing of that

caliber tends to be rather abbreviated because there isn't much choice of loads on dealers' shelves. Since the cartridge was announced, Winchester has offered only one load, a 230-grain full metal jacket. Just this past year Pro-Load ammunition of Burbank, California, introduced a 240-grain hollow-point.

Testing was hand-held due to the non-availability of Ransom Rest inserts. Nevertheless, by using the solidly-braced sitting position off of a concrete bench (as described in Chapter 15) I was able to shoot the big automatic with commendable accuracy.

The factory 230-grain hardball load, which uses what appears to be the standard .45 ACP bullet, went across the chronograph screens at 1138 feet per second, with a standard deviation of 12. The Pro-Load round, using the 240-grain Sierra JHP, was hotter at 1380 with a standard deviation of 14.

The best news is that both were very accurate. The Pro-Load put five in 1.631 inches, but the factory ammo went a tight 1.012 inches. There are lots of so-called match .45 autos that won't do that well.

I can't find much to fault about the Grizzly. It's accurate; it handles well; it's well made and it shoots some powerful rounds. Considering the second caliber option available via the company-supplied conversion units, the Grizzly makes a lot of sense. I hope to be able to work with the cartridges and guns more in the future.

Section Two

HANDGUN AMMO & RELOADING

THE GUNS, THEMSELVES, ARE NOTHING WITHOUT AMMUNITION AND TODAY'S HANDGUNNER HAS MORE AND BETTER AMMUNITION TO USE THAN EVER BEFORE. HE CAN CHOOSE FROM A WIDE VARIETY OF FACTORY AMMUNITION. HE ALSO CAN ROLL HIS OWN, USING A VARIETY OF FINE HANDLOADING TOOLS AND CHOOSING FROM A VARIED ARRAY OF COMPONENTS. IN EITHER CASE, TODAY'S SHOOTER ENJOYS LOTS OF OPTIONS, WHICH WE'LL SURVEY IN AN INITIAL CHAPTER ON HANDGUN AMMUNITION IN GENERAL.

ONE OF THE MORE INTERESTING DEVELOPMENTS IN HANDGUN AMMUNITION IS THE INTRODUCTION OF TWO DIFFERENT BRANDS OF SHOT LOADS FOR THE OMNIPRESENT .45 AUTO; WE'LL LOOK AT BOTH. WE'LL ALSO DO AN IN-DEPTH EVALUATION OF EVERY FACTORY LOAD FOR THE .41 MAGNUM, FIRING EACH IN FOUR DIFFERENT HANDGUNS. ANOTHER CHAPTER WILL BE A POTPOURRI OF INFORMATION ON RELOADING TOOL DEVELOPMENTS.

THE FINAL CHAPTER IN THIS SECTION IS UNUSUAL AND INTERESTING. TWO AUTOMATIC PISTOL CARTRIDGES ARRIVED ON THE HANDGUN SCENE WITHIN THE PAST FEW YEARS AND THE COMPETITION BETWEEN THEM IS EXCEPTIONALLY INTERESTING. THEY ARE THE 10MM AUTO AND THE .41 ACTION EXPRESS.

HANDGUNS 89

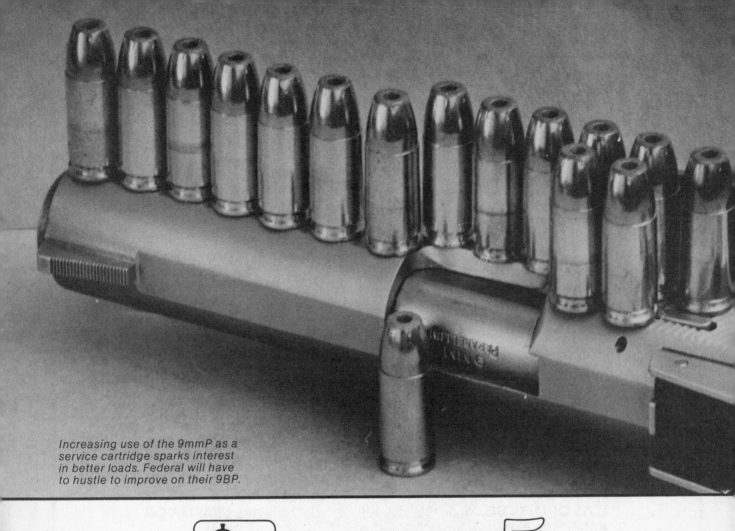

Increasing use of the 9mmP as a service cartridge sparks interest in better loads. Federal will have to hustle to improve on their 9BP.

CHAPTER 5
HANDGUN AMMO SURVEYED

An Overview Of Ammunition For This Year

IF WE have it good in this Golden Age of Handguns, we aren't doing so bad where handgun ammunition is concerned. Never before has there been so much variety in available factory ammunition, new calibers and even reloading components. Today's handgunner can buy or make a wide variety of different fodder for his pet handguns.

A good bit of the credit for all of this variety in handgun ammunition comes from the pioneering efforts of a fellow named Lee Jurras. Jurras was the first contemporary ammo maker to see the handgun as a true high-performance firearm. Twenty years ago, his Super Vel ammunition company produced a line of high-velocity handgun ammunition in a variety of calibers. Jurras reached these velocities by using bullets of somewhat lighter weight and smaller diameter, plus lots and lots of powder. He was a pioneer, responsible for a definite trend in the industry.

Some of the ammunition sold today is for exotic new calibers, but the majority is for the same popular old favorites. Two decades or so back, most of the big makers offered

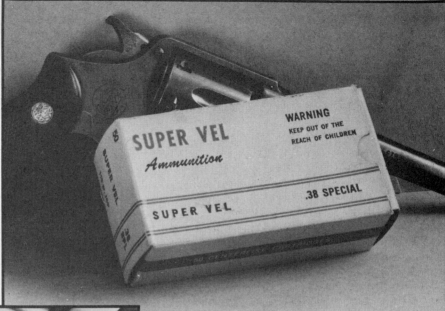

Sequence of operations in making the exotic new 357/45 Grizzly Winchester magnum. From the left: 7mmBR brass; 7BR necked to .357; necked-up case run through sizer die; trimmed to length; loaded with an appropriate slug.

maybe four or five loadings of the most popular calibers, such as the .38 Special. Last year's catalog shows Remington offering thirteen different .38 Special loads, from a 95-grain ultra-speedy JHP to the old standard 200-grain lead roundnose. Still, in just .38 Special, the variety from Winchester includes three different weights of Silvertips plus nine other kinds.

Where once there was one kind of 9mmP ammunition offered by each of the makers, demand has forced them to broaden the variety. Federal has a current advertisement showing two rows of different 9mmP ammunition. CCI and Hornady offer gobs of different loads, five or six each, and the rest of the makers are just about the same.

Even the bellerin' magnums have a broadening variety of loads. You can buy factory-loaded .44 magnums with 180-grain bullets from several makers and weight options range upward to the hard-kicking 300-grain JSP load from Barnes. Once we were concerned about the future of the .41 magnum, but Chapter Seven of this book reports favorably on the status of the cartridge, as interpreted by ammunition makers' offerings.

The message is clear. Handgunning is here to stay and the people who make ammunition are fully — and commercially — aware of that fact. I believe the widening variety of available handgun ammunition also stems from greater use of economically-produced ammunition made in basement and garage handloading shops from Maine to

California. With so many new handgun shooting sports, the ammo makers have to hustle to keep up.

The most significant part of the ammo story for this year is the sudden wide availability of 10mm ammo. For several years, we've had two kinds of Norma, period. Now there are three other makers offering six other kinds of ammunition. This interesting cartridge — and its competitor, the .41 Action Express — are the subject of a separate chapter.

There were several new handgun chamberings offered in the course of this year, but only one of them has factory ammunition made for it. That's the new 9mm Federal. It is a unique version of the basic 9mmP. The basic difference between the regular 9mmP and the 9mm Federal is simply that the latter round has a rim of just about the same dimensions as the .38 Special. In other words, it is a parabellum with a revolver rim. The rim makes the cartridge totally unsuitable for use in autos. It will chamber and fire in a special Charter Arms revolver and a derringer from American Derringer Corp. There also may be a Ruger for it at a later date.

You might be tempted to pass off the cartridge as a sort of 9mm Auto Rim, but the headspacing arrangements in the

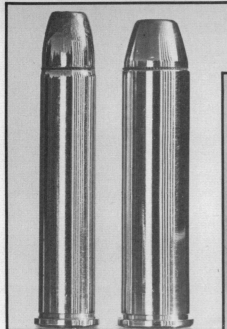

Left: More variety in cartridges today than ever before as evidenced by Elgin Gates' newest semi-wildcat. The new .445 Super Mag on the right, compared to the .357 Super Mag (.357 Maximum). Virgin brass is available.

Above: Thousands of rounds of .38 Special go downrange every year and lots of them are in bullseye matches. A hard-working researcher could probably come up with a hundred different factory loads for the old favorite.

There is also no shortage of different loads for the old .45, either. Remington makes a special version of the 185-grain JHP for the police. Sad to say, they need it.

revolvers won't allow the use of anything but 9mm Federal ammunition — you can't use 9mmP in any form. The available ammunition is loaded pretty hot and its right there with 9mmP ammunition if you realistically consider the barrel lengths involved. We'll have to wait and see how this one does in the marketplace. I haven't put any of this stuff over the chronograph screens yet, but I doubt that it will out-perform the hotter .38 and .357 loads.

Another interesting new chambering is the .357/.45 Grizzly Winchester magnum, as discussed in the section of Chapter Three dealing with the L.A.R Grizzly pistol.

The cartridge is a bottleneck design, with a case length from 1.295 to 1.303 inches. When produced at the L.A.R. plant, they start with .308 Win brass by Federal, cut off the surplus, size it in the .357 GWM die, ream the necks with a .3535-inch reamer and go on to load it. The .357 GWM can be made from 7mm BR Rem brass by expanding the mouths to .357-inch, resizing in the .357 GWM die and trimming to 1.300 inches.

Cases made from the 7mm BR Rem take a small rifle primer, while those from the .308 Win and similar calibers use the large rifle primer. Usually, there is no need to inside-ream case necks when making the .357 GWM from 7mm BR Rem brass. After loading, the diameter at the case neck should not exceed .382-inch, the diameter of the L.A.R. factory load at that point.

Out of the Grizzly, the .357 GWM shows fine accuracy and it will put a 160-grain bullet out of the ten-inch barrel at 1919 fps, according to the chronograph. Factory rating on that load is 1724 fps. I think this is one of the most promising hunting loads to come along in many a year.

Another new wildcat which uses a similar approach is the 9mm Action Express, or 9mmAE. This round stems from the new .41 Action Express, a rebated rim cartridge intended for high-capacity automatics. .41 Action Express brass is exceptionally strong, particularly in the important head area. Necking down to .355-inch produces a stubby little case with enough capacity to hustle typical bullets downrange at velocities over 1600 feet per second. Since the case is so strong, there is not the usual concern about blowing the case head over the feed ramp.

Elgin Gates, out there in Idaho, is wildcatting once again. His most famous effort was the .357 Super Mag, termed the .357 Maximum by the ammunition makers. That round was a stretched .357 magnum, fired in special revolvers with extra-length cylinders and frames. This time Gates took the same concept and applied it to the .44 magnum, producing something called the .445 Super Mag. Handloading members of IHMSA are spared the tedious business of making brass, since Elgin ordered ample supplies of factory stuff from one of the big brass mills. The early reports on the cartridge show a lot of promise. A .41

version, the .414 Super Mag, currently is under development.

Apart from completely new cartridges, wildcat or factory, we have several brand new loadings in the old familiar rounds. One of the best is from Federal. It is a load that establishes quite clearly the fallacy of an oft-repeated litany in the ammo business — the 9mmP won't shoot.

For reasons that defy logical analysis, it is widely accepted that the 9mmP cartridge is somehow inherently inaccurate. Until fairly recent times, we haven't had a lot of match experience with the cartridge. But the new U.S. service pistol is the M9 Beretta and it is a 9mmmP. The service pistol matches will be fired with 9mmP ammunition soon and the bullseye shooters won't settle for poor ammo. Federal introduced a 9mmP load that will fill the bill.

It is called 9mm Luger Match (coded 9MP) and features a 124-grain jacketed truncated-cone bullet at velocities just under 1100 feet per second. The stuff is exceptional. I fired twenty-shot groups from several of my more accurate 9mmP pistols and got clusters measuring just over an inch. The best, from an H&K P9, was a superb 1.023 inches. This is a convincing reply to the argument that the cartridge is deficient.

We also have a considerable interest going in high performance ammunition for defensive purposes. All of the ammunition companies experiment with various types of hollow-point bullet designs. Federal has gone one better by breathing new life into the Hydra-Shok bullet concept. This bullet had a hollow-point cavity with a central post formed in the swaging process. The post protrudes from the bottom of the cavity and tapers toward the tip of the bullet. The theory behind this complicated design contends that fluid-filled tissue will fill the cavity upon impact. It's likely to be under considerable pressure, which presses inward on the middle post from all sides. The post is equally stabilized and cannot collapse, therefore forcing the pressure outward on the wall of the bullet. The result is expansion. Federal will have the ammunition on dealer's shelves by the time you read this, but none was available when we went to press. It will be made in several of the popular pistol calibers.

If you want violent, almost explosive, results from your defensive ammunition, consider Joe Zambone's MagSafe ammo. It is made by pouring an especially developed epoxy into a bullet jacket containing a number of shot. The number and size of the shot varies with the caliber, but the epoxy hardens to form a hard matrix. It is a light bullet, which Zambone loads to some impressive velocities. On impact, the bullet fragments with the force, creating a large cavity and deep penetration. It's pretty impressive ammunition and suffers only from the fact that it isn't widely

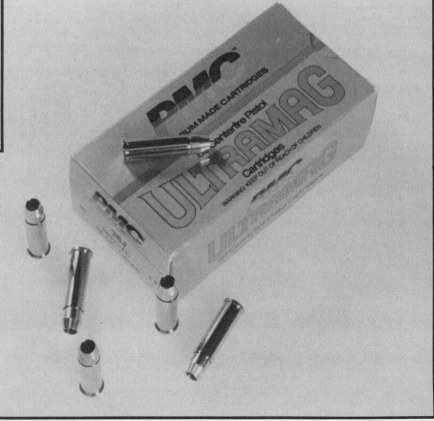

Based on the experiments of Abraham Flatau, the PMC Ultramag load uses a tubular bullet. There is a plug at the bottom of the bullet in order to seal the bore, but it drops away in flight. The tubular bullet penetrates well in tissue. It's said to be an effective combat load.

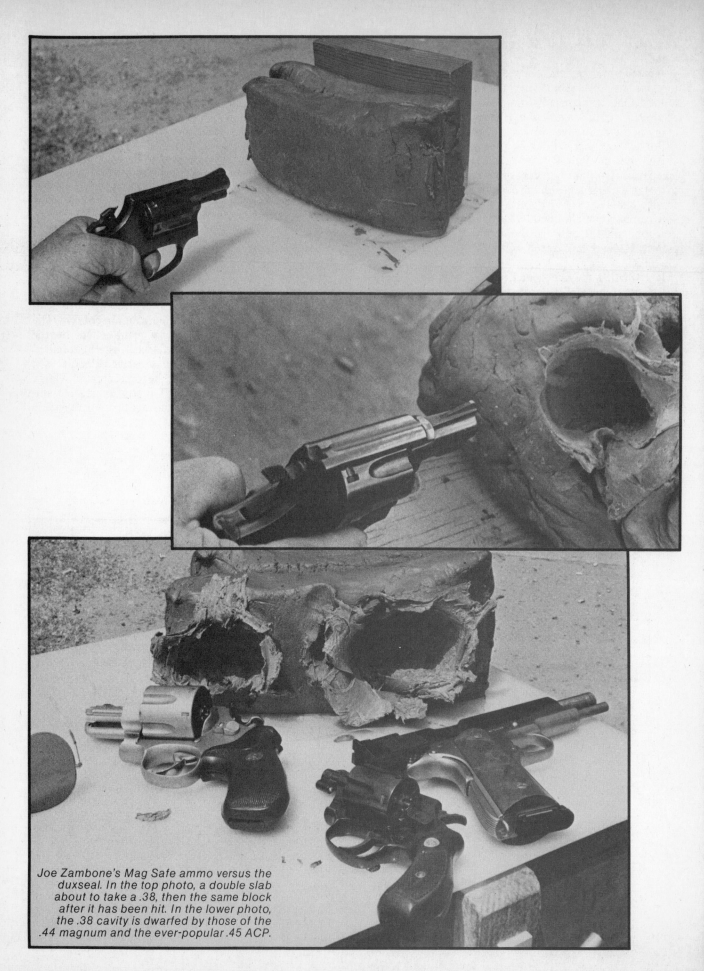

Joe Zambone's Mag Safe ammo versus the duxseal. In the top photo, a double slab about to take a .38, then the same block after it has been hit. In the lower photo, the .38 cavity is dwarfed by those of the .44 magnum and the ever-popular .45 ACP.

distributed and is expensive. Each bullet is virtually made by hand.

Glaser Safety Slugs are still here. The little clear plastic six-packs are in every gun store I visit these days. They have been simplified and improved since the early days, but they still have the ceramic nose cap over a bullet jacket full of fine shot. The early Glasers suspended the shot in aqueous teflon, but shot in the current ammo is teflon-coated. Glasers are a bit expensive, too.

The next type of ammunition to look at is not so expensive. It's PMC's Ultramag with an unusual tubular bullet. Made competely from bronze, the bullet is a perfect tube, except for the nose area, which has an ogive of sorts for in-flight stability. The base of the tubes has a light plastic cap riding over the powder. This feature insures the bore will be obturated or sealed, until the projectile exits the muzzle, at which time the base cap will drop away.

Since the bullet is light, it can get up a good head of steam with conventional powder charges and pressures. Upon impact, the bullet acts like a cookie cutter and slices out a long, cylindrical section of tissue. Presently available only in .38 Special and .44 Special, the tricky little bullets avoid the bullet ban because they won't penetrate a policeman's vest.

There is a great deal of thought and effort going into this business of combat ammunition for the police and security

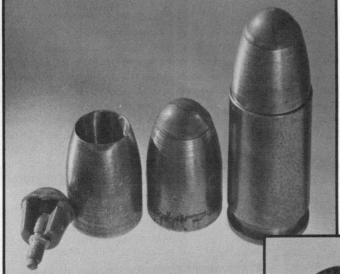

forces. Much of the dogma influencing handgun ammunition design is in the process of review. Some influential people in large law enforcement agencies are slowly changing their position on what works and what doesn't.

We have long been told to choose handgun ammunition that will deliver the largest temporary wound cavity. In this light, velocity is king and the lightweight hollow-points that turn up balloon-shaped cavities in ballistic gelatin are often chosen. But it is a fact that many instances occur where that kind of ammunition doesn't work. To summarize the results of a recently-conducted seminar on the matter, it now appears the bullet that penetrates to and hits the central nervous system, doing as much tissue damage in the process as possible, will be the best choice. The pendulum swings toward penetration.

One of the best kinds of ammunition on the market for this purpose is the exotic GECO Action Safety (GAS) 9mmP round. It is sold in the United States as the BAT (Blitz Action Trauma) bullet, made in West Germany by GECO, in response to a mandate of the government. It is really unusual stuff.

The bullet is all copper and weighs 86 grains. Profiled like a conventional round of ball ammunition, the BAT bullet is different inside. It has a cavity that passes completely through the bullet and is sort of umbrella-shaped in cross-section. The cavity is plugged with a plastic cap, the larger end of which is toward the muzzle. When the round is fired, the bullet heads down the bore while gas pressure flows through the central hole and forces the plug out ahead of the bullet. Just a short distance away from the muzzle, the asymetrical plug drops away.

The sharp-edged BAT bullet continues at approximately 1400 fps. It will fold back slightly when it hits tissue, creating a small rotary saw of sorts. Sharp, hard fingers slice through all kinds of material. The BAT bullet has seen extensive use in South America, where it earned an awesome reputation for performance. One of the side

The Geco Action Safety (GAS) bullet is arguably the best of all the performance 9mmPs. Capped with a plug of plastic, the bullet is hollow. Made of solid metal, the bullet weighs 86 grains and travels at 1400 fps.

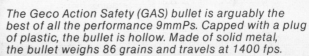

The white box .38 Special load from several years ago was one of the first of the performance loads for law enforcement. The new 147-grain JHP in 9mmP comes in a plain brown wrapper. The Feds are looking it over.

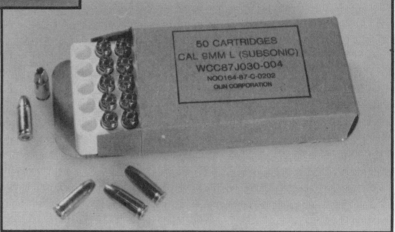

The sketch of the GAS bullet shows how the German import works. The key is the plastic nose plug, which is not symetrical. GENCO of North Carolina makes special bullets for handloaders. They have hollow points and shot-filled cores. No ricochets!

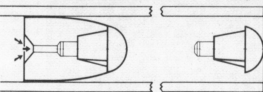

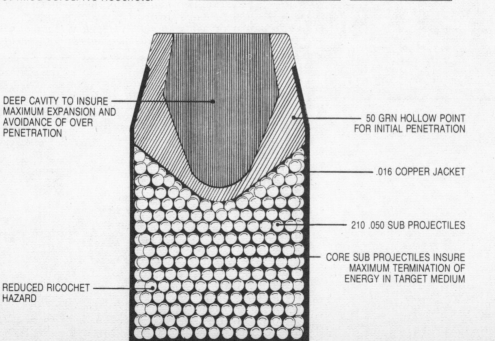

DEEP CAVITY TO INSURE MAXIMUM EXPANSION AND AVOIDANCE OF OVER PENETRATION

50 GRN HOLLOW POINT FOR INITIAL PENETRATION

.016 COPPER JACKET

210 .050 SUB PROJECTILES

CORE SUB PROJECTILES INSURE MAXIMUM TERMINATION OF ENERGY IN TARGET MEDIUM

REDUCED RICOCHET HAZARD

benefits is that the bullet is the best thing ever made for deflating tires. It cuts a tight cookie of material from the tread and the tire deflates pronto.

It's too bad that life in our times forces the ammunition makers to be preoccupied with such grim matters, but they must. Even in the area of handloaded ammunition, several makers are heavily into special-purpose bullets for hunting and defense. Genco of North Carolina is one such maker and their bullet is unique. It is a conventional bullet jacket filled with fine shot. Atop the shot is a nose plug swaged into a hollow-point. The idea is to give the shooter the best of two worlds, a hefty hollow-point for initial expansion and the pre-fragmented main bullet for heavy tissue destruction.

Probably the biggest news in the handloading component area is the almost overnight availability of 10mm bullets. There are two from Sierra (150-grain JHP and 180-grain JHP), three from Hornady (155-grain JHP, 170-grain JHP and 200-grain FMJ), two from Barnes (170-grain JHP and 200-grain FMJ) and two from Norma (170-grain JHP and 200-grain FMJ). Nosler and Speer are likely to have their bullets on line soon. Last year at this time, you'd be lucky to find a box of Norma 200-grainers on your dealer's shelves.

One of the more interesting aspects of the ammo scene in the United States is the rise of smaller ammunition companies. Once they were called commercial reloaders, but that's actually unfair. The scale of operations might be smaller than at Remington or Winchester, but there is nothing shoddy or second-rate about the product. I have fired enough of the ammo from two of these companies to speak affirmatively for them.

In California there is a small outfit that puts up ammunition in red and black boxes marked Pro-Load. The ammo is assembled in a spotless factory using the best of components and carefully selected load data. In a couple of places in this book, I have referred to Pro-Load ammunition. They make a wide variety of pistol ammo, including some exotics like 240-grain JHP .45 Winchester magnum and 180-grain JHP 10mm. Look at the adjacent picture of the 10mm group and tell me it isn't first-rate ammo.

In similar vein, Black Hills Shooters Supply of Rapid City, South Dakota, offers an even larger variety of ammunition. I have used their products in lots of test projects and have had nothing but good results. Their .44 magnum stuff is particularly accurate. Most of the time, ammo from the smaller makers carries a lower price tag. At least in the case of these two makers, I don't believe you can go wrong.

There is another category of ammunition that we can't logically get into. That's the special stuff made for law enforcement use under controlled circumstances. Since you can't buy most of it, there isn't much point in discussing it. Still, it's good to know that the principals in a vigorous market are producing some fine stuff for the belabored men and women who enforce the law. There's no real shortage of good ammo and components for the rest of us.

All of the good factory ammo doesn't come from the big companies. Pro-Load 10mm put eight shots in less than an inch. The company makes a variety of ammo, some of which is unobtainable from the other makers.

Black Hills ammo is likewise excellent. Author Clapp shot some exceptional groups with their .44 magnum .45 ACP and 9mmP ammunition. Also, their 125-grain .357 magnum JHP is a true tack-driver in some guns.

CHAPTER 6

NEW .45 SHOT LOADS

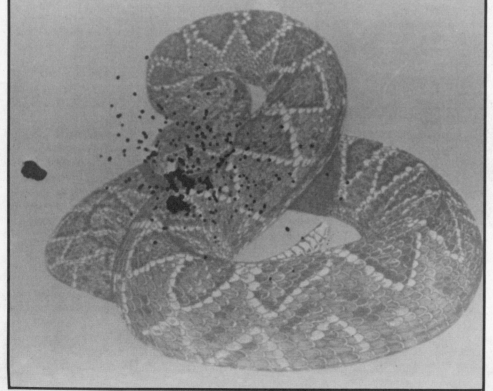

Evaluating

The Newest In

Snake Medicine

Author's testing pretty well established these new .45 shot loads to be close quarters propositions. It's also a good idea to double-tap ol' Fangs. In the above photo the paper snake got two rounds of the Remington load at ten feet. There may be enough in the head to do it,...

...but look at all the misses! Facing page, top: The CCI load with heavier shot produced a much tighter pattern with two shots at ten feet. At the bottom, there's yet another pair of the CCIs. This time, it is two shots at six feet and there's no doubt about the effect on target.

THE HABU is a relative of the American rattlesnake, a nasty flat-headed pit viper that has neither the equipment nor the disposition to give warning before he puts the fangs to you. In my salad days as a Marine lieutenant, I pulled a tour of infantry duty in habu homeland, the bush country of Okinawa. We encountered the slithery things with marked regularity as we went about our snoopin' and poopin' in the bush.

In view of the possible injury — or even death — associated with a losing battle with a habu, officers and senior NCOs were ceremoniously issued a "habu round" for their .45. You only needed one, because the M15 .45 shotload would not feed through the action of a .45 automatic. I would have approached trips to the field with my beloved machine-gun platoon far more confidently had I had a few rounds of the ammo at hand.

CCI and Remington both introduced .45 ACP shotloads in 1988 and both types work quite nicely through .45 automatics. The old M15 GI shot cartridge was labeled as usable for small game, but it is pretty clear what the CCI and Remington loads are meant for. There's even a picture of a rattler on the Remington box and a comment "excellent for dangerous pests at close range." These are snake loads, with a possible secondary use against rats and mice. In the latter role, the rounds may have advantages in their low potential for ricochet.

The two rounds are completely different in the way they're made. The CCI round is put up in the inexpensive aluminum cases first used in Blazer ammunition. With a special size of Berdan primer, the case is not reloadable. The aluminum case has the contour of a blunt-nosed round of .45 ammunition, with the case mouth roll-crimped over a clear plastic top wad. You can see the topmost shot pellets through the wad.

The box bears an inscription to the effect that the ammo is intended for use in .45 autos and should not be used in revolvers, since cylinder lockup might occur. It isn't clear whether the lockup might happen with the round being fired or the one adjacent to it busting its payload loose from cylinder inertia. I remain convinced that the Good Ol' Boys know what they're talking about, so I didn't try it.

The Remington load, on the other hand, has no such

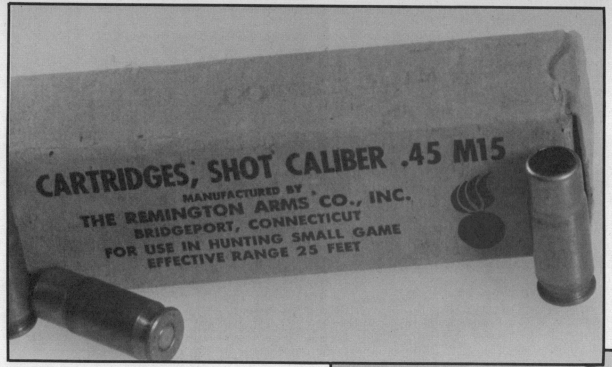

The old GI issue .45 shotload was made by Remington for use in survival kits. It was a fairly effective load, but was not shaped correctly to feed through the action of M1911 pistols. Therefore, the first shot was often the only one. This was the Okinawa Marine's Habu load.

admonition and might even work through a revolver. It uses a conventional cartridge case rolled into a six-point star crimp. A short, blunt little round, the Remington obediently slithered up the feed ramp of the stock .45 uses as the test pistol.

The CCI round houses one-third ounce of #9 shot, according to the label; approximately 210 pellets. The Remington load carries a payload of 650 #12 shot. According to my references, #9 pellets are .08-inch in diameter and #12s run to .05-inch. It would seem that the Remington load carries a payload of between a quarter and a half ounce of shot. The two shells are roughly equivalent in payload weight, with the CCI using fewer of the heavier #9s.

But will they work? I had to build a paper snake as a target. Art director Denise Comiskey conjoured up the gray snakes you see nearby by her magical printing techniques and I was away to the range to find out how the new loads worked.

The coiled paper snake on the target measures about twelve by nine inches, which I believe is pretty accurate in any location other than Texas. I tried a single shot from a stock Colt .45 auto at a measured ten feet. The CCI load patterned into about twelve inches at this range and about half of the pellets were in the snake's body with the head used as an aiming point. Two shots did not increase the size of the pattern, but the number of hits in the body was a lot more encouraging.

Using the Remington load with the smaller #12 shot, I produced a markedly larger pattern, nearly eighteen inches

The Remington .45 ACP shot load is new. It has about 650 ±12 shot. The pattern photos on the previous page show the Remington load to pattern quite widely when compared to the CCI. The Remington load might be the better choice for survival hunting of small game birds.

in diameter and with a significantly larger number of pellets missing completely. Two fast shots didn't cause the pattern to grow appreciably and I did get a few more than double the number of hits where they would count.

I believe that trying to stay ten feet away from the snake and kill him with one or two shots would be a hopeless

Remington and CCI loads contrasted, below. The CCI on the left has a non-reloadable aluminum case. There is enough contour for the straight-walled case to feed without a problem. The Remington load uses a six-point crimp in an essentially conventional case. Both feed.

proposition. Faced with this task, I think I would choose the CCI load with its tighter pattern of heavier pellets. I also would empty the magazine of seven and adjourn to wherever I could find the nearest sawed-off 12-bore with a proper load of BBs or the like.

All of which brings up a pretty good question. If you are ten feet away and *know* the snake is there, why not just go around and leave Ol' Fangs to go about his business in peace? Asssuming that you are in field or forest (his turf), I believe that's the best course of action. Nevertheless, snakes can and do get into outbuildings and areas where there are pets and children and are notoriously unwilling to relinquish the right of way. An efficient snake-killing load may not be such a bad idea.

If you choose a .45 auto, I think I'd move inside ten feet and use the CCI #9 shot load. I tried a double-tap of that stuff at six feet. It absolutely hashed the paper snake's head. Presumably, a real life habu would have likewise succumbed.

You have to get close to make either load work. The CCI version has fewer pellets, but they are larger and heavier. These will not work in revolvers, which limits them somewhat. In his omnipresent Commander or S&W 645, the author would choose the CCI load for snakes.

CHAPTER 7

.41 MAGNUM AMMUNITION

This Ammo Survey Looks At The Middle Magnum In All Its Forms

Below: This is the full variety of .41 magnum ammuniton. There are ten kinds available. Four makers load ammunition in this caliber.

Above: Ruger's Bisley Model is one of several typical revolvers available in .41 magnum. This .41 wheelgun shot the smallest group.

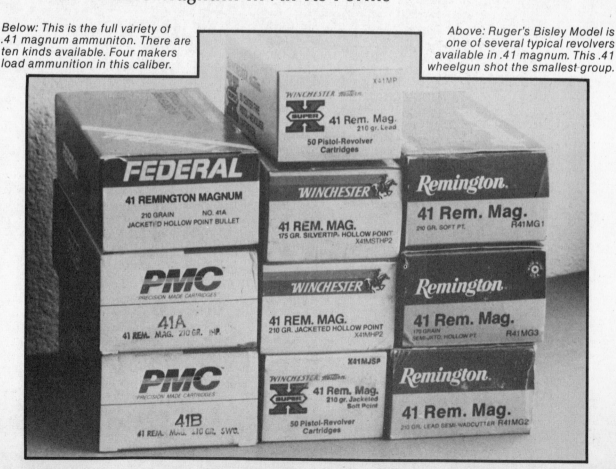

SOME OF us were getting worried a few years ago. It looked like our pet handgun cartridge was going to die off from a lack of interest and a resulting lack of ammunition. The .41 magnum had not lived up to the advance billing of its promoters and there was only a single manufacturer of the ammunition and brass. Usually, that means a cartridge is on its way out, that it will no longer be made. But in a few short years, we have seen a resurgence of interest in what some have called the "middle magnum." Anyone who investigates carefully will quickly find out that the .41 magnum is one of the most useful and accurate handgun cartridges.

In this chapter, you'll find a detailed examination of the available commercial loads for the .41 magnum. We'll check them out in a variety of typical handguns chambered for the cartridge and show you the tabulated results, which are nothing short of startling.

All ten of the commercial loads averaged under three inches, with only one going over the three-inch mark. The high-velocity, jacketed-bullet loadings of the cartridge averaged 2½ inches at twenty-five yards. The best groups out of individual guns are at the 1½-inch mark. And when I say group, I mean a twice-around-the-cylinder group, *twelve shots from the machine rest.*

The .41 magnum is a fine cartridge, with origins in the early Sixties. Policemen of that day became dissatisfied with the performance of the almost universally used .38 Special cartridge. There was a minor clamor of sorts and the matter came to a head at an NRA convention when Elmer Keith and Bill Jordan went to the executives at Smith & Wesson and Remington and demanded a new gun and cartridge.

After a remarkably short gestation period, the .41 was born. Smith & Wesson's contribution was a pair of revolvers: Models 57 and 58. Some of the early proponents of the cartridge, such as Skeeter Skelton, had hoped for an intermediate-sized gun, but the 57s and 58s were built on the time-tested N frame which dates to the Triple-Lock of 1907. More than anything else, the size of the S&Ws reduced the chance of wide acceptance in the police market — the guns were large and heavy.

The ammo half of the equation came from Remington in the form of two loadings of the new cartridge. Bullet diameter for both was an even and honest .410-inch. Case length for the new rimmed, straight-sided case was 1.290 inches. Remington offered a 210-grain jacketed soft-point loading at a velocity of about 1200 feet per second and a lead bullet police load, a 210-grain semi-wadcutter at about 900 fps. There was trouble right away; too many cops ended up with the hard-kicking high-velocity load and the popularity of the gun-cartridge combo suffered. As police armament, the .41 died in a matter of a few years.

That left the sporting market, where magnum revolvermen were in their second decade of a love affair with the .44 magnum. The smaller magnum had a rough row to hoe and nearly died off. But when the silhouette game burst on the scene and when handgun hunting became a fact of life,

For many years, Remington was the only source for .41 ammunition. Then Winchester got on the bandwagon and Federal followed suit. PMC is the latest maker to offer ammunition. These groups were fired with Remington's stuff and you wouldn't likely go wrong with any of it. Look at the group directly below — Damn that flyer!

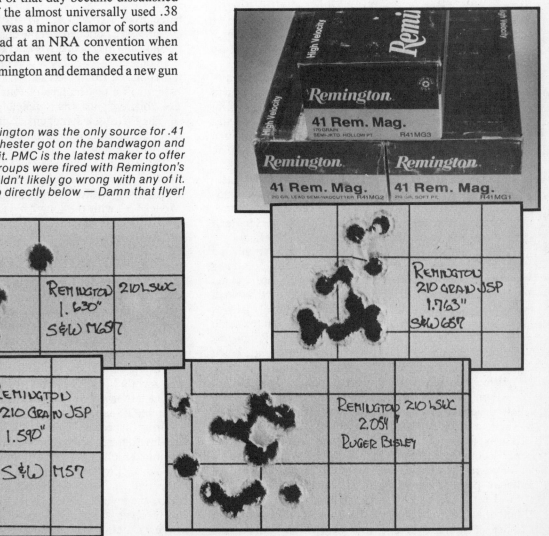

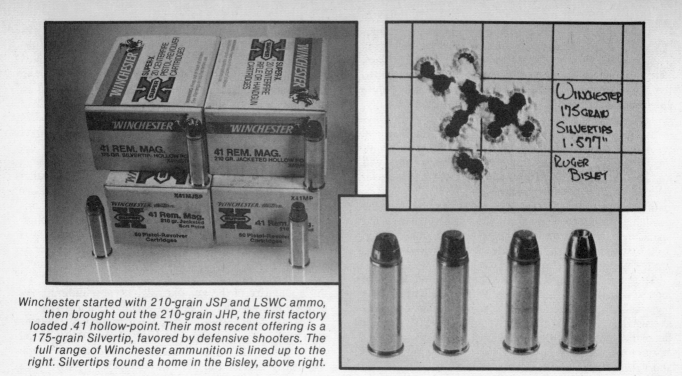

Winchester started with 210-grain JSP and LSWC ammo, then brought out the 210-grain JHP, the first factory loaded .41 hollow-point. Their most recent offering is a 175-grain Silvertip, favored by defensive shooters. The full range of Winchester ammunition is lined up to the right. Silvertips found a home in the Bisley, above right.

(handwritten on target) WINCHESTER 175 GRAIN SILVERTIPS 1.577" RUGER BISLEY

lots of shooters looked around for more options. The .41 was a logical thing to try and when they discovered a high level of accuracy, the middle magnum got a new lease on life.

The real stamp of approval came when a second ammuniton maker got into the act. Olin-Winchester began to market .41 ammunition in the late 1970s, offering several different loads including a hollow-point design. A third maker was added when Federal introduced a load with a hollow-point 210-grain design in the early 1980s. The newcomer to the scene is PMC, with a pair of loads using lead semi-wadcutter and jacketed hollow-point designs.

Four manufacturers presently make ten different kinds of ammunition in .41 magnum. All of this ammunition is first-rate stuff in terms of accuracy, affording the shooter a wide range of velocities and terminal ballistic effect.

In the first few years, only Remington made ammo and not a wide choice at that. The 210-grain soft-point was quite accurate and performed well in sporting use, but the 210-grain lead semi-wadcutter had an undersized bullet in too many lots and tended to lead the barrel badly. It was not particularily accurate in the early years, but the same load, as tested today, leaves little to be desired. Remington now has announced a 170-grain hollow-point load, which has the distinction of being the speediest .41 load available.

Winchester opened with loads matching those offered by Remington: 210-grain LSWC and JSP. Later, they introduced the first factory .41 hollow-point, a 210-grainer. Their most recent offering is the 175 Silvertip, a flashy fast-expanding performance round that exceeds 1200 feet per second in most guns.

Federal has but a single load, a 210-grain jacketed hollow-point that sizzles out of most handguns at over 1300 fps. Lastly, there's PMC with a pair of loadings. They're both the 210-grain type, a LSWC and a JHP. That's the range of ammo available: four loads from Winchester,

three from Remington, two from PMC and one from Federal. We obtained sample quantities of each, collected up the guns and headed to the range.

In order to accurately report on the available variety of ammunition, I obtained samples of all ten kinds. Then I assembled a test battery of four different .41 revolvers. Each of these guns was completely typical of all others like it. They're stock handguns in good condition, without fancy rebarreling jobs or other extra (and non-standard) aids to accuracy.

The four guns were a Model 57 Smith & Wesson with a four-inch barrel, a Ruger Blackhawk with a 4⅝-inch barrel, a Ruger Bisley with a 7½-inch barrel and a Smith & Wesson Model 657 with the long 8⅜-inch barrel. The four had varying degrees of mileage, but none was either brand new or on its last legs. All were stock revolvers, well broken in.

All four were fired in Ransom Rests. The amount of firing to be done would have strained the attention span of the most devoted bench marksman and the recoil of this much magnum ammunition would not have been kind to his anatomy. As written elsewhere in this volume, the Ransom Rest is a device that is quite consistent in positioning the handgun in the same location from shot to shot. Perhaps more importantly, the Ransom Rest responds to the torque and recoil of firing with utter consistency.

The test procedure called for twelve rounds of each type of ammunition to be fired in each revolver. The sequence of firing placed the high-velocity jacketed types ahead of the three different lead semi-wadcutter loads. Twelve rounds of ammunition — or twice around the cylinder — usually is enough to produce an accurate picture of a revolver's potential accuracy. With each of the six chambers used twice, the revolverman ends up with a good idea as to how his revolver will perform.

Test shooting was uneventful, taking the better part of

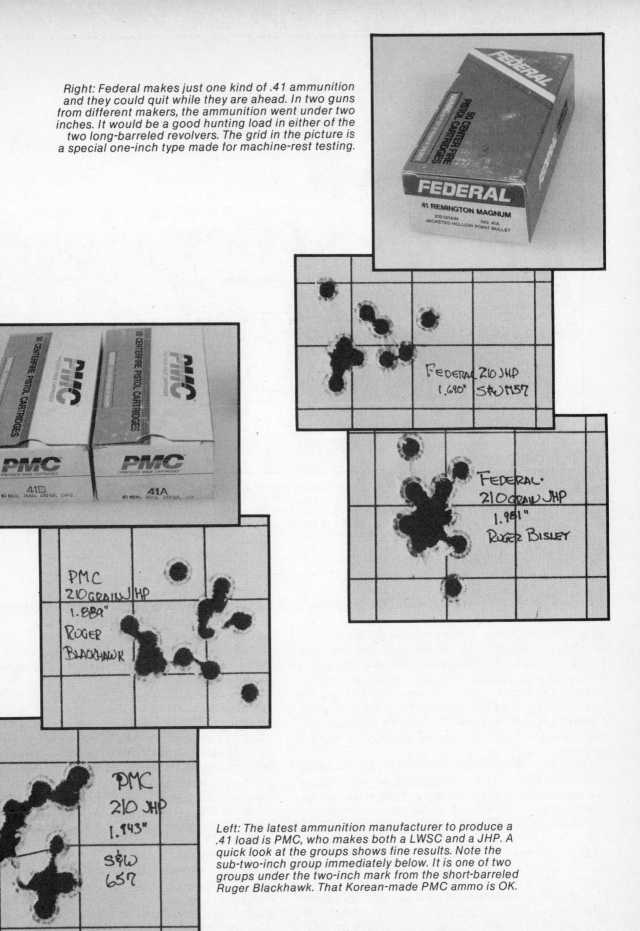

Right: Federal makes just one kind of .41 ammunition and they could quit while they are ahead. In two guns from different makers, the ammunition went under two inches. It would be a good hunting load in either of the two long-barreled revolvers. The grid in the picture is a special one-inch type made for machine-rest testing.

FEDERAL 210 JHP 1.690" S&W M57

FEDERAL 210 GRAIN JHP 1.951" RUGER BISLEY

PMC 210 GRAIN JHP 1.889" RUGER BLACKHAWK

PMC 210 JHP 1.943" S&W 657

Left: The latest ammunition manufacturer to produce a .41 load is PMC, who makes both a LWSC and a JHP. A quick look at the groups shows fine results. Note the sub-two-inch group immediately below. It is one of two groups under the two-inch mark from the short-barreled Ruger Blackhawk. That Korean-made PMC ammo is OK.

These two .41 magnum revolvers are currently owned by shooting partner Stan Waugh (but negotiations remain in progress). We used them in the course of writing the data portion of another DBI book on handgun reloading. They're typical revolvers without special modifications.

the morning. Each of the seven jacketed performance rounds went through the first pair of test guns, followed by the three lead bullet types. The second pair of guns were inserted in our side-by-side machine rests and the same sequence followed. At the same time, I recorded the statistical summary — extreme spread of velocities, average velocity, and standard deviation of velocities — as measured and calculated by a pair of side-by-side Oehler 33 chronographs. In short order, I had a pile of targets with twelve shots in each and a page of tabulated data in my notebook.

There is no doubt that the .41 is an inherently accurate cartridge and that the four ammo makers all produce first-rate ammunition. The best evidence of that is the average group size of all seven kinds of jacketed ammunition as fired through four different guns. It is an exceptional 2.52 inches. Remember, that is twelve shots in each group.

For an average to run that tight, there must be some really exceptional groups. A number of the groups went under two inches, but the best, from the Ruger Bisley, was a 1.577-incher with Winchester Silvertips. It was closely followed by a 1.590-inch group from the four-inch Smith & Wesson with Remington's 210-grain JSP. That latter load, the first one ever produced for the .41 magnum, is the

accuracy leader. By a small margin, the Remington 210-grain JSP is the most accurate ammo available, at least for the four guns tested.

The three lead semi-wadcutter loads all shot well, but they just aren't as accurate as the so-called performance loads. The margin is not great — 2.70 inches versus 2.52 — but it does exist. The highest velocity load is the brand new Remington 170-grain JHP. This lightweight speedster broke the 1500 feet per second mark in the Ruger Bisley at 1524. It also produced the highest velocity in every gun.

One curious phenomenon did come to light in the course of the testing. The Ruger Bisley, shooting next to the S&W M657, consistently produced higher velocities than its long-barreled neighbor. The barrel length disparity is 7½ inches to 8⅜, nearly an inch, but the Ruger shot every single one of the ten loads to a higher velocity. This could only result from some characteristic of the Ruger's bore and rifling specifications.

Having fired considerable quantities of factory ammunition in a variety of handguns in the past few years, I can speak with some authority on the matter. I don't recall any caliber that consistently shoots the available range of ammunition this well. In all journalistic objectivity, I cannot declare the .41 the most accurate revolver cartridge

.41 MAGNUM JACKETED AMMO TEST

	PMC 210 JHP	WINCHESTER 210 JSP	WINCHESTER 210 JHP	WINCHESTER 175 STHP	REMINGTON 170JHP	REMINGTON 210JSP	FEDERAL 210 JHP	
ES	50	76	66	112	99	84	49	M57 4"
AVG	1207	1251	1331	1177	1367	1083	1199	
SD	13	18	21	38	54	26	15	
GS	3.411	3.495	3.124	3.312	3.443	1.590	1.690	
ES	76	40	48	41	101	52	87	RUGER 4⅝"
AVG	1265	1325	1236	1232	1386	1194	1302	
SD	23	13	15	13	26	18	25	
GS	1.889	3.375	1.870	3.382	3.101	3.370	3.102	
ES	88	62	28	24	49	42	104	RUGER BISLEY 7½"
AVG	1344	1420	1345	1296	1524	1322	1386	
SD	41	18	10	17	13	14	24	
GS	1.823	2.930	2.225	1.577	2.034	2.035	1.981	
ES	112	137	77	70	109	61	62	S&W M57 8⅜"
AVG	1315	1391	1304	1262	1476	1214	1339	
SD	28	36	21	17	32	21	17	
GS	1.943	2.197	2.119	2.021	3.384	1.763	2.567	

ES = Extreme Spread. AVG = Average Velocity. SD = Standard Deviation
GS = Group Size in inches.
Test conducted at 25 yards in the Ransom Rest. All groups are 12 shots.

made. I haven't had the chance to do the same thing for all other cartridges and the range of available ammunition is much larger for some of them.

This doesn't change the fact that I know what I'll be holstering when I head north to Oregon for a whitetail hunt with my buddy Chuck Karwan this fall. It'll be that fine Ruger Bisley with a good handload. If I don't have the time at the handloading bench, I'll use the old original .41 magnum load, the Remington 210-grain JSP. Nothing is more accurate.

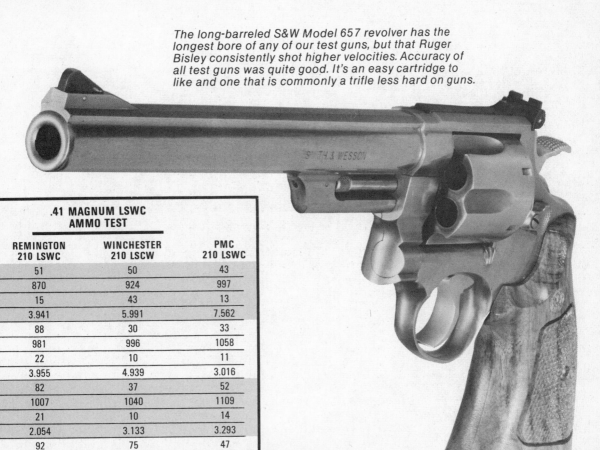

The long-barreled S&W Model 657 revolver has the longest bore of any of our test guns, but that Ruger Bisley consistently shot higher velocities. Accuracy of all test guns was quite good. It's an easy cartridge to like and one that is commonly a trifle less hard on guns.

.41 MAGNUM LSWC AMMO TEST

	REMINGTON 210 LSWC	WINCHESTER 210 LSCW	PMC 210 LSWC
ES	51	50	43
AVG	870	924	997
SD	15	43	13
GS	3.941	5.991	7.562
ES	88	30	33
AVG	981	996	1058
SD	22	10	11
GS	3.955	4.939	3.016
ES	82	37	52
AVG	1007	1040	1109
SD	21	10	14
GS	2.054	3.133	3.293
ES	92	75	47
AVG	969	1019	1075
SD	25	18	15
GS	1.630	3.576	2.723

CHAPTER 8
RELOADING TOOL MISCELLANEA

The BC-800 is a cleanly engineered little machine that anneals case necks with great consistency. The manual that comes with the BC-800 describes the use of the machine in plain language. It is a help to the reloader.

I AM NOT the sort of handloader who regards the business of assembling ammunition as dumb drudgery. To me, it is downright fun to sit down at the loading bench and crank out a batch of whatever. This does not mean that I am unwilling to look at labor-saving devices. As the saying goes, I may be dumb, but I sure ain't stupid.

What we'll look at in this chapter is an assortment of various tools with which I have been working over the past year or so. Some of them are rather complex devices, others are the very soul of simplicity. All of them are alike in the sense that they make better ammunition possible, usually with a saving in time.

We might as well begin with a gadget that solves a problem you may not have known you had. The device is the BC-800 Case Neck Annealer and it does two things for your brass. Properly annealed brass will last longer and deliver better accuracy.

Before the blue-collar sport of handgun silhouette burst on the scene several years ago, most case neck annealing was done by avid wildcatters and guys who were working with brass in such precious small quantities that it had to be preserved at all costs. Annealing is the process of heat-treating metal to alter its metallurgical properties. As applied to cartridge brass, it means applying heat to the case mouth area in order to make it softer.

Everyone who reloads has encountered the phenemenon of the split case neck. When the brass cartridge case goes through the loading and firing cycle a number of times, the mouth becomes work-hardened to the point that it will eventually split. When it does, the case is usually ruined and must be discarded. Proper annealing can extend case

Richard Beebe and his wife Sherri run Redding-Saeco and they do a hell of a job of it. Their dies are chosen by the IHMSA crowd more often than others. Redding is often the first to produce loading dies for new rounds.

One of the best special-purpose dies available is the Redding Profile crimper. This die is simple. It insures that the crimp in a revolver case is heavy as well as even. It centers case and bullet in the die for crimping.

longer life and that appeals to the IHMSA ramslammers as much as the increased consistency.

The BC-800 is a modern adaptation of an older armory-type device built for the same purpose. Basically, the device is a motor-driven wheel with holes drilled to accept cartridge cases and hold them upright. The motor cycles the brass through the flame of a pair of propane torches in such a way that the mouths of the cases are subjected to exactly the right amount of heat to anneal them. Earlier systems are grossly inconsistent in the amount of heat they place on the case mouth. Properly adjusted, the BC-800 will give every case that cycles through exactly the same dose of flame. It is one hundred percent repeatable. As the name implies, the BC-800 will do up to eight hundred cases per hour.

Setting up the machine is a little complex and I don't have space for a complete description of the process. The manual that comes with the machine is an absolute jewel. If every manual for every device we deal with in this complicated modern life were half as well written, we'd all be a lot better off. Harvard Pennington wrote the thing and not only justifies his product, but describes its use — all in the simplest possible terms.

If the BC-800 is a device of belts, motors and moving parts, the next gizmo is at the other end of the scale in complexity. Redding's profile crimp dies have no moving parts.

life, but few reloaders appreciate the fact that there are tangible benefits to annealing beyond the obvious economies.

The basic advantage of annealing is that it will keep cartridge case mouths at a relatively consistent degree of tension. This means they will grip the bullet in the same way from one loading to the next. Consistent bullet pull is the fundamental reason that many reloading operations are performed. As mentioned earlier, annealed brass has a

They just sit there in a reloading press and make good ammo better. The profile crimpers apply a different sort of crimp to a revolver case.

Die manufacturers know they have to leave a little slack in a seater-crimper die to allow for varying case neck thicknesses and bullet diameters. At the end of the stroke in a revolver crimper die, an internal shoulder rolls a crimp into the case mouth, solidly engaging it into the cannelure or crimp groove of the bullet. The slack in the die means that the crimp may not be even all the way around the case. In other words, it won't have a good profile.

Enter Richard Beebe with the Redding profile crimp die. It can't be used in a seat-and-crimp operation, but if you seat your bullets separately, the die will crimp it perfectly. The main feature of the Redding die is a short, tapered section just before the case mouth encounters the crimping shoulder. As the seated bullet approaches the crimping shoulder, it is gently guided into a perfectly centered spot

Hornady achieves a breakthrough in economy with the New Dimension pistol reloading dies. The costly insert of tungsten carbide has given way to plating. By using a coating of titanium nitride, the sizing die costs less.

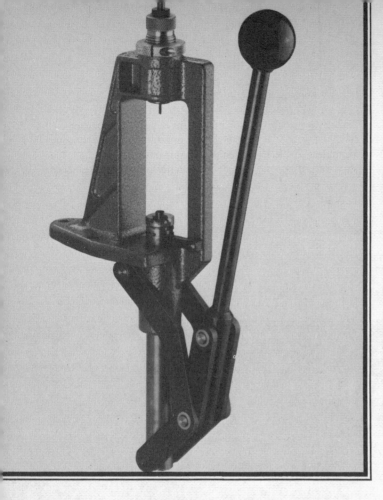

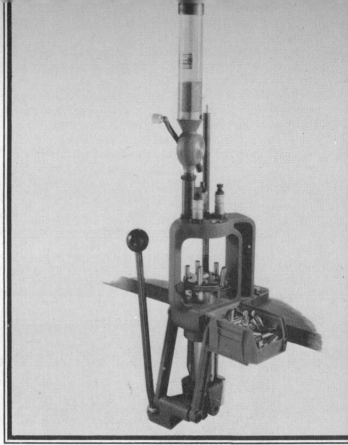

It was a year for both simpler and more complex tools. RCBS came out with a Partner (top left) and Lyman countered with the Accu-Line (bottom left). Both are low-cost single die tools. The newly automated RCBS 4x4 (bottom left) is a progressive and so is the Hornady Pro-Jector (top right). Not shown is any one of the several popular and widely used tools from Mike Dillon.

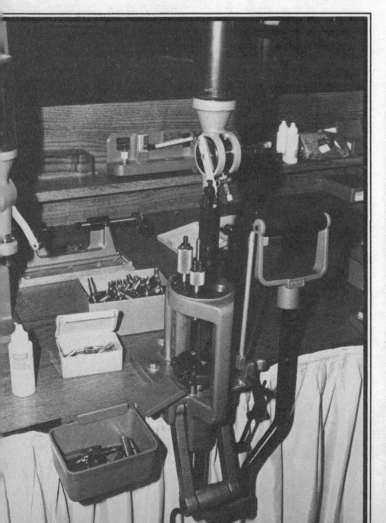

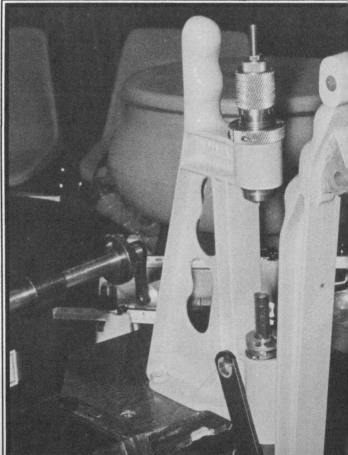

in the die, thereby allowing the die to crimp perfectly, all the way around the case. It's possible to adjust the die for more or less crimp, but it will always be evenly profiled.

Is it worth the added expense and effort? I think so and not solely on the basis of theory. In the course of producing the load data for last year's *Gun Digest Book Of Handgun Reloading,* I used the die to load ammo for a particularly accurate GP100 revolver. With one memorable combination, the gun shot six shots into less than a half inch at twenty-five yards. I have since loaded the same combination without the special crimp die and the result was a group over an inch. It's worth it.

Speaking of loading dies, we have another breakthrough. For most of my reloading experience, handgun handloaders have been gritting their teeth over the cost of the delightful tungsten carbide sizing dies. They are so nice to have because they allow the reloader to squeeze the case back down to shape without the mess and bother of sticky lubrication. Tungsten carbide is so bloody hard that a ring of the stuff cemented into the die mouth where the case bears will not scratch or deform. Therefore, no need to lube.

Hunky-dory, except that the die costs like hell. Hornady offers a viable alternative to the expense of tungsten carbide inserts. They call their dies New Dimension and they use a coating of a substance called titanium nitride at the case mouth to accomplish the same thing. It is far less expensive than the insert system and does exactly the same job.

For many years, Lyman produced the M die for discriminating shooters. The die has an unusual expander plug and was originally intended for preparing cases to take cast bullets. The plug uses a section nearest the case mouth which is stepped to a greater diameter. As the plug goes into the case mouth, it expands with the minor diameter section. When the step enters the case mouth, it takes it out a couple of thousandths more, before the mouth is actually flared.

One of author Clapp's favorite pieces of loading gear is the Lyman Multi Expand Powder Charge Die. It uses hollow M die expander plugs of the popular diameters. With a measure on top, powder charge drops through.

When the reloader seats bullets in these cases, the bullet starts easily, as well as straight. In using M dies in my own reloading, I am usually careful to trim all cases to the same length. Then I adjust the depth off the expander plug in such a way that there is virtually no flare, just the M die step. Bullets seat easily, usually with a positive snap. This tells me that the base of the bullet has engaged the step and is sitting perfectly straight with the case, ready to be seated to full crimp depth. Crooked ammo shoots crooked — straight ammo doesn't.

There is more to this happy circumstance in the form of Lyman's newest version of the M die. It is called the Multi Expand Powder Charge die. It consists of a universal die body into which the loader inserts whatever expander plug is correct for the case he's reloading. The plug has the characteristic M die step and screws onto a drop tube, which fits into the die body.

What's the advantage? Simply that the top of the die body is threaded ⅞x14, so that you can screw a powder measure into place. The expander plugs are drilled through, as you may have guessed, and they allow powder to drop through the plug. The advantage is that a sized and primed case can be expanded and charged with powder in one operation. The handloader places a case in the shell holder, raises the ram to full height then strokes the top-mounted powder measure handle and withdraws a charged case.

It may not seem such a big deal until you try it a few times. The new Lyman M Die system is a delight to use. It saves time and effort. Such simple little economies make the whole business so much more appealing — and it was fun at the start.

CHAPTER 9

AMMO FOR
.40 and .41 AUTOS

**Testing The
Available
Ammo
For The
Medium-Bore
Automatics**

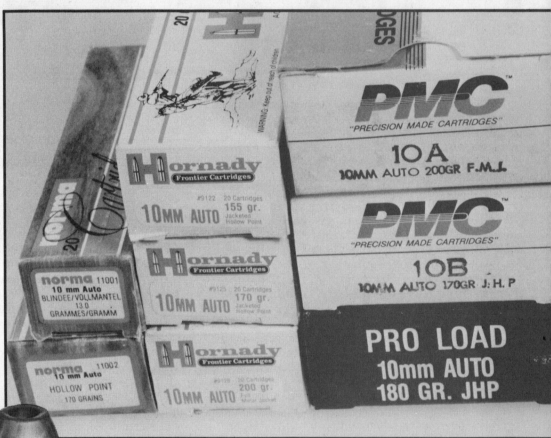

The cartridges under consideration in this chapter are seen to the left, with the 10mm auto on the far left and the .41 Action Express next to it. Bullet diameters of the two are .400 inch and .410 inch respectively. They are the two most recent automatic pistol cartridges. Above: In the case of the 10mm, we already have at least this variety of ammuniton.

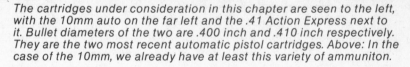

LIKE SO many other things in the gun business, there is nothing new about the idea of a mid-sized automatic pistol cartridge. Almost as long as there have been automatics, there have been attempts to make a medium-bore cartridge to work in them. The idea is an engaging one, particularly in a time when there's such intense interest in the automatic pistol as a defensive weapon. The benefits of such a thing are legion.

CAUTION

This product is intended for use in firearms warranted by the manufacturer of the firearm to have been proof load tested at pressures in excess of 53.300 psi and having a valid proof mark on the firearm. The ammunition contained herein is factory loaded to develop a mean pressure of 37.000 psi with a maximum pressure of 44.400 psi plus or minus industry tolerances.

THIS STATEMENT IS EXPRESSLY IN LIEU OF ALL OTHER WARRANTIES EXPRESSED OR IMPLIED INCLUDING WARRANTIES OF MERCHANTABILITY AND FITNESS FOR USE.

im Auto 20 NORMA CARTRIDGES • 20 NORMA CARTOUCHES • 20 NORMA PATRONEN

At the top of the page, there's the troubled Bren 10 pistol. It was the first pistol chambered for the 10mm cartridge. Not having a test Bren, we used one of Colt's new Deltas, equipped with a Bar-Sto barrel. You'd be hard put to find a more accurate automatic. The lower picture shows the back of a box of Norma 10mm ammunition. Note the pressure figures.

A mid-sized cartridge in a conventionally-sized automatic would have lots of advantages. Conceivably, it would be capable of producing velocities close to those of the smaller bores, but with bullets weighing close to those of the bigger bores. The actual bullet diameter would be about .400- to .410-inch. That's just about in the middle of the road between the 9mm and the .45s. We have that today, in the form of two different cartridges called the 10mm auto and the .41 Action Express.

There is really nothing so terribly difficult about asking such a thing in the pure mechanical sense. It requires appropriate tooling for the pistol and the same for the ammunition. The problem is in the business sense, where speculative manufacturing start-up costs are not popular with investors. In this light, it is surprising that we have the two cartridges in question.

But we do have them and they show great promise. Actually, we have had the 10mm for four or five years, but there was little by way of firearms from which to shoot the ammo. The .41 Action Express dates to 1986 and, until recently, there weren't that many guns from which to shoot it. But with ammunition available, it would seem the makers will be offering guns in greater variety.

In the modern sense, the 10mm cartridge started in the early 1970s when magazine writer Whit Collins reported a series of experiments using rifle cases cut back to pistol length. The pistols used were modified versions of the venerable Browning Hi-Power, with special barrels made by Irv Stone of Bar-Sto Precision.

Collins' first efforts centered around the .25, .30 or .32 Remington rounds, all of which share the same case head size. It was fairly easy to cut these rounds down to an appropriate size. One of the first stumbling blocks was the lack of stable bullets. That one was solved by using a Remington 180-grain JSP slug intended for use in the .38-40 revolver round. While the Collins experiments did not lead to immediate acceptance of the cartridge, they drew a lot of favorable attention. There were also some subsequent experiments with one of the Weatherby belted magnum cases, modified by lathe-turning the belts from same.

By the late 1970s or early 1980s, the gun world buzzed with talk of the Bren 10. This was a special modern pistol made by Dornaus & Dixon of Huntington Beach, California. The pistol was strongly influenced by input from handgun authority Jeff Cooper, who also assisted in the design of the ammunition which would be made by Norma.

The effective life of the cartridge almost ended when the pistol fell on hard times. For reasons I have never com-

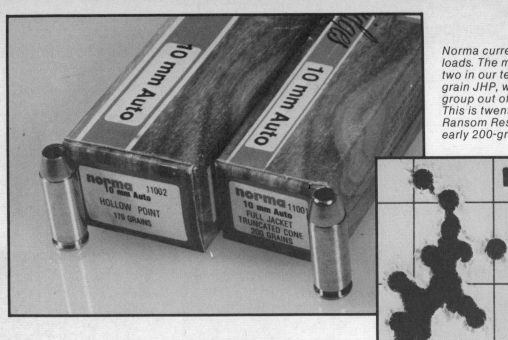

Norma currently makes two 10mm loads. The more accurate of the two in our testing was the 170-grain JHP, which produced this group out of the Bar-Sto Colt. This is twenty shots, fired in a Ransom Rest at 25 yards. The early 200-grain didn't do as well.

NORMA
170 GRAIN JHP
1.123"

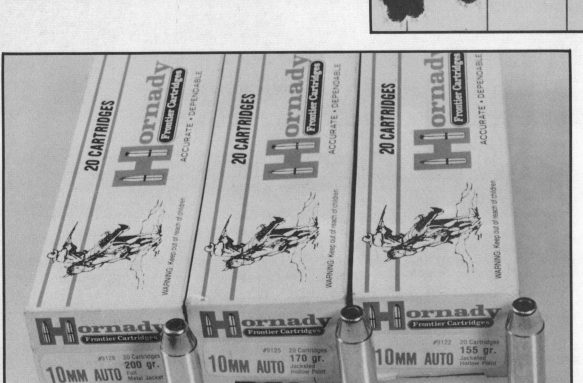

Hornady makes three kinds of ammunition for the 10mm and all of it is good. However, look at the group fired with the 170-grain JHP. Twenty shots in a group that is comfortably under an inch at twenty five yards from the Ransom Rest is just plain outstanding. The target is printed with a one-inch grid for reference purposes.

HORNADY 10mm
170 GRAIN JHP
.981"

25 YARDS
20 SHOTS
RANSOM REST

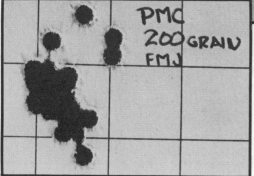

PMC, the Korean-based ammunition firm, makes a wide variety of ammo, including two 10mm loads. The 200-grain variety was the most accurate, shooting twenty into this group which measured 1.898 inches between the centers of the most widely spaced shot holes. The velocity of this load averages 1069 feet per second.

pletely understood, the gun's maker was unable to keep the pistols going out and the money coming in. After a few years of effort, the company ceased production of the pistol. It was a bitter disappointment to a great many people, because the Bren 10 had a lot going for it.

Norma made many thousands of rounds of the new 10mm ammunition. It used a bullet weighing 200 grains and measuring .400-inch in diameter. It was a full metal jacket slug in truncated cone form with a healthy flat point. The Bren 10 makers quoted ballistics of approximately 1200 fps in the Bren 10 pistol. In fact, the ammo would actually turn up about 1150 fps, as determined by actual chronographing in two different pistols. The box containing the ammunition stated the ammo was loaded for use in a firearm proof load tested at over 53,300 psi and that the ammo was made to develop a mean pressure of 37,000 psi.

The more common means of expressing cartridge pressure is in copper units (c.u.p.=copper units of pressure), so the use of psi does not relate directly. Nevertheless, it should be clear we are dealing with a very hot automatic pistol cartridge. In time, Norma also chose to make a 170-grain JHP load.

Shooters certainly liked the idea of the new round. It had great promise as a flat-shooting, penetrating, high-velocity automatic pistol cartridge. It is assuredly not comparable to a big-bore revolver magnum round, but the closest cartridge to the 200-grain 10mm load is the .41 magnum. There is further appeal to the round in the sense that the cartridge is dimensionally small enough to go into a double-column magazine.

But the Bren 10 was dead and the 10mm round had no home. After some fitful false starts, Colt introduced the Delta Elite pistol. It was a version of the old standby Government Model, suitably strengthened to take the 10mm round. People bought them and looked around for something to shoot. There was an almost overnight demand for ammunition.

Two more makers also introduced pistols for the cartridge. Springfield Armory brought out the Omega pistol and L.A.R. introduced the Grizzly. Both of these are heavy handguns and both are also variations of the Colt GM. They're both better able to handle 10mm pressures, but they are larger than the Colt Delta. Neither of the latter guns is well suited for use as a combat pistol, if carrying the gun on the person is a factor.

At the present time, the 10mm leader is pretty much the Colt, which has all of the legendary virtues of John Browning's timeless design. For this pistol, we have a much wider variety of ammunition than ever before. In preparation for this report, I obtained shooting samples of everything

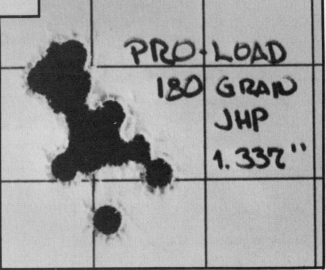

Surprise! The second most accurate load in our 10mm testing is John Koppel's Pro-Load 180-grain JHP. Made with the Sierra bullet and custom-made brass, the Pro-Load ammo put twenty well under an inch and a half at twenty-five yards. This would be a dynamite hunting or defense load; the bullet is moving at an average of 1216 fps at the muzzle.

currently available on the market. This adds up to eight different loads from four different makers. Shooting the ammo under controlled conditions produced some results that border on the astonishing.

In order to give the ammunition the best chance possible, I fired it in the best possible pistol I could find. It was a near-new Colt Delta Elite fitted with a Bar-Sto barrel. The pistol went out to 29 Palms, California, where Irv Stone personally installed a Match Target version of this famous stainless steel barrel. Stone's rifling specifications call for one turn in sixteen inches, the same as Colt's. After a few shots to settle everything into place, the Bar-Sto Colt performed superbly.

Results of the testing are shown in the accompanying chart. In order to remove the human element of marksmanship from the equation, I placed the pistol in the Ransom Rest and measured velocities with the Oehler 33 chronograph. Having adequate supplies of ammunition on hand allowed me to shoot twenty-shot groups as described in Chapter 15. The results show the range of 10mm ammunition in a realistic and objective light.

To the best of my knowledge, 10mm is loaded currently by the four makers listed: PMC, Hornady, Pro-Load and Norma. I began with PMC 200-grain FMJs and followed with their 170-grain JHPs. Then it was the three Hornady loads: 155-grain JHP, 170-grain JHP and 200-grain FMJ.

The single Pro-Load round was next. It is a 180-grain JHP, built around the Sierra bullet. Last were the two Norma loads, a 170-grain JHP and a 200-grain FMJ. The results of the test show that there is a high potential for pure accuracy in this 10mm cartridge.

In a good barrel, properly fitted to a good pistol, a number of different 10mm loadings will shoot twenty consecutive shots under two inches at twenty-five yards. None of these loads was any sort of mid-range matching loading of the 10mm; all of them turned up some pretty steamy velocities. The best is the absolutely exceptional group produced with twenty of Hornady's 170-grain JHP. It measured .981-inch, the best twenty shots from any automatic pistol I

have yet fired. John Koppel's Pro-Load 180-grain JHP wasn't that far behind. It popped twenty into 1.337 inches which includes a single flier that spoiled an otherwise one-hole group.

At a later date, I had an opportunity to do a fairly serious handloading session with a number of different 10mm bullets and with different powders. Groups here were limited to ten shots, but I was able to shoot several groups under one inch with several different bullets and at several velocity levels. The message is clear to me — the 10mm cartridge is highly accurate and may even end up the most accurate of them all.

There's only one fly in the ointment. The 10mm is terribly hard on the pistol. The recoil spring guide on my pistol is battered all to hell and needs to be replaced. This problem is discussed in coverage of the Delta Elite pistol in Section One of this book. The Ten must have a new home, in a pistol engineered to hold the action closed a nanosecond longer, thereby allowing pressure to drop. Joe Peters' Omega system looks like the best way to go, but

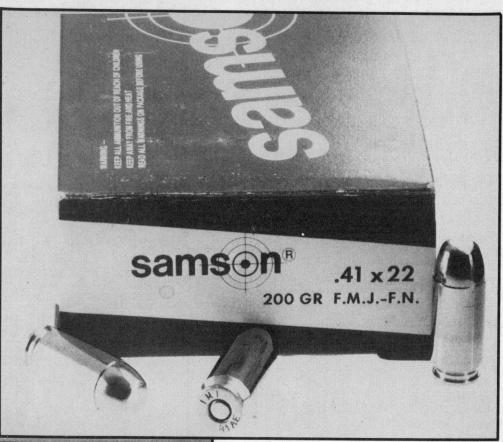

samson ®
.41 x 22
200 GR F.M.J.-F.N.

Only one maker of .41 ammunition at the present time, unfortunately. Guns for the cartridge aren't in every store and the ammomakers are reluctant to tool up for the round when there's a limited market. Nevertheless, the .41 Action Express is potentially one of the most promising cartridges you'll ever find. It does not have the horrendous pressure problems of the 10mm and it is acceptably accurate. We used another Bar-Sto Colt here.

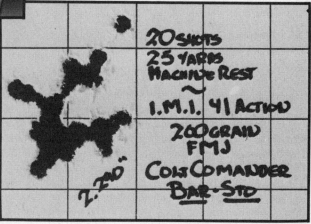

20 SHOTS
25 YARDS
MACHINE REST
~
I.M.I. 41 ACTION
200 GRAIN
FMJ
COLT COMANDER
BAR-STO

let's get it down to the point where the pistol can be carried.

A carrying gun for a mid-bore auto round is exactly what Evan Whildin had in mind when he came up with the .41 Action Express round. He wanted a pistol cartridge that would interchange in most any double-column 9mmP handgun. After some head-scratching, Whildin hit on the idea of turning down the rim of a shortened .41 magnum. Busy at running Action Arms in Philadelphia, Whildin turned the concept over to engineer Bob Olsen.

After a certain amount of developmental work, Olsen had the cartridge ready to go. Quantities of brass, bullets and loaded ammo came from the plants of Israel Military Industries and a special version of the CZ75 pistol came from a Swiss factory. The whole works was announced at the SHOT show in New Orleans in 1987. It was an auspicious beginning.

The cartridge is really interesting. It holds a bullet of .41-inch diameter, just like the .41 magnum. The case is a little shorter than the 10mm at .866-inch. The tricky part is

10mm AMMUNITION TEST				
AMMO USED	ES	AVG	SD	GS
PMC 200-gr. FMJ	56	1069	18	1.898
PMC 170-gr. JHP	36	1172	11	2.305
Pro-Load 170-gr. JHP	29	1215	10	1.337
Hornady 155-gr. JHP	61	1331	14	2.122
Hornady 170-gr. JHP	89	1263	22	.981
Hornady 200-gr. FMJ	31	1066	8	3.284
Norma 170-gr. JHP	56	1325	12	1.923
Norma 200-gr. FMJ	24	1202	6	2.627

Test conducted at 25 yards, Bar-Sto Colt Delta, Ransom Rest.
Groups are 20-shot, measured center spread with dial caliper.
Abbreviations: ES = Extreme Spread;
AVG = Average Velocity; SD = Standard Deviation;
GS = Group Size

the case head, which is exactly like the 9mmP at .394-inch. The body of the case is larger, measuring .434-inch. The rim is rebated; actually smaller than the body of the case. The theory was to have a cartridge that would interchange in a double-column 9mmP pistol by simple substitute of a new barrel. In practice, it just hasn't worked out that way.

Most pistols are turning out to be a bit balky about feeding the stuff without a special magazine made for it. Action Arms sells conversion units for Colt GM pistols and even markets the Uzi pistol for the round. My last information on the subject of .41 Action Express guns is that an updated AT84 (CZ75) will be available soon, called the AT88. I hope so, because this cartridge is almost as interesting as the 10mm.

It will accomplish almost what the 10mm will do at somewhat lower pressures. With no guns yet on the market, the ammo makers aren't trying to put the .41 Action Express on dealers' shelves. Therefore, we have only the original 200-grain Samson load as test ammo. Action Arms did produce a small run of 170-grain JHP ammo, but I wasn't able to get a test quantity.

To give the cartridge the best of chances, I did with it just what I did with the 10mm. I sent a Colt Commander with an extra 9mm slide out to Irv Stone and he fitted up a Bar-Sto barrel. The pistol shoots the .41 stuff without a hitch, using a 10mm Colt magazine. I've been told that other writers have attempted the same stunt with poor results, but I can only say that I have yet to have a problem with three or four magazines in my Bar-Sto Commander.

I wish there were more to say about .41 Action Express ammo variety, but there isn't anything out there except the 200-grain IMI Samson load. Out of the machine-rested Commander, twenty shots went into 2.290 inches at twenty-five yards. Lots of other calibers and guns won't do that on the best day they ever had.

The major problem for the .41 Action Express cartridge is a lack of a proper home. When someone comes up with a really viable pistol in compact and carriable form, the ammo makers will respond with a wider variety of loads. If the whole concept of the .41 Action Express remains tied to full interchangeability in fundamentally 9mmP pistols, the round won't last. If Action Arms can produce quantities of the gorgeous little AT88P, the round will become one of the best defense gun choices we have. If that happens, other makers will likely offer guns for it and the ammo race will be on.

The .41 Action Express' main competition is the 10mm and that cartridge needs a home just as badly. If someone can put together a carry gun that will take 10mm pressures and hang together, the ammo is already around and we know it's accurate and powerful.

We'll have to wait and see.

Section Three

HANDGUNNING THIS YEAR

THIS WAS A YEAR LIKE NO OTHER, A YEAR IN WHICH AMERICANS BROADENED THEIR HANDGUNNING HORIZONS CONSIDERABLY. LOTS OF MEN AND WOMEN TOOK UP THE COMPETITION HANDGUN FOR THE FIRST TIME, SO OUR HANDGUNNING COVERAGE BEGINS WITH A SURVEY OF THE MAJOR TOURNAMENTS. OTHER SHOOTERS TOOK THEIR HANDGUNS AFIELD IN PURSUIT OF VARIOUS KINDS OF GAME. WE OFFER A PAIR OF CRACKERJACK CHAPTERS ABOUT THE FAST-GROWING SPORT OF HANDGUN HUNTING.

THERE ARE OTHER SIDES TO THE HANDGUNNING PICTURE. WE HAVE TO CONSIDER THE DEFENSIVE USE OF THE PISTOL AND THIS YEAR'S COVERAGE WILL DEAL WITH THE MATTER OF CHOOSING A BUSINESS GUN. MOST KINDS OF HANDGUNNING INVOLVE A HOLSTER, SO WE WENT TO IDAHO AND WATCHED ONE OF THE BEST COME TO LIFE ON THE MAKER'S BENCH. FINALLY, THERE MUST BE A BETTER WAY TO MEASURE THE MERITS OF THE VARIOUS HANDGUN MAKES AND MODELS, SO WE'LL SPEND SOME TIME ON TESTING TECHNIQUE.

HANDGUNS 89

HANDGUN COMPETITION

 **C**HAPTER **10**

"Friendships born on the field of athletic strife are the real gold of competition. Awards become corroded, friends gather no dust." — Jesse Owens

The Major Tournaments In Perspective

By Kerby Smith

WHEN YOU TALK to top pistol champions Bill Blankenship, Allen Fulford, Gary Wrigley and others, they admit they like to win matches. But all of them say the real value of pistol competition is the friends they have made over the years. Now there are more shooting games for handgunners than ever before; therefore ways to make friends.

For years, the only pistol game in town was bullseye. Then in the fifties and later, in the seventies, two new forms of pistol competition emerged. The first was practical shooting and the second was long-range silhouette shooting. But it all started with bullseye.

NRA OUTDOOR PISTOL

Traditional one-handed shooting at a white paper target with the center scoring rings colored black (the bullseye target) is still the most dominant form of pistol marksmanship in this country today. The distances are moderate, with competitors standing shoulder-to-shoulder on the firing line and the targets at 25 to 50 yards.

The National Rifle Association (NRA) National

Championships at Camp Perry, Ohio attracted 1,047 entries in 1987. The National Pistol Champion is the grand aggregate winner of 12 matches. The matches are shot with three different guns; the .22 caliber pistol, the centerfire pistol (any pistol .32 to .45 caliber), and the .45 caliber pistol.

The basis for all of the matches is the National Match Course. The first portion of the National Match Course is called slow fire. A competitor has ten minutes to fire 10 shots at a 50-yard target with an 8-inch sighting bull which includes the X, 10, 9, and 8 rings. The next two portions of the match, timed and rapid fire, are fired at 25-yard targets with 5½-inch sighting bulls which include the X, 10, and 9 rings. The timed fire stage of the match consists of two strings of five shots each. Each string is fired in 20 seconds. The rapid fire stage of the match also consists of two strings of five shots each, but the time for each string is cut in half to 10 seconds.

At Camp Perry, the National Matches are a three-day championship round. The .22 Caliber Championship is held on the first day. Competitors start out on the the 50-yard line. They shoot the Slow Fire Match, which is 20 shots for a possible 200 points. Then they shoot 10 shots in the slow fire stage of the National Match Course. Next, they move to the 25-yard line and complete the National Match Course, shooting 10 shots of timed fire and 10 shots of rapid fire. Then there's the Timed Fire Match with 20 shots for a possible 200 points. The last match shot is the Rapid Fire Match, and it too consists of 20 shots for a possible 200 points. The .22 Caliber Champion and winner of the Walker Trophy is the shooter with the highest aggregate of all four matches. There are 900 possible points.

On the second day, the competition is for the Center Fire Championship or the Clark Trophy. The course of fire for the four matches is repeated, except this time a centerfire pistol or revolver is used to fire another 90 shots for a possible point total of 900.

On the third day of competition, each shooter fires 90 shots with a .45 caliber handgun. The competitor with the best score out of a possible 900 points wins the Orton Trophy and the .45 championship. After three days of competition, the National Pistol Champion and winner of the Harrison Trophy is the shooter with the highest aggregate score of the three gun championships. He will have the highest score out of a possible 2700 points.

The 1987 National Matches at Camp Perry saw the Ohio countryside heat up to 95 degrees, with 90 percent humidity and winds blowing at steady speeds of 20 to 25 m.p.h. Army reservist SSG. Darius R. "Doc" Young got off to a fast lead in the three-day championship when he posted a score of 892 to win the .22 Caliber Championship and the Walker Trophy. Civilian shooter Allen Fulford of Vienna, Georgia, came in second with a score of 890.

By the second day of the competition, some people felt that the hot, humid weather was beginning to affect the shooters. "Doc" Young shot an 865 on the Center Fire Championship and Army MSG Eric Buljung shot an 871 to pull within one point of him in the aggregate standings. Young lives and trains in the cooler climate of western Canada while Buljung, who is stationed at Fort Benning, Georgia, is used to shooting in a southern steam bath. The Clark Trophy was won with an 872. Bernard Janosko, a

civilian Expert from Pocono Summit, Pennsylvania, bested Buljung's score by a point. And Georgia shooter Allen Fulford, who is used to hot weather, fell 10 points behind Darius' pace.

On the third day of the championship tournament, the weather did not let up and neither did the Army master sergeant. Buljung shot another 871 aggregate in the .45 Caliber Championship, but again he would be denied a trophy. Army reservist Capt. Fred Wright of Indianapolis, Indiana, shot an 876 to claim the Orton Trophy.

But Buljung was not disappointed. His grand aggregate totaled 2627, winning him the most sought-after trophy of the National Pistol Championship, the Harrison Trophy. Buljung was the new NRA National Pistol Champion. Sgt. Mitchell R. Reed finished second with a 2622, and Young finished third with a 2619. Fulford would claim the Manchester Trophy, going to the Civilian Champion with a 2608. Olympic silver medalist and Army Reserve SSG Ruby Fox would win the Alexander Trophy to once again become the Woman Champion with a 2570.

On the facing page, we have the firing line at Camp Perry. This has been the site of the National Matches since before World War II. The pistol shooting is pure bullseye, one-handed and standing. Below: The Civilian champion thinks about his next shot. Allen Fulford had a great year, winning both at Camp Perry as well as at the Masters. Photo courtesy of the NRA and J. Roberts.

PRACTICAL SHOOTING

The beginnings of practical pistol shooting grew out of the quick draw competition at a ski lodge in Southern California. Jeff Cooper organized the first Big Bear Leatherslap in 1956. Drawing a gun from a holster and shooting at targets at close range was not only fun to do, it was fun to watch. The event, held at a ski resort during the off season, was so popular that a club, the Bear Valley Gunslingers, was formed to hold monthly matches. While the popular sport of quick draw tended to emphasize speed for speed's sake, with competitors switching from live ammunition to wax bullet loads, Cooper had other ideas.

He wanted to use this new form of pistol competition as a laboratory to find out the best way to shoot a handgun. As secretary of the Bear Valley Gunslingers, Cooper saw to it that full-power ammuniton was mandated for the matches. The rules were simple: ".38 caliber and up, serviceable leather, all contests from the leather, premature starts disqualified, varied ranges, varied hand clearance, varied targets. Annual points based on placement, number of entries and Hatcher rating (power factor)."

What made this form of pistol competition different from traditional competition was that the matches were varied and *unrestricted.* There were no restrictions on the handgun, holster, ammunition or technique. The matches varied from simple exercises in speed shooting to matches designed to test tactical problems. The freestyle matches were a lot of fun as Cooper and his friends experimented with new ideas and concepts. Soon, other clubs sprang up in Southern California and a league was formed to schedule these new practical shooting matches. Cooper, who was handgun editor of *Guns & Ammo* magazine, was a vocal advocate of the new kind of pistol competition.

USPSA MATCHES

Almost twenty years later an organization would be formed to regulate the sport of practical shooting. The International Practical Shooting Confederation (IPSC) was formed to regulate the sport and host periodic World Championships. The United States Practical Shooting

In this NRA/Roberts photo, Allen Fulford grins widely as he is awarded the Manchester trophy, emblematic of the National Civilian Outdoor Pistol Championship. Fulford is a cotton agronomist from the Deep South.

Association (USPSA) was formed to regulate the sport in the United States.

Each year USPSA holds a National Championship. In 1987, the 10th U.S. Nationals were held at the Pike-Adams Sportsmen's Alliance (PASA) Park in Barry, Illinois. Since practical shooting is a freestyle sport, there is no set course of fire fired year after year like there is at Camp Perry.

The 10th U.S. Nationals had eight stages with targets varying in distance from 2 yards to 45 yards. The total course of fire for all stages required that a competitor fire a minimum of 173 rounds of ammunition. There were four days of shooting for 378 competitors and a shoot-off on the fifth day for the top eight women and top 16 men.

The competitors were grouped into squads with approximately 16 shooters on each squad. The top men and women shooters in the country are placed on the Super Squad and the odds are that the men's and women's titles will go to shooters on the Super Squad.

The first day of competition saw the Super Squad shooting standard exercises. In IPSC competition, this stage of the match is not a standard course of fire, but rather a course of fire testing standard skills that a practical shooter should have. The 1987 standard exercises were some of the most difficult exercises ever seen in U.S. competition.

There were six separate strings of six shots each with a maximum score of 180 points possible. The targets were three standard IPSC silhouette targets. The IPSC target is tan cardboard with perforations on the target to indicate scoring zones. The targets were turned away from the shooter and appeared for 5 seconds on each firing string. The first string was shot standing at 45 yards. On the signal to start, the competitor drew his pistol from its holster and engaged the targets with 6 rounds. The second string was shot from the kneeling position and the third string was shot from the prone position.

On the fourth string, the competitors moved up to 20

The overall winner at Perry was Army Master Sergeant Erich Buljung. It was marksmanship skills plus stamina that carried the senior soldier to victory. The title goes to the highest three gun aggregate and Buljung held on to post a 2627. Photo courtesy of NRA and Joe Roberts.

Above: Jerry Barnhart is seen here hard at work with a Springfield Armory .45. The scene is the USPSA/IPSC Nationals. This gun has been extensively customized by Steve Nastoff, a pistolsmith who builds some of the best.

yards. On the signal to start, the competitor drew his pistol from his holster and engaged the targets with two rounds each, using his strong arm only. On the fifth string, the competitors moved up to 15 yards. On the signal to start the competitor again drew his pistol, but this time transferred it to his weak hand and engaged each target with two rounds, using his weak hand only. The sixth string was also shot at 15 yards. On the signal to start, the competitor drew his pistol and fired one shot on each target freestyle and then had a mandatory reload, engaging each target with one more round.

No shooter came even close to cleaning this stage of fire. Jerry Barnhart, an electrician from Michigan, won this stage with a top score of 150 points. Right behind him was Federal Revenue Agent Rick Castelow from Tennessee. Four-time National Champion and reigning World Champion Rob Leatham from Arizona had disaster strike when his gun stopped working on the stage. Scoring only 115 points on this stage, Leatham would never catch the front runner in the match.

The other seven stages of the championship match consisted of four speed matches and three field courses which were all scored by the Comstock method (score divided by time). A complex computerized scoring system was used to score the match.

With Leatham out of contention, the match soon became a race between Barnhart and Castelow. The two battled back and forth over the four days of competition. The shadows were growing long as they climbed the hill to the last stage they would shoot at the U.S. Practical Shooting Championship. The stage was a field course called "El Pariso Barracks."

The week before the match it had rained heavily in central Illinois, and range engineer George Metcalf and the PASA club members had trucked load after load of sand in to keep the range from turning into a mudhole. The sand was ankle deep and earlier contestants on the course had complained that they couldn't get any speed running in the sand.

Above: The main competition in the USPSA/IPSC Match came from Rick Castelow, who fought Barnhart down to the last shot. Note the intense concentration evident on the shooter's face. Also note two empties in mid-air.

Even though no one knew their exact standing, Barnhart sensed that he was behind Castelow. Luck was with Barnhart as he drew the first run on the squad. His feet flew across the sand as if it were hard-baked clay. Shot after shot hit the A-zone of the IPSC targets.

Castelow was last man up on the squad. It was cold and the light was fading. He knew he didn't have to beat Barnhart's blazing run, all he had to do was shoot smoothly and consistently. He looked smooth on the first part of the course, but he pushed it too hard on the back part of the course and dropped a shot. When the USPSA computer had made its last calculation, Barnhart was the new National Men's champion by a mere nine points.

In IPSC competition, women shooters compete on the same course as men do, and not all of the top shooters are on the Super Squad. Debby James, an unknown shooter from Connecticut, finished 151st to become the U.S. National Female Champion.

BIANCHI CUP

In 1979, holster magnate John Bianchi wanted to establish the professional sport of practical pistol shooting. He collaborated with Ray Chapman, one of the original Bear Valley Gunslingers and practical shooting's first World Champion. The event they designed was called the Bianchi Cup and it became one of the first big money matches where shooters could earn cash as well as prizes.

The NRA realized the popularity of practical shooting competition. When the opportunity arose in 1985, it took over the Bianchi Cup and launched its action shooting program with a nationally approved program of tournaments and championships. Despite its late entry into practical shooting competition, the NRA Bianchi Cup is perhaps the best known of the modern pistol sports. The NRA has seen ESPN coverage on national TV. The match is held on Chapman's range in Columbia, Missouri, as it has been from the beginning, but it is now the NRA Bianchi Cup Action Shooting Pistol Championship.

Unlike IPSC, which varies its courses under the NRA Action Pistol Shooting Rules, there are ten approved courses of fire as well as a Tyro Course which is designed as an option to allow tournament sponsors to test the proficiency of a brand-new shooter. Courses like the Los Alamitos Pistol Match, the International Rapid Fire (Modified), the Advanced Military Pistol Match and the Flying "M" are time proven courses which were popular in the early days of practical shooting.

Above: This NRA photo shows John Pride, the Action Shooting champion from Los Angeles PD in the act of firing one of the shots that contributed to his win in the Bianchi Cup. Pride studies marksmanship in depth.

Below: Rob Leatham won the special Colt Speed Event at the Bianchi Cup. Note the unusual targets and the varying heights at which they are placed. The challenge here is to shoot flawlessly, but also at extreme speed.

The rules and courses of fire at the Bianchi Cup are such that lots of revolvers are used. These competitors are in the process of shooting the Baricade event. The event is sponsored by Tasco scopes. While the original Bianchi Cup was run by holstermaker John Bianchi, the match is not the NRA Action Shooting championship.

The four courses of fire that decide the Bianchi Cup are the Practical Event, the Barricade Event, the Moving Target Event and the Falling Plate Event. Each of these requires 48 shots for a total possible score of 480 points. The four matches have a possible score of 1920 points. No one has ever shot a perfect Bianchi Cup.

In addition to these events, the top 20 finishers in the Bianchi Cup are eligible to enter the Speed Event. The Speed Event, sponsored by Colt, is one of two events at the Bianchi Cup that use falling metal plates for targets. The Falling Plate Event has an eight-inch diameter steel plate. The Speed Event target resembles a large ice cream cone that stands twenty-eight inches high. The top of the cone is a circular twelve inch diameter plate.

The targets for the other three events are beige cardboard targets that resemble tombstones. Known as the NRA D-1 targets, they have low visibility scoring lines. The X-ring is four inches in diameter. The A-ring is eight inches in diameter and counts ten points; the B-ring is twelve inches in diameter for eight points. The remainder of the target is worth five points.

Match I, the Practical Event, was sponsored by Action Arms, Ltd. and is the standard exercise portion of the Bianchi Cup. It is shot at ranges of 10, 15, 25 and 50 yards. All strings are shot after drawing from the holster, and at 10 yards there is a weak-hand-only string. The record for this event was established by John Pride of the Los Angeles Police Department at 480-37X. The 1987 winner of this match was Roger Burris of Mitchellville, Maryland, who set a record with a 480-43X. Pride finished in seventh place with a 478-33X.

Match II, the Barricade Event, was sponsored by Tasco.

The match gets its name from the 2x6-foot barricade which the competitor stands behind, waiting for the two turning D-1 targets to flip toward him. Strings are fired at 10, 15, 25 and 35 yards. The previous Bianchi Cup record was set by Paul Liebenberg at 480-41X in 1986. 1986 Bianchi Cup Champion Riley Gilmore was favored to win the 1987 Bianchi Cup and he won this match, tying Liebenberg's record.

In past years Match IV, the Falling Plate Event sponsored by Winchester, was the decisive event in the championship. This year the schedule was arranged to make Match III, the Moving Target Event, the deciding event in the aggregate. The scoring on the falling plates is simple: hit the plate and knock it over for ten points. If it doesn't go down — nothing. Losing one plate, ten points, is disastrous. A perfect score on this stage is 480-48X. In 1987, a dozen top shooters cleaned the plates, shooting strings at 10, 15, 20 and 25 yards.

To determine a winner on Match IV, those top shooters went into an "X-count" stage. However, plates shot in this stage only count for winning the match, they do not apply to the overall championship aggregate. The record for this event is shared by Bill Rogers and Tom Campbell at 480-155X. Brian Enos, the 1985 Bianchi Cup Champion, won this stage but did not break the record with his score of 480-153X.

Thus Match III, the Moving Target Event sponsored by Aimpoint, became the decisive match at the 1987 Bianchi Cup. A single D-1 target travels 60 feet in six seconds. The target is exposed for fifty of those feet and the competitor will shoot strings at 10, 15, 20 and 25 yards. It is a difficult course to shoot a perfect 480 on, but it has been done, and

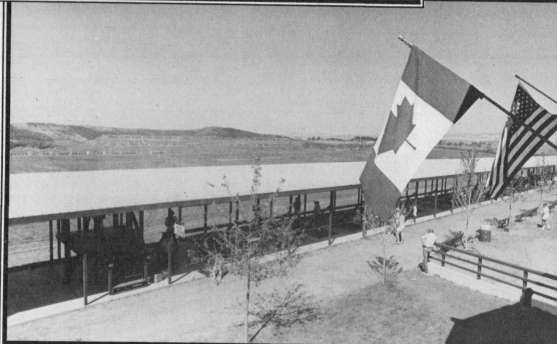

One of the larger, but lesser known shooting events is the IHMSA Nationals. The silhouette shooters are all avid handloaders, who burn up lots of ammo in matches and practice sessions. They also have built one of the best ranges in existence. These are two views of the facility in Idaho Falls, Idaho. There is also an Eastern range, where the '87 championships were held. With some targets as far away as 200 meters, it's a hefty challenge.

Cyril Rosel won the event with a 480-24X.

Rosel was not in contention to win the aggregate and the Bianchi Cup. John Shaw, one of four shooters to have shot all nine of the championships was and he shot a 476-31X. Shaw finished the aggregate at eight points off perfect with a score of 1912-147X

Riley Gilmore, the 1986 Bianchi Cup champion, was in the perfect spot to win back-to-back cups. He had won the Barricade Event, shot clean in the Falling Plate Event and was down two points in the Practical Event. The pressure was intense. The ESPN TV cameras were on him, his sponsors were watching him, the crowd was watching him, and instead of shooting a new record he dropped a shot and

posted a 470 on Match III. He would finish fourth with an aggregate of 1908-147X.

Burgess had won the Practical Event and came into the final event, Match III, down eight points. If he cleaned the mover, he could tie Shaw's score and possibly beat him on X-count. He went for it and the attempt was valiant, but he came up two points short with a 478-24X. His aggregate would leave him in third place with a 1910-152X.

Pride was the last challenge to Shaw. Although the LAPD firearms instructor had not won any of the other events, he was only four points down coming into Match III. Pride's best finish in seven trips to Columbia had been a second. He wanted to win the Bianchi Cup. Pride, who practices self-hypnosis, was confident that his armor could not be pierced the way Gilmore's had been. He shot the mover clean at seven and fifteen yards. But at twenty yards he let two shots slip out of the 10 ring and he finished the match eight points down to tie Shaw at 1912. But Pride had four more tie-breaking Xs. He was the new NRA Action Shooting Champion with a score of 1912-151X.

HANDGUN METALLIC SILHOUETTE

In the seventies, two other forms of pistol competition requiring heavy handgun loads emerged at opposite ends of the handgunning spectrum. One was long-range metallic silhouette shooting and the other was close-up shooting of bowling pins.

Shooting metallic silhouettes of chickens, pigs, turkeys and rams was a popular Mexican rifle sport which slipped across the border in the sixties. The NRA was persuaded to adopt the game and the first NRA National Rifle Silhouette Championships were held in Tucson, Arizona, in 1973.

Shortly thereafter, Lee Juras, the founder of Super Vel and originator of the Outstanding American Handgunner Award, got the idea of holding a long-range handgun match to promote handgun hunting and the Auto Mag pistol. The First National Handgun Championships for Metallic Silhouette were held in Tucson, Arizona, in 1975.

The following year the International Handgun Metallic Silhouette Association (IHMSA) was formed to promote and regulate the sport. In 1978 the NRA Silhouette Committee adopted rules for Long Range Pistol and Short Range Pistol. The latter was renamed Hunter's Pistol.

Metallic silhouette targets, whether they are used for rifle or handgun competition, are the same. Made out of ⅜-inch steel plate, they are life-size cutouts of chickens, pigs, turkeys and rams. The difference between the two courses of fire is the distance at which the targets are placed. In handgun competition, the chickens are set at 50 meters, the pigs at 100 meters, the turkeys at 150 meters and rams at 200 meters.

To score a hit in silhouette shooting, a target must be knocked over. The rams weigh 50 pounds and a bullet that hits it, but does not topple it off its stand, is scored as a miss. It takes a powerful handgun cartridge to propel a bullet 200 meters and have enough energy to knock a 50-pound ram off its feet.

The course of fire in a standard silhouette match is 40 targets, ten targets of each type of animal shot in banks of five. A competitor has two minutes to shoot each bank of five targets. At the IHMSA International Championships, the target count is doubled to 80. One target equals one point and a perfect score in any category is 80. Ties are broken by shoot-offs consisting of ten targets shot in two banks of five. The shoot-off targets are half-sized and one bank is at 150 meters and the other bank is at 200 meters. To date, no one has shot a perfect 10 in a shoot-off.

The categories of competition are Standing, Production, Revolver and Unlimited. Guns used in the Standing, Production and Revolver categories must be out-of-the-box factory models with no modifications or non-standard parts. The only modification allowed to the handgun is a trigger job.

The Unlimited class permits any kind of modification to the gun as long as it does not weigh more than 4½ pounds or have a barrel longer than 15 inches. Guns in all categories must use iron sights. Optics of any kind are not permitted.

The 1987 IHMSA International Championships were held at their brand new eastern range facility at Oak Ridge, Tennessee. The overall IHMSA champion is determined by the shooter's aggregate score of all four categories. Thirty-nine-year-old Gary Wrigley shot a perfect 80x80 in Unlimited, but wound up in 26th place with a shoot-off score of 4x10. He shot a 79x80 in the Production for a 24th place finish in that category. His Revolver score of 77x80 was good for 16th place there. But where Wrigley's strength is as a competitor is in the Standing category. Standing is the most difficult of the IHMSA disciplines, and his score of 62x80 not only won the category for him but pushed him over the top in the overall championship.

The NRA National Long Range Pistol Silhouette Championships do not declare an overall winner. But if they did, in 1987 Lon Pennington of Canon City, Colorado, would have been the champion. He entered five of the six matches and won them all. His score in Conventional Revolver was 77x80, Conventional Single Shot was 79x80, Unlimited Freestyle was 80x80, Conventional Standing was 51x80, and Unlimited Freestyle (½-size) was 79x80. The only event he did not enter was Unlimited Standing, and it was

The targets are bowling pins and the match is one that everyone loves to shoot. Richard Davis conjured up the idea and still runs the unique event. It is named for the Davis Second Chance protective vest, used by many cops.

The Second Chance match was so popular that it quickly exploded in size. It's a fun shoot, one that doesn't have delusions of grandeur about its relevance. The prizes are considerable. In this photo, Ken Tapp, on the left and Jerry Barnhart on the right are going head-to-head in a Master Blaster shoot-off. This was at the 1987 Match.

won by Robert Jackson with a 62x80. In the NRA Hunter Pistol event, Larry Weir of Dallas, Texas, dominated the matches. He won both individual matches with a total aggregate score of 113x120 to become the 1987 NRA National Hunters Pistol Silhouette Champion.

BOWLING PINS

1975 was also a significant year for the birth of another handgunning sport. Richard Davis, the inventor of concealable soft body armor, held the first Second Chance Combat Shoot in Central Lake, Michigan. In contrast to the long-range metallic targets of handgun silhouette shooting, Davis' match was shot at 25 feet and the targets were bowling pins. Five wooden bowling pins were placed on a 4-foot by 8-foot table. The object was to see who could knock the pins off the table in the fastest time. The shooter's time starts with a shot from a starter's gun and ends when the last pin hits the ground. The competitor gets to shoot six tables of five pins each. His score is an aggregate of the five best out of six times.

Unlike silhouette shooting, the success of Second Chance match did not lead to the formation of an organization to oversee the game. Davis' prime interest was operating his company, and his original intent with the bowling pin shoot was to say thank you to the people who bought his vests, not to create a new sport.

Despite Davis' intentions, bowling pin shooting has become a world-wide sport. And like other forms of competition, special guns have been developed to handle the hot loads that it requires to drive a bowling pin back three feet and off the metal-topped tables.

The Second Chance Combat Shoot is an annual event and attracts over 500 shooters every year to the small town in northern Michigan. Davis believes in keeping the rules to a minimum and he said, "Rule number one is, I get to change any rule anytime I want to!" Because he did not have to deal with organizational bureaucracy, Davis has been able to readily cope with changes in the sport.

When it appeared that the average shooter was being pushed out of the competition by shooters using expensive custom compensated semi-automatic pistols, Davis quickly split the competition into two categories. One category was created for Pin Guns and one for Stock Guns.

The rules for a Pin Gun are simple: "Hand weapon where the barrel can be of any length weighing no more than 64 ounces with an empty magazine. No optical sights allowed, no laser beams, gyro-scopes, etc. Neither can the shooter wear weighted wristwatches, sap gloves or place feet in cement."

The Stock Gun rules are equally explicit. "Any semiauto handgun with a barrel no longer than five inches and having a weight no more than 44 ounces with an empty magazine. No extended sights, weighted wrist straps or weighted gloves. Also, any revolver that has a barrel not longer than 6½ inhces and total weight not exceeding 48 ounces. The only exception will be the 7½-inch Redhawk. Mag-na-port jobs are allowed, but no extended muzzle brakes or weighted magazines.

In addition to having classes for different guns, there are two different classes of shooters at Second Chance, Ordinary Standard Shooters (OSS) and Master Blasters (MB). The 1987 Shoot saw 54-year-old Ken Tapp from Kentucky repeat his 1986 win in the MB Pin Gun Class with a aggregate time of 17.5 seconds. Jerry Barnhart was having a great year as a shooter, and won the MB Stock Gun class with an aggregate of 17.8 seconds.

Denny Shackelford, the 1986 North Carolina IPSC State Champion, won the OSS Stock Gun Class with an aggregate time for 23.4 seconds. And Canadian Nick Alexakos won the OSS Pin Gun aggregate with a time of 20.2 seconds.

STEEL CHALLENGE

In 1981, two Combat Masters from the Southwest Pistol League, Mike Dalton and Mike Fichman, founded the World Speed Shooting Championships, better known as the Steel Challenge. The tournament was hosted by the Southwest Pistol League and designed to promote pro-am shooting as inspired by the Bianchi Cup. Speed shooting is an outgrowth of practical shooting. The competitors draw from a holster and shoot at steel plates at varying distances. The targets are steel plates varying from 8-inch diameter round plates to 18-inch by 24-inch rectangles. There are a maximum of five targets in any stage. The distance from the shooter to the targets varies from 6 yards to 40 yards.

The scoring is all based on time. At the start signal, the shooter draws his pistol and shoots the plates. They do not have to be knocked over, they just have to be hit. Missing a plate is a five-second penalty. Timing is done with electronic timers which measure the elapsed time in hundreths of seconds.

The Steel Challenge, like other major shooting events, was an instant hit. The World Speed Shooting Association (WSSA) was formed to promote steel matches similar to those shot in the Steel Challenge. But the rights to the Steel Challenge were owned by the Southwest Pistol League, not the WSSA. Without title to the major event that sparked interest in the game, the WSSA has made slow progress in promoting speed shooting around the country. However, the Steel Challenge is such a popular event, it draws almost 300 competitors every year and winning it is one of the most coveted titles in the action shooting world.

The match is well named, because no one has ever won the speed shooting championship twice. John Shaw won the first Steel Challenge in 1981 and he wanted to win it again. The 1987 Steel Challenge had six different stages. After two days of competition, Shaw was three seconds ahead of the field.

On the last day of the match, Shaw faulted on his first string of a very fast stage called "Triple Threat." It caused him to slow down on his remaining runs, and Jerry Barnhart caught Shaw and gained an advantage of .19 of a second.

Shaw and Barnhart would duel it out on a stage appropriately called "Showdown." Barnhart shot first and posted an aggregate time on the stage of 11.49 seconds. A fast time, but not an unbeatable time. Shaw came to the line. His goal was to hit each plate with one shot. Missing a plate and having to pick it up with another shot cost precious time. Shaw missed three plates and posted an aggregate time of 12.02 seconds on the stage. Barnhart won the 1987 Steel Challenge by less than three-quarters of a second. His winning time was 72.80 seconds.

THE MASTERS

For years Roy Jinks dreamed of a match that would test all aspects of a handgunner's shooting ability. In 1986, with the support of Smith & Wesson and other members of the firearms industry and community, The Masters International Shooting Championship was inaugurated.

Held at the PASA range in Barry, Illinois, The Masters challenges the three major disciplines of handgun competition in reactive-style competition. The Precision Event draws from the traditional NRA Bullseye and International Shooting Union styles of shooting, using the Olympic Biathlon reactive-style target system. The shooter is required to hit extremely small targets (1.77 and 4.5 inches in diameter) at 25 to 50 meters. The Long-Range Event calls for contestants to fire at heavy, round steel plates (6, 9 and 12 inches in diameter) at ranges from 75 to 200 meters. The plates must be struck with enough force to knock them over. The Action Event is patterned after practical shooting events. Contestants draw from a holster and

The Masters International Shooting Championships comprise a difficult three-gun affair. In this Precision event, the targets are small and the shooter has to hold hard, follow through. Olympic-type score boards have spectator appeal.

The Long Range event at the Masters has targets as far out as 200 meters. This event is also a challenge to pure marksmanship skill, without onerous time limits. In the photo below, the match winner, Allen Fulford, has just let one go with a favored custom XP-100 single-shot.

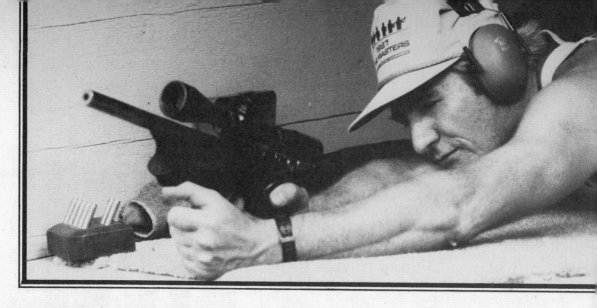

shoot at steel targets of various sizes and shapes at relatively close distances. The fastest time wins but, unlike the Steel Challenge, the plates must be knocked over.

After only two years, The Masters has become the premier pistol competition in the world in the eyes of some shooters. The challenge of each event is so difficult that no one yet has shot a perfect score.

The 1987 Masters saw the record on the Long-Range Event pushed up to 36 plates out of a possible 40 by Al Sinclair of Rock Hill, South Carolina, using a scoped and custom stocked T/C Contender. But the real story on the Long-Range course was Allen Fulford, who shot 34 plates

In the space of two short years, the Masters has come to be accepted as the premier pistol match in America. The man who wins must be capable in several styles of shooting. This year, the Master was Allen Fulford.

The record for the Masters Long Range event fell with a resounding clang as Al Sinclair took down 36 out of 40 plates. The South Carolina shooter used a Custom Contender. He also used his optical sight option here.

with iron sights on his custom stocked Remington XP-100. At The Masters, competitors are allowed to use an optical sight in only one event, but the shooter gets to make the choice.

Fulford, a 56-year-old retired cotton agronomist from Georgia, had already won the Manchester Trophy at Camp Perry. He started action shooting a few years before and he was hoping that he would be fast enough to stay in the running when he would shoot his favorite Precision event. The Action event was dominated by IPSC speedsters such as Rob Leatham and Brian Enos, but it was Jerry Barnhart, winner of the Steel Challenge, that would win the Action Event with a time of 25.15 seconds. While Fulford's time of 37.36 seconds was slow in comparison, it was fast enough to keep him in contention with about a half-dozen other shooters.

Fulford holds the record on the Precision Event at 27 plates. Other top shooters opted to use their scopes on the Long-Range event. Fulford was in his element with his Aimpoint-equipped High Standard pistol, the same pistol he had been shooting for over ten years. The pressure was on; Fulford had never shot for big prize money before and there was over $10,000 in cash and prizes if he could shoot straight.

He shot straight. Fulford knocked over 26 of the little plates, one less than his record. Allen Fulford became pistol shooting's new Master. For Fulford, pistol competition is a game where he has a lot of friends. So it was quite gratifying for him to have his friend and fellow Georgian, Jim Fulwood, win the Precision Event with 27 plates.

Everyone wants to be a winner. And Gary Wrigley said it nicely after winning IHMSA International Championship. "Don't get me wrong," he said. "I like to win. But really, the most enjoyable part of it for me is the people you meet and the friends you make at the Internationals." Competitive pistol shooting is a sport of friendships. There are more opportunities today than ever before to enjoy shooting and make new friends.

ABOUT THE AUTHOR

IT'S HARD to say where Kerby Smith is most at home: behind the mainspring housing of a much-modified Colt auto, behind the viewfinder of a modern single-lens reflex camera or even behind the keyboard of a word processor. Few people in the shooting business have assembled such a complex assortment of skills and held them in such balance. Kerby Smith bills himself as a "shooting photojournalist."

As a journalist, he has worked for such diverse publications as the New York *Times* and the *National Geographic,* contributing both well-written stories and superb photographs. From his California headquarters, he regularly sallies forth to the major handgun tournaments where he writes coverage that will appear in several different magazines. He invariably manages to shoot the match, typically with commendable results.

Kerby Smith is currently a contributing editor to Petersen's *Handguns* and a regular contributor to *Shooting Times Handguns Quarterly.* He is well qualified to comment on the Handgun Competition scene in the United States.

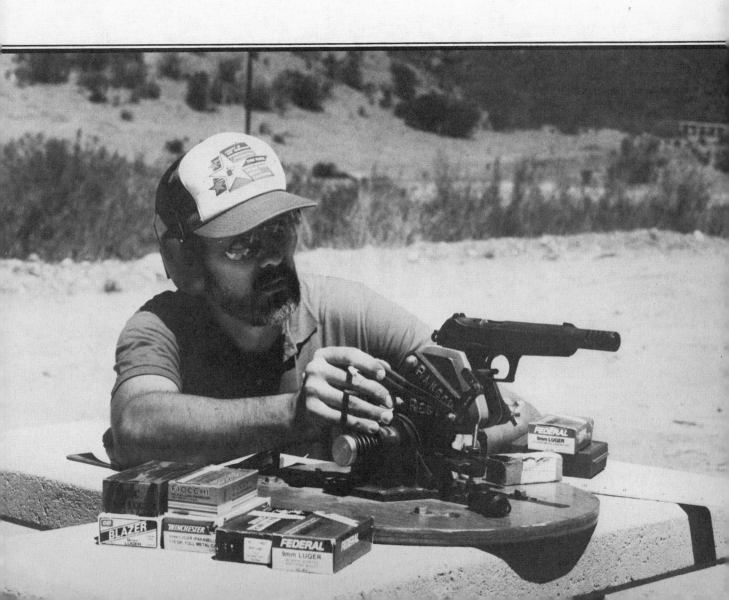

CHAPTER 11

HANDGUNS AND JAVELINAS

Arizona's Desert Ghosts Are Elusive Quarry

By Bob Davis

SOME lines just seem to stick with you. I can't help but remember Robert Ruark's classic lines in his book, *The Old Man and the Boy.* He wrote, "March is a fine month for remembering. I suppose that's because there is really nothing else you can do in it."

Arizona handgun hunters would disagree with that statement. March is the month for hunting javelina. All it takes is one handgun hunt for Arizona's desert ghost and you'll agree that March is really the month for making memories.

By the end of February in the mountains of Northern Arizona, we've had three months of nasty winter weather. Even though there are plenty of javelina within minutes of my house, I'm ready to head for the lower desert elevations and warmer temperatures. Armed with only a handgun, stalking the javelina on his native desert turf is an experience that thousands of Arizona hunters consider the only game in town.

When I think back over my years of hunting with a handgun, one element stands out in my mind. In order to be successful, you have to get close. A hunt three years ago reminds me of just how uncomfortably close you often get.

It was already the third day of the hunt when my partner and I decided to split up in order to work a series of ridgelines overlooking Roosevelt Lake in central Arizona. We had seen pigs on both of the preceding days, but had been unable to work in a position for a shot.

This was the same area in which my brother-in-law had taken a nice boar out of an exceptionally large herd. It was a little after eight o'clock in the morning and I couldn't help remembering previous years. Eight to nine o'clock had been good times for spotting javelina.

The morning silence was shattered by a shot. Then another. Raising my binoculars, I scanned the distant ridgeline where I had last seen my partner. I couldn't believe my eyes.

Through the binoculars it appeared as though the top of the ridge was moving. I was actually looking at the largest herd of javelina I had ever witnessed. A quick count revealed at least seventy pigs. As incredible as the sight

---

Facing page: He's an improbable little animal, one that you'd never figure to be nicknamed "The Desert Ghost," that is until you try hunting him. The javelina has that uncanny skill to appear and disappear, almost at will. All veteran hunters respect the little porker immensely.

Author Bob Davis has tried a variety of handgun models and calibers for his desert hunting. One of his current favorites is a compensated .45 auto, shown below. The Aimpoint 1000 sight is exceptionally practical for the quick shots that present themselves in desert hunting.

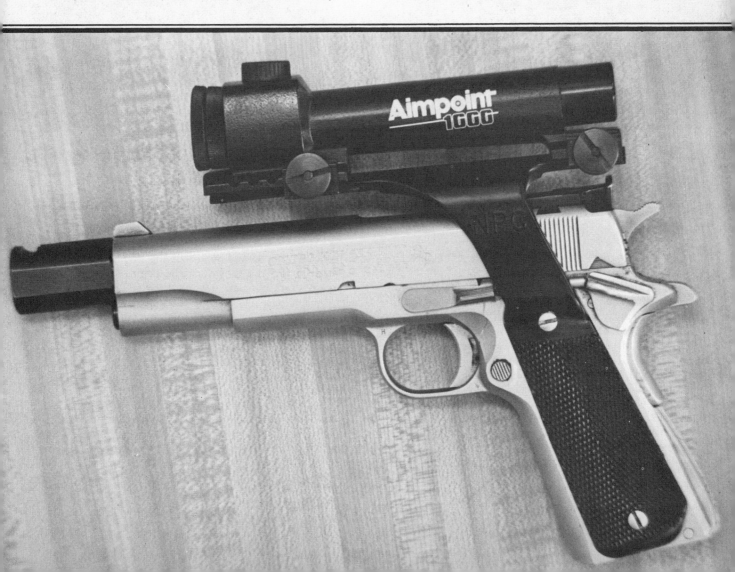

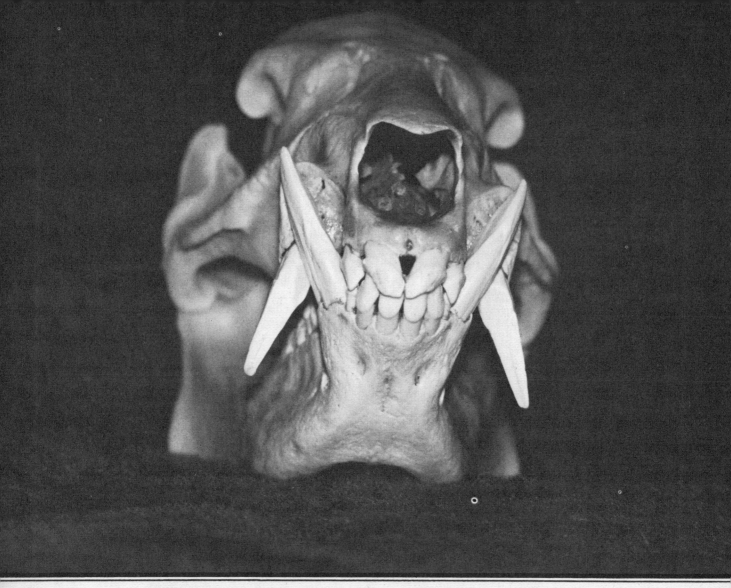

Javelina may not be as big and mean as Russian boar, but they are far from wimps. A front view of a cleaned javelina skull displays those nasty tusks and suggests the kind of trouble the desert pig can dish out. It's also wise to reflect on the fact that they travel in packs. It is smart to use a powerful handgun, don't you think?

was, I knew that this wasn't the time for sightseeing, especially with two ridgelines separating me from the pigs. Judging from their speed, it wouldn't take them long to be in the next county.

I've hunted javelina for twelve years and have found that the only predictable thing about them is their ability to be unpredictable. They will line-out and run for a mile one time, but will scatter like a covey of quail the next.

My best hope for success was to intercept them at the bottom of the wash as they made their final descent from the top of the ridge. Few experiences are quite as memorable as a high-speed cross-country run through the desert in the morning. Even at full speed, I could see that I wasn't going to make it into position ahead of the pigs.

I was relieved to see that most of the herd had formed a single line that meandered down the side of the hill. The animals in the lead appeared to be turning to my left in the creek bottom. I angled to where I thought the front of the herd would pass and knelt beside a small Palo Verde tree. At less than ten yards from the bottom of the wash, I would have an unobstructed shot at any animal passing.

After waiting about a minute, more than enough time for the pigs to be filing past, I realized that something was wrong. Over my right shoulder, I heard the grunt of a javelina. Instead of turning up the wash, they had lined-out again and were headed up the side of the canyon I had just come down. I knew that the whole herd had enough time to be well ahead of me by now. I couldn't believe my bad luck again. If I were to ever catch them, it would involve another foot race.

Even before I had run ten yards, I realized my mistake. A quick glance to my left revealed at least thirty javelina starting to bed down in the wash. The remainder of the herd, the ones I had run into the middle of, scattered in every direction.

Having made a mistake twice in just a matter of minutes, I decided that the most prudent thing to do was to just stop and see what happened next. Most of the pigs did what I expected. They ran like hell as far away from me as they could. The remainder of the herd was still milling around in the wash. One old boar caught my attention.

A big javelina will weigh forty pounds. Not only was this the largest javelina I had ever seen, but his tusks were so long they were exposed even with his mouth closed.

I slipped the safety off. At fifteen feet, the range was so close I knew that any fast movements would result in a once-in-a-lifetime opportunity vanishing into the ocotillo and greasewood.

Easy does it. Remember the front sight and don't jerk. Carefully squeezing the trigger, I felt the .45 fire.

The pig didn't move. I knew he had been hit hard. *Hit him again.* As the action cycled on the second shot, the big boar arched his back, grunted and dove into the wash out of sight.

I could only hope the 185-grain hollow points had opened up enough to provide a good blood trail. Going directly to the spot where the pig had been standing, I found his tracks but not blood. Could I have missed? I thought back on my sight picture and remembered how the boar arched his back on the second shot. I was sure that both shots had been good.

A policeman's service revolver in .357 caliber makes a fine javelina gun. It's the sort of gun that carries well in a variety of holsters. Fairly light in weight, this S&W Model 686 has plenty of power for the job at hand. The lower photo shows an assortment of cartridges for various automatics that can be fine pig-shooters. On the left, there's the 9mmP, followed by .38 Super, then 10mm Auto and .45 Auto.

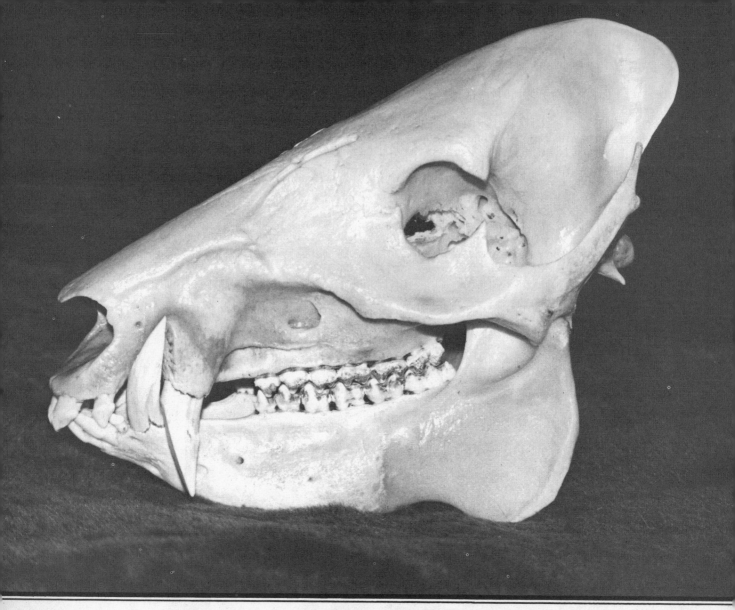

The author's own words say it best: "...couldn't help but remember those teeth. You only have to see two boars fighting over a sow in heat one time to develop a healthy respect for their ferocity...a set of dentures that could rip your leg to pieces." This is a side view of the same skull and the jaw length is apparent.

Even without seeing visible blood, I knew the pig couldn't have gone far.

On my hands and knees, I searched the area where he had been standing. After several seconds, I found coarse hairs that had been cut when the bullet struck the animal's side. Still on my hands and knees, I lined up the tracks where the pig had gone into the wash. His only avenue of escape was a thick patch of "wait-a-bit" thorns on the opposite side of the wash. He had to be in there.

I couldn't help but remember those teeth. You only have to see two boars fighting over a sow in heat one time to develop a healthy respect for their ferocity. Even the winner of the fight is often seriously wounded. This fellow I was about to crawl into a thorn thicket with had a set of dentures that could rip your legs, or anything else he got a

hold of, to ribbons. To make it worse, he was wounded. I replaced the magazine in the Colt with a fresh one.

As I started into the thicket, I spotted movement. He was headed out the opposite side. Relieved that he was going to retreat instead of taking the seemingly ineffective wounds personally, I moved to cut him off from the safety of the wash. As the boar broke for the creek bottom, I stopped, held the front sight on the front of his shoulder and emptied the gun. It was impossible to tell if the boar had been hit as he dropped down the embankment into the wash.

Standing there with my slide open, I couldn't believe that he could still be moving so fast after taking the punishment the .45 was dishing out. As I moved to the edge of the wash, I recharged the Colt with my last magazine. The boar had made it to the bottom of the wash, but he was down; this time for good.

In Arizona, any centerfire handgun is legal for hunting javelina and, in any camp you walk into, you are apt to find quite a conglomeration of firearms and ammo. Last year in our camp alone, there was a Smith & Wesson Model 25 in .45 Colt, a Sig Sauer P-226 in 9mm, a Ruger Super Blackhawk chambered for the mighty .44 magnum, a Colt Python .357 magnum and a Ruger P-85 9mm. During the course of the hunt, I observed several hunters carrying Thompson/Center Contenders and another hunter with a scoped Remington XP-100.

I have personally used a .45 auto, a 9mm, a .357 magnum and a .44 magnum, all equipped with conventional sights, to hunt javelina. Due to the close-in nature of the hunting, I haven't found that you gain that much by going to a scope. Were longer shots available, the scope would be more beneficial. I will have to admit that I was seriously considering using an Aimpoint Electronic sight on either a Colt Government Model chambered for the .45 Auto or the .38 Super for this year's hunt. Once you get used to picking up the Aimpoint's red dot, hitting moving targets is a lot easier than trying to line up conventional sights.

While you are apt to find nearly any type and caliber of firearm in the field, I don't think that I would be comfortable with anything smaller than the 9mm or .38 Special for javelina hunting.

My brother-in-law uses cast bullets in his .45 Colt and he has never had a problem in bringing down a javelina. I'm not sure that just any cast bullet would work as well as the

In Arizona, any centerfire handgun is legal and lots of old-timers get pressed into service when March rolls around. This is a Colt Police Positive Special and, with the right .38 Special ammo, it will do. Common cartridges for revolvers that go afield for javelina: .357 magnum, .41 magnum, .44 Special, .44 magnum, .45 Colt, from the left to right in the lower photo. There's plenty of power in this bunch.

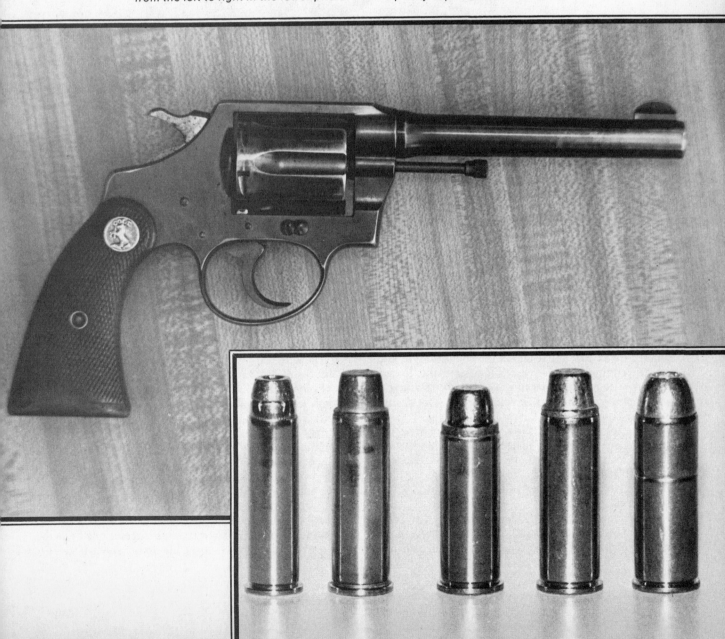

The author's brother-in-law poses with a trophy javelina. That's a healthy-sized animal. This hunter uses hard-cast lead slugs in that Smith & Wesson Model 25-5 .45 Colt and usually anchors his pig quickly. Note the background country. It's a high desert setting, fairly open but with lots of little arroyos and deep canyons.

Hensley and Gibbs 200-grain semi-wadcutter that he uses. Round nose bullets, unlike the semi-wadcutter style, don't have the cutting edges necessary for clean kills. I used a Keith-type semi-wadcutter in a six-inch .44 magnum the first couple of years I hunted javelina. I have since changed to hollow point bullets.

Any jacketed bullet, with the exception of full metal jackets, are legal for javelina. I've been experimenting with the Nosler 125-grain jacketed hollow point bullets loaded to about 1300 feet per second in my .38 Super. At the higher velocities, this bullet shows excellent expansion as well as penetration.

My informal polls in the field show that about half of the hunters reload their own ammo. The other half use factory loads. Recently, I've noticed a number of handgun hunters using the new Winchester Silvertip. I've used the Remington jacketed hollow points on several pig hunts with excellent results both in the .45 and 9mm calibers.

Before taking off on a handgun hunt, I try to spend at least several weeks preparing. One of the most common mistakes handgun hunters make is over-extending their ability to shoot their handguns effectively. Using life-sized animal targets is a good way to measure your skill level. If you can't put your shots into a predetermined kill zone at the practice range, it's a safe bet you won't be able to do it in a hunting situation either.

A good source of animal targets is Freeman's Archery and Animal Targets located at 2553 W. Morris Street in Plainfield, Indiana. Their javelina target is one of the best I've ever come across. Using life-sized targets also allows the potential hunter to better estimate range. While the point of impact doesn't vary that much from zero to twenty-five yards, once you get past the twenty-five-yard mark, range estimation starts to become critical.

Unless the hunter is used to shooting at extended ranges with a handgun, he owes it to the game he is hunting to impose limitations on the shots he will take. You can increase the number and types of shots you are qualified to take by practicing.

Running shots are another problem for the handgun hunter. Practicing a running shot is not as difficult a task as it seems. I use an old tire that has a piece of cardboard that has been inserted into the center. By having a shooting buddy roll the tire down a hill, you can gain valuable practice that would not normally be possible. As your skill level increases, the tire can be rolled faster and over rougher terrain, simulating a running game animal. With a little practice, you'll be surprised at how easy it is to hit moving targets.

The most difficult problem facing the handgun hunter is learning how to get close to his quarry. While this is a problem, getting close is the very essence of hunting and is one of the main reasons why handgun hunting is so popular. Being a skilled marksman is not enough. You have to be a skilled woodsman as well.

Learning to use available cover to prevent the animal from seeing your approach is just one of the skills necessary for success. The proper use of camouflage and learning to stay down-wind of your quarry is just as important. Most big game animals have incredible senses and for good reason; their survival depends upon their ability to detect approaching predators.

Another popular handgun 'mongst Arizona handgunners is the Commander. This one has been tricked up with extended safety and MMC sights. The little .45 carries so easy and has such respectable power that it can't be left out. Lower photo is Mr. Javelina at mealtime. This particular javelina is part of a herd that Davis can usually approach without trouble. When he came to take their picture, they shied.

You may not get a lot of shots on a javelina hunt, so practice in the off-season. Davis has high praise for the life-sized target from Freeman's. The heart-lung area is marked but it isn't very large. The aspiring javelina hunter needs to get himself a good gun, quality ammunition and these targets, then practice, practice, practice.

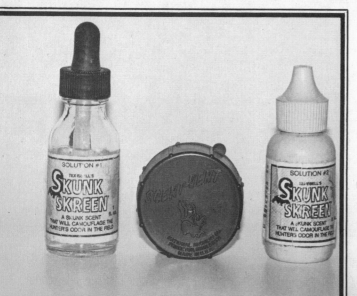

While their eyesight is poor, the javelina have excellent noses. That means that products like these, discussed in the text, are practical. Davis also uses a bath in baking soda to remove the human scent that alerts javelinas.

The javelina has the reputation of having terrible eyesight. Judging from my own experiences, I think the reputation is well deserved. While his eyesight may leave something to be desired, his other senses, especially his sense of smell and hearing, are quite acute. One whiff of human scent and he's gone!

In many hunting situations, you can't depend upon the wind direction and velocity remaining constant. There are two schools of thought on scent. My preference is to disguise my scent with a stronger, more natural outdoor odor. One of the strongest, most naturally occurring outdoor odors is that of a skunk. Tex Isbell's Skunk Skreen is the best (and strongest) skunk scent I've ever found. When placed in equal proportions in a "Scent-Vent" (a plastic capsule that vents itself when the lid is unscrewed), Skunk

Skreen creates an eye-watering solution that will camouflage even the heaviest human odor. If you prefer going the more natural way, bathing in baking soda kills body odor quite effectively as well. It is a natural deodorant.

I thought that I had covered all the bases pretty well on javelina hunting with a handgun until I got home the other day and checked the mailbox. I realized that I had forgotten one thing.

Arizona works off a drawing system for allocating big game hunt permits. You have to fill out a hunt application for each species you want to hunt. All the applications go into the computer and it selects who will be hunting (and who won't). If you are selected, your permit is mailed to you. If you are not selected, you will receive a rejection notice or a "pink slip" in the mail.

I had been rejected for the spring 1988 javelina hunt! Ruark had been right after all. At least in the Davis' house, March of 1988 would have to be "a fine month for remembering."

ABOUT THE AUTHOR:

BOB DAVIS, who hunts javelina every March (when his number is picked!) is a tall and lanky transplanted Kansan. He now lives in the beautiful juniper and redrock country of northern Arizona, where hunting of all types is just a mile or two away from town. Davis makes his living as a senior patrolman with the Arizona Highway Patrol, an organization of which he is deeply and vocally proud. Davis' background includes service with the Navy as a Medical Corpsman treating U.S. Marines wounded in Vietnam.

Bob is an avid hunter and outdoorsman who keeps his shooting skills honed razor-sharp in the competitive arena. An active competitor in several shooting disciplines including Service Rifle and IPSC pistol, Davis handloads most of his own ammunition. He is forever fiddling with his loads and that experimentation has attracted the attention of shooting editors. Bob has published a number of recent articles in *Shooting Times* magazine. Anyone who reads what he writes quickly comes to understand that he knows what he's talking about and says so in the plainest terms possible. It's a pleasure to have his work gracing the pages of this edition. — *WC*

CHAPTER 12

WHEELGUNNING AFRICA...

Where The .454 Casull Is Right At Home

THE TRACKERS had made several serious mistakes when they built the grass blind at the lion bait. They had chosen the base of a large anthill to erect the blind, which would place us between the lions to our front and the water hole to our backs. Beyond the water hole was where we would have to park the Land Rover when we approached the blind. Apparently, with the anthill to our backs, they had felt it was not necessary to completely surround us with the blind and they only built a grass wall six feet high and eight feet long.

Late in the afternoon, we parked the Land Rover about a mile from the blind and made a quiet approach. The lions — two males and several lionesses — were on the bait. Professional hunter Craig Hunt and I both realized, as we approached the blind, that where and how it was built could become dangerous in a hurry. As I settled into the blind, I tried not to think about Cape buffalo being a staple in the lion's diet! With a name like Kelly, you'd think I'd pay more attention to Murphy's Law: "If something can go wrong, chances are that it will." Craig Hunt, our tracker

Facing page: That's the author, his professional hunter and one very dead Cape buffalo. Kelly took the buffalo with a special revolver shown above. It is the Freedom Arms .454, probably the most powerful factory-produced handgun in the world. The handloaded ammunition uses a special 300-grain, thick-jacketed slug at about 1700 feet per second. Recoil is heavy, but manageable, and Kelly took a wide variety of African game with the gun.

and I were about to become believers in said law!

I was in Africa for my ninth safari, with professional hunter Don Price and one of his men, Craig Hunt. Price runs Busanga Trails in Zambia. For the past fifteen years, as a professional hunter, he has been involved extensively in culling buffalo and elephant, as well as problem animal control, particularly lion. I've hunted with Price before and am impressed with his ability, especially in his handling of dangerous game.

Most of my hunting has been done with custom Rugers, custom Smith & Wessons and J. D. Jones' .375 Handcannon by SSK Industries. This time, I was testing a new gun, the .454 Casull by Freedom Arms. The .454, of course, is not new, but it was the first time I'd used one on a hunt and I was anxious to find out what this gun could do.

Sometime back, I became acquainted with Wayne Baker of Freedom Arms and one of his staff, Ron Ptashkin. Ron impressed me as quite a gun man, as well as a businessman, and had something I admire in a man: common sense. He had approached me at the annual Safari Club Convention regarding a limited edition gun based on my thirty years of hunting with a handgun. I was flattered and impressed with the way the edition was to be offered. Like the .454 itself, it was to be top-drawer in quality. I told him I'd think it over.

I'd seen a good deal of the work that came out of the Freedom/Custom shop, such as the Handgun Hunter Hall of Fame guns, and knew Ptashkin would give it his best shot.

Several months later, he flew to the Mag-na-port facility in Mount Clemens, Michigan, and handed me one of the prototype guns for the edition. The gun was a .454 Casull that duplicated the custom Stalker I had developed for big-game handgun hunting. It had my favorite barrel length of 8⅜ inches. I prefer this length, as it balances well

and points well for me. It also had four-port Mag-na-porting, an inverted muzzle crown, a smoothed action with three-pound trigger pull, sling swivels and a sling, a 2x Leupold scope in their excellent mounting system, black micarta grips and resting places in the cylinder for five of the most powerful revolver cartridges in the world. If this gun performed as well as it looked, I was going to say, "Yes," to the edition.

Many of the .454s had passed through my employees' hands to be Mag-na-ported and they continually remarked on the gun's quality. I was interested in the gun but was sure that a gun with the power of the .454 was going to kick like a mule. That's why I had avoided it for so long. I don't like recoil! I can't see being abused when I'm shooting a handgun for sport or pleasure. That's the reason I experimented with the porting of guns and ultimately founded Mag-na-port. You need a big, heavy, powerful cartridge for big-game, but you don't need a gun that hurts you when it goes *bang!* I was in for a pleasant surprise. The Mag-na-ported .454 didn't have nearly the recoil I had expected. In fact, it was quite controllable.

I had asked for a heavy jacketed 300-grain bullet with a velocity of around 1700 feet per second. Most commercially-produced jacketed bullets for handguns have a .012-inch thick jacket and soft-lead core. The factory premium bullets from Freedom Arms have a .032-inch thick jacket and a hard-lead core. Dick Casull discovered early in the development of the .454 that standard jacketed bullets would not stand up to the pressures generated by this round. This is a bullet that leaves nothing to be desired. It performed so well for me that, as I continue to use the .454, I doubt I'll ever change this load. I had complete penetration on almost every animal I shot, including Cape buffalo. This is exactly what I want in a bullet. You need a heavy, tough bullet to penetrate the hide and bone of the big ones

The story behind the hunt for this young male is enough to make your heart stop. The lion is a dangerous game species and Kelly halted this one at a too-close range.

and a large exit hole was generally a bonus with this round. But I'm getting ahead of myself...

I had already experienced a sampling of Murphy's Law when, having already taken three Kafue lechwe (one of which will tie for second place in the Safari Club International record book) I was standing in the back of the Land Rover as it raced across the Kafue Flats. Animals were everywhere. Wildebeest, hartebeest, lechwe, zebra, running alongside the Land Rover. It was a scene straight out of *National Gerographic.* I felt like a king; the wind in my face, in the midst of thousands of animals — however there's one hole on the Kafue Flats, and we hit it at 60 mph. The Land Rover became airborne and wrenched my grip from the roll bar with enough force to throw me against the bar, fracturing my left rib cage so that it shifted and pressed

against my left lung. I knew I was seriously hurt but didn't know the extent of the damage; neither did the doctor at the hospital in Lusaka, as the X-ray machine hadn't worked for some time. After poking me, he said, "I don't know if you have internal injuries, cracked ribs, or what." Great! I could have told him that. It was a good thing the safari outfit had pain pills, because the doctor didn't.

Now what? Should I go back home for proper medical care or try to continue the hunt? Did I have internal injuries — would I die here?

"Kelly," I said, trying to dredge up some courage, "you came here to hunt, so let's get on with it."

I was in pain for the rest of the hunt. It hurt like hell when I raised my left arm and I didn't do my best shooting, but I did manage to salvage the hunt.

The .454 was a good killer of plains game and it was time to try it on the ones that bite back. As we needed lion bait, and a local chief had requested hippo meat, we decided to take two of them. Many people don't realize that a hippo is a dangerous animal. They are responsible for more deaths than any other animal in Africa. The hippo, for all its size, presents a small target when in the water, and, generally, all you have for an aiming point are the eyes and ears. This requires precision shooting.

We found a huge bull about sixty yards from shore. I took a rest, aimed between his eyes, and squeezed the trigger. The impact of the bullet actually jerked his head up and out of the water. It looked as though, had he not been in the water, it would have knocked him back on his haunches. The second hippo was much the same; another one-shot kill, with spectacular results.

While natives were skinning the hippo, Don Price and I headed downriver to try for a big croc. I spotted one swimming that would go twelve or thirteen feet. Price said, "Take him!"

I put the cross-hairs on his head, led him a bit and squeezed off. The croc arched his back on impact, his mouth open as he rolled over and sank like a battleship. Generally, when you shoot a croc, the tracker will not retrieve it; they are frightened of the huge reptile only being wounded. There was no doubt in their minds about this

one, as they immediately took to the water to retrieve it. By the time they were halfway there, the croc had already sunk and was not to be recovered. I was becoming more and more impressed with this .454.

I was more than satisfied with the performance of this gun and decided it was time to try for a Cape buffalo. We needed a couple of buff for lion baits and weren't trophy hunting, but I did want to take a good representative buff with the gun.

Price and the trackers found a large herd in a large open area called a dambo. As we checked the wind and circled to make our approach, we knew there were lions in the area, as the buffalo were nervous, shuffling around and continually looking over their backs. We also were looking for lions — being in the tall grass stalking a herd of Cape buffalo, while they are also being hunted by lions, is a sure way of not collecting your social security. We couldn't see any lions and the buff had settled down somewhat, so we began to stalk. We caught up with the herd at the edge of a thicket and I got to within sixty-five yards. As we weren't trophy hunting, it was agreed that after I shot, if it looked as though we'd have to chase the buff, Price would drop him with his .458. At the shot, the buff dropped, shuddered all over, then regained his feet and took off running away from the herd — a sure sign of a good hit. Price hit him again with his .458 and the buff was down for good.

Right: this photo gives idea as to size of the .454 round. From left, the regular .45 ("Long") Colt, the .454 and the .45 Winchester mag. The .454 is longer by significant and obvious margin.

Africa's "river horse" or hippopotamus is big enough and mean enough to be responsible for thousands of deaths in Africa every year. Author Kelly took this one with a single shot from the reliable .454 Casull revolver.

But we didn't need Don's shot; the .454 had smashed the near shoulder, gone through both lungs, clipped the aorta, smashed the far shoulder, then had come to rest under the skin on the far side of the animal. This was the one bullet I recovered on the hunt. All exposed lead ahead of the jacket was gone, with the rest of the lead still in the jacket that hadn't deformed much. I couldn't ask for anything better than complete penetration on a Cape buffalo that went 1800 to 2000 pounds; a good trophy with a thirty-seven-inch spread.

I was hunting with Craig Hunt when I took the second buffalo. The herd was feeding toward us and one was a nice

bull. I was behind an anthill in a cramped position and could barely move my left arm, the pain was so intense. The bull was broadside to me and walking slowly. I put the cross hairs behind his shoulder and squeezed, or rather, jerked the trigger. The buff stumbled and took off, following the rest of the herd. Gut shot! I consider a wounded Cape buffalo that has its adrenalin pumping to be the hardest animal in the world to stop. As he ran off, I put another .454 about an inch off his exhaust port, called the O-ring in Africa. The bull ran into the brush with the rest of the herd. I replaced the two rounds in the .454 and we went in after him. After about one hundred yards, Craig Hunt spotted the bull in the bush about eighty yards away, looking right at us. The tracker had a stick, which I used as a rest. I cocked the hammer on the .454 and got a bead under his nose, and as I did — out he came! Just as he charged, I busted him. Well, he just disappeared from view. I knocked him right on his O-ring. He started bellowing, which I took to be the death bawl that a buff makes just as he dies. I turned to Craig and said, "Boy, I knocked the .... out him, didn't I?"

Hunt declared, "Hey! He's mad!"

"What do you mean? He's dying!"

"No, he isn't, he's roaring mad!"

Hunt was right, but the buff was apparently hit too hard to do anything but stand there and roar. We circled to the left of the animal and I put one through his neck and that was the end of that. This was a big beefy bull with a forty-inch spread. If you've ever had to take a front-on shot at a charging Cape buffalo, you'll know what I mean when I say I awed at the power of the .454 Casull when it stopped him. We now had our lion bait.

A lion always goes to water after he feeds. Great! The water hole was behind us and the Land Rover behind that. It was getting close to dark, and, at best, if the lions went to water after dark, they'd be between us and the Land Rover.

Add to this the fact that, rather than being totally enclosed by the blind and having only a grass wall in front of us, the cats just might be a bit upset as they pass the flimsy curtain and discover uninvited dinner guests. When a blind completely surrounds you, it's like a false security blanket. It won't keep a lion out, but it will deter the cat, as it isn't quite sure what's inside. While it's trying to decide when and where to come in, you can shoot through the blind.

Here comes Murphy's Law! The big male got up, moved to the right — out of my line of sight — and headed for the water hole. I couldn't see him to shoot and, as I looked back at the bait, four of the lionesses had decided that there was something wrong at the blind. The big male was somewhere behind us, and the lionesses — their bellies to the ground and ears flattened — were circling the anthill to make false charges at the blind. We were in trouble, and the situation was getting worse by the minute!

Craig Hunt and the tracker — with a .458 and .375 respectively — guarded our back and sides. I was at the bottom of the anthill, looking through the peephole to watch the younger male. During all this, he just lay there, watching it all. The lionesses were getting braver and braver. At the side of the blind now, low to the ground, they were rush-

Not all of Kelly's hunting was of the big ones that bite. This lechwe has a beautifully shaped set of horns. The .454 Casull was more than enough gun for the job. There is lots of variety in the shape of African game horns.

ing the blind and backing off again. I looked back through the hole in the blind at the young male, and he got up, kind of stretched and yawned — then charged right at the blind!

I stuck the .454 out the hole and only had time to yell, "Lion coming!" Craig Hunt was above me and had no way of seeing through the blind, but he could hear the lion coming. The lion was in the scope, coming full-bore at us. When he was six or seven feet from us, I fired and hit him in the chest. It, literally, blew the lion over backwards. It was like he went straight up in the air, clawing at his chest. As he went over backwards, his rear paws kicked dirt and sticks all over the blind and Craig, not able to see what was happening, cut loose with his .458 at the sound. He missed the cat that was already down and somewhat to the left of the spot that Craig had shot at.

It didn't make any difference though — that cat was dead when it hit the ground. Craig wanted me to put another one into the lion, so I stood up where I could see over the blind and put an insurance shot into him. Then out stepped a lioness that apparently was either behind us, or lying off to the side. I'm not sure which. She was a big mama. She walked to the young male, nudged it and started to make noises like she was crying. I said to Craig, "She's crying." He said, "No, she isn't." I said, "She crying." He said, again, "No, she isn't." Then the lioness turned and glared at us with a look that I'll never forget as long as I live! There was nothing but hate in that look. "She's coming," I said and Craig didn't say anything. The tracker, Craig and I were shoulder-to-shoulder. The tracker was watching our back, while Craig and I riveted our attention on the lioness, when we heard the Land Rover coming. The driver, having heard the shooting, was coming to pick us up. When he got close to us, we jumped in, fired several shots to scare the lioness, drove to the dead lion, threw him in the Land

Below: The scoped .454 is a massive handgun, but it is effectively dwarfed by the size of the tusks on this warthog. This animal may be one of the smaller of the African game animals, but it isn't easy to kill. Author's big .454 got it done.

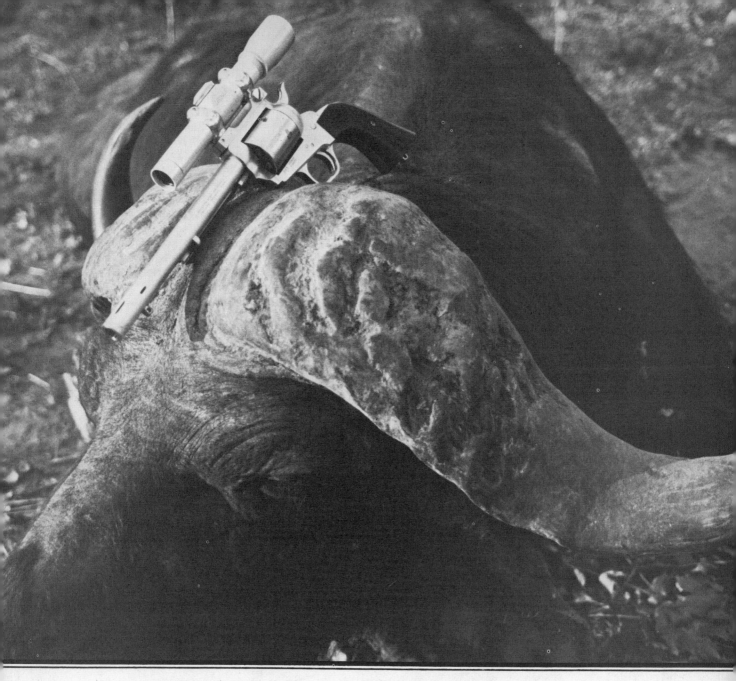

Kelly's buffalo is no midget of an animal, either. The beefy revolver sits atop a hefty boss of horns. This view shows a pair of ports on the left side of the gun's barrel. They are a Kelly innovation and make shooting the .454 downright bearable.

Rover and got the hell out of there. Upon examining the lion, we found the .454 had entered his chest and exited just ahead of the rear leg.

The .454 had proven itself in Africa as accurate, dependable and capable of taking any animal on earth. I was more than happy to put my name on this gun.

I had planned to hunt another lion in South Africa, as well as a sitatunga, which to my knowledge, had never been taken with a handgun, but Murphy wasn't through with me yet. I had not taken my malaria pills before leaving for Africa and had not built up immunity to the disease. By the time I had remembered to take the pills, I discovered I had left them at a previous camp. I was down for the count!

While I was in the hospital undergoing treatment for malaria, tests showed I had a disease called bilharzia. This is a parasite that lives in a snail in the African waters and attacks the internal organs. Since I had been bathing and wading in these waters for several years — the last four of which I was constantly ill — I believe I've been infected for some time now.

I'd like to warn those who may be planning a trip to Africa to be certain to take their malaria pills for immunity and, as I've been to many doctors and hospitals stateside and none of them discovered the bilharzia, I'd like to alert them to the fact that it is a disease that cannot be diagnosed in normal medical circles in this country.

ABOUT THE AUTHOR

LARRY KELLY is one of those rare fellows who managed to make a business out of a pleasure, or perhaps vice versa. A number of years ago, Kelly took a technology common to precise machine shop work and applied it to the gun business. The procedure was EDM, the cutting of precisely shaped and burr-free holes in metal by electrostatic discharge. Kelly cut holes in barrels in such a way as to vent powder gasses upward and thus control recoil. As you read this, the Mag-na-port company has tamed vicious recoil for thousands of shooters. Thus, business from pleasure — or vice versa.

Calming the abrupt rearward movement of magnum handguns enabled Kelly to pursue a goal of promoting handgun hunting as a real and viable sport, both here and abroad. He currently heads the Handgun Hunter Museum and Hall of Fame and has been closely associated with the Outstanding American Handgunner Foundation. He still finds time to actively hunt all over the world. Happily enough, he also finds time to write about his adventures. The accompanying story gives the reader an insight into the thrill of handgun hunting, as well as the dedication and skill of Larry Kelly. — WC

As the century opened, the choice in defensive handguns was almost always one of the revolvers of the late 19th Century. The Colt SAA did not persist as a fighting tool; the Webley lasted through WWII.

CHAPTER 13

CHOOSING THE COMBAT HANDGUN

Considerations Of Defensive Tools — A 20th Century Phenomenon

By Ken Hackathorn

(EDITOR'S NOTE: A conversation with this author is an education in many ways, but inevitably leads to a discussion of choices in combat handguns. Ken often begins his commentary with what I call the Hackathorn Hypothesis — "What if you were in a dark room and knew that a succession of homicidal terrorists was going to come through the door, one at a time, each with a razor-sharp machete in his hand? What if you were allowed to choose either a .45 auto with a magazine of seven rounds or an M9 with seven? What would you choose?"

Clearly, Ken Hackathorn has his reasons for making his choice. But it is important to understand that the choice is an informed one. For that reason, we have to consider his discussion of the evolution of the combat handgun as a prelude to making a choice.)

THE SERVICE sidearm is one of the more interesting fighting arms of the Twentieth Century. While other arms have changed the nature of warfare far more, the role of the pistol as a means of personal defense remains as solid today as it was in the first years of this century. Virtues and weaknesses of the handgun as a fighting tool have been modified little with the passing of time. Service sidearms remain close-quarters combat tools. Close-quarters battle relates to ranges from arm's length to twenty-five meters. Most combat pistol work is at ranges of ten meters and less. For such use, the fighting handgun in proper form has few equals. A service pistol, be it revolver or autoloading pistol, is easy to carry, powerful, reliable and easy to shoot with only one hand.

By the year 1900, some changes had begun in the concept of a service pistol. Only with active combat experience do we really begin to understand just how good a particular service pistol really is. Handgun design and concepts are often slow in changing. While there have been hundreds of pistols and revolvers manufactured for service use, only a relatively small number have stood the test of time.

With the dawn of the present century, a couple of service revolvers dominated the field. Both the Colt Single Action Army and British Webley had gained real regard. The Colt SAA .45 was put into service in 1873 and remained popular into the first quarter of the Twentieth Century. Many a lawman of our great Southwest still packed the Colt SAA well into the 1930s. George Patton went off to hunt Pancho Villa with a Colt SAA .45 in his holster and still packed the same sidearm during his march across Europe during the Second Great Hate. The excellent balance and reputation of the Colt for its Indian Wars utility added to the attitude that the Colt was a real man's fighting sidearm.

The Webley .455 Mk I was adopted initially in 1887 and served the British, with a variety of modifications and models, until 1926. The Mk VI .455 Webley was still in issue during the Second World War. During this period of time, the Webley served the Crown in a vast number of conflicts and was one of the most combat-tested revolvers of its time.

The Webley offered a fast reload ability and double-action firing mode. When the Webley was mated to the Prideaux quick loader — an all-steel speed loader — the Webley offered recharging of the revolver in combat with

The major advantage of both of these 19th Century guns is their caliber. Both of them are .45s, throwing a big chunk of lead at a decent velocity. The Colt was slow to reload, but the Webley was faster than most modern revolvers. The single-action revolver died with the Colt.

far greater speed than any other sidearm of the day. The Webley was certainly far better suited for close-quarters combat than the Colt SAA, but due to the lack of the romantic exposure in the British tabloids, the Webley never gained the popularity of the Colt SAA, which captured the glamour of the American Wild West.

Belgium-made and -designed Nagant revolvers found great success with much of the European military of the late 1890s. Chambered for 7.5, 8 and 9mm, the Nagant set

Interestingly enough, the Nagant system attempted to resolve what was seen to be the major disadvantage of revolvers — barrel to cylinder gas loss. Since there was nothing in the same caliber to compare it to, the issue was never really resolved. The Colt was probably better.

Right at the end of the 19th Century, a number of truly practical double-action revolvers appeared. Here's the Russian Nagant and one of the early Colt DA .38s. The Nagant hung on to the one-at-a-time ejection of Colt's SAA, but the DA Colt used an early swing-out cylinder.

the trend for smaller medium-bore service revolvers. Also, the trend to double-action trigger systems had begun and the Nagant was a popular sidearm partially for this reason.

In 1892, the French adopted the Lebel 8mm revolver which offered not only double-action trigger design, but also the swing-out cylinder to provide fast emptying and reloading capabilities. At the same time, the United States adopted the Colt .38 double-action revolver. This Colt .38 DA was given great hope, since the U.S. Cavalry wanted

This muscular young shooter with his custom Hi-Power in practical leather would have been an object of much curiosity on a shooting range around the turn of the century. In those days, defensive shooting was unheard of. Marksmanship was all bullseye, one-handed standing.

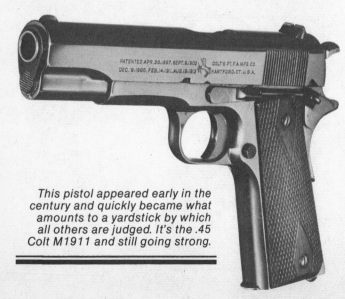

This pistol appeared early in the century and quickly became what amounts to a yardstick by which all others are judged. It's the .45 Colt M1911 and still going strong.

a much-faster-to-operate sidearm. The Colt .45 SAA always had suffered from the weakness of slow reloading. In most nations, the calvary had the final say in handgun use, since the handgun was considered the primary tool of the horse-mounted trooper.

By the turn of the century, the Colt SAA and Webley still were popular fighting arms. The Nagant and Lebel remained in use for decades, but the winds of change had begun with the introduction of the autoloading pistol.

While the service sidearms of the 1890s and 1900s remained quite basic, the major reason for this was not the availability of the weapons, but to a greater degree, the techniques of using the sidearm. Handgun skill was limited purely to target shooting form. Anyone learning to shoot a handgun was limited to the strict bullseye target shooting technique. Tradition was maintained along the lines of the shooting schools of the mid-1800s at which proper gentlemen were taught the art of pistol shooting to enhance their odds of survival in a "duel."

Dueling was the first truly handgun oriented "martial art." Rules were quite strict and a stance, with a one-hand firing position, was developed to provide a small target profile. This dueling shooting stance was a product of the mid-1800s and remained not only as the proper way to fire a sidearm in the early 1900s, but is with us today in the formal NRA or UTI pistol discipline.

Any individual wanting to learn pistol skills in the late 1800s or early 1900s was forced to join a target club or pistol shooting association, many of which had sprung up over much of the USA and Europe. The Bisley tradition was established in England, and the American revolver club became the norm in pistol training. A skilled sidearm user of the early years of this century would stand in the classic dueling stance, cock his revolver in the single-action mode and fire a careful deliberate shot. Any notion of firing a sidearm in any other manner was not allowed.

Popular sidearms of the era reflected this approach. Long barrels were favored not only for the use of burning the black powder in the cartridges, but because the extended sight radius was of assistance in target shooting. Even with the popularity of the newer double-action revolver, the established manner of shooting dictated that the revolver be cocked manually and fired in the single-action mode.

In the 1890s, the first practical autoloading pistols began to appear. Of course, the Mauser military pistol of 1896 was one of the first auto pistols to gain acceptance. While many autoloading pistols were introduced, few gained any acceptance. By 1900, the Swiss had adopted the Luger Parabellum pistol in 7.65mm.

Autoloading pistols showed great promise as a military pistol and, once again, the cavalry tactics that dominated military pistol thinking of that era created excitement about the idea of an improved fighting tool. John Browning had started things rolling in the United States with his M1902 .38 Colt Military pistol.

The U.S. Army recognized the appeal of giving the cavalry trooper a pistol that was easy to shoot, fast to reload and had a cartridge capacity greater than that of the revolver. American military experiences had established the fact that .45 caliber was the most desirable in a fighting pistol. John Browning went to work to develop a .45 auto pistol. His M1905 was the first step and the later M1910

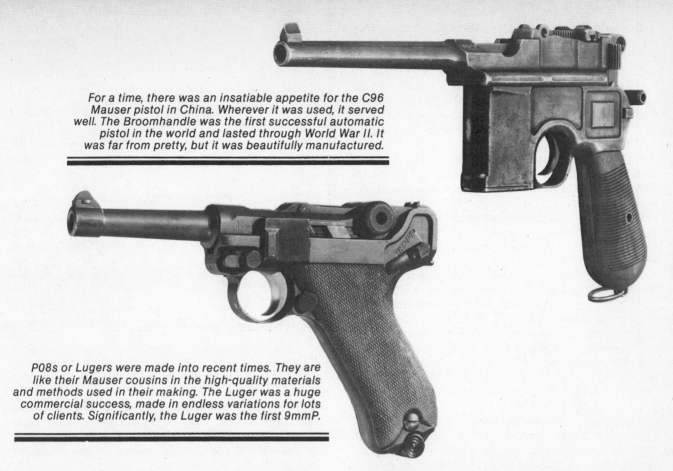

For a time, there was an insatiable appetite for the C96 Mauser pistol in China. Wherever it was used, it served well. The Broomhandle was the first successful automatic pistol in the world and lasted through World War II. It was far from pretty, but it was beautifully manufactured.

P08s or Lugers were made into recent times. They are like their Mauser cousins in the high-quality materials and methods used in their making. The Luger was a huge commercial success, made in endless variations for lots of clients. Significantly, the Luger was the first 9mmP.

.45 Colt pistol became the U.S. Army M1911 .45 ACP pistol.

At about the same time, the German Army took an interest in the Parabellum pistol. They preferred a caliber greater than the 7.65mm, and the 9mm Luger pistol was adopted in 1904 for German Navy use. By 1908, the German Army had standardized the 9mm Luger pistol as their official sidearm.

Much of Europe made the change to self-loading pistols in the first decade of the Twentieth Century. England stayed with the .455 Webley and much of America — par-

ticularly the police and civilian populace — preferred the revolver. To most Americans, the autoloading pistol was a gadget, certainly not the sort of thing on which one would stake his life. While the new generation of service revolvers offered swing-out cylinders and double-action trigger systems, few shooters took advantage of these features. The new auto pistol, with greater cartridge capacity and faster reloading modes, was not popular either; the one-handed, slow-fire target shooting technique of the era called for none of these assets. Any advances in the weapon's combat potential were ignored totally.

The big Webleys were so popular that they led to little Webleys. This reflects the trend to smaller, more compact ammunition that crept into combat weaponry doctrine.

By the beginning of the second decade of this century, the storm clouds of war had begun to gather over Europe. For the most part, fighting pistols were intended for cavalry use. The tiny sights on service pistols reflected the concept that a pistol was to be used at nearly arm's length or a distance slightly beyond that of the saber. Regardless of intended use, the service pistol of the era was subject to training that dictated dueling-stance bullseye target shooting.

When the First World War broke out, the Imperial German Army was issued the Luger pistol. This P08 was highly regarded as a service pistol. Austria had the M1911 Steyr Hahn and Hungarian Cavalry units issued the M1907 8mm Roth Steyr. The British had their battle-proven Webley .455 revolver, and France was armed with the M1892 8mm Lebel revolver. When the U.S. entered the war, Colt's M1911 .45 ACP pistol was the standard military sidearm.

Shortages of sidearms were noted by all combatants. The U.S. put the Smith & Wesson large-frame Hand Ejector revolver series into service with such modifications as are incorporated in the M1917 .45 ACP revolver. This revolver was modified to shoot the .45 ACP cartridge with the aid of special steel half-moon clips. Colt adapted their New Service revolver to use the same half-moon clips to fire the .45 auto pistol cartridge. These M1917 Colt and S&W revolvers were issued in large numbers to make up for shortages of the M1911 pistol.

The Colt New Service had been adopted in 1909 in .45 Colt caliber as the new U.S. service revolver. The U.S. Marines favored this big Colt, but adoption of the Colt .45 ACP pistol in 1911 ended the 1909 New Service revolver as an issue sidearm. Smith & Wesson had improved upon their medium-bore First Model Hand Ejector and pro-

Combat pistolcraft got back on track in the 1920s and 1930s when Fairbairn of Shanghai began serious study of the matter. The stance of the bullseye shooter, as seen here, changed to reflect real gunfight situations.

duced the "Triple Lock" in .44 Special in 1907. These large N-frame S&W revolvers were to become top choices of professional gunmen and lawmen for the next three decades.

With the end of the so-called Great War in 1918, the trend in service pistols was well established. The autoloading pistol had proved itself more than rugged enough for combat use. The revolver, while still in use in some nations, was now history as an army-issue weapon.

While the armies of the world were busy adopting auto pistols, civilians simply did not take to the self-loader and

In World War I, there weren't enough .45 automatics to go around. The War Department bought over 300,000 of these Colt and Smith & Wesson 1917 revolvers. The big revolvers used .45 ACP ammo with the half-moon clips.

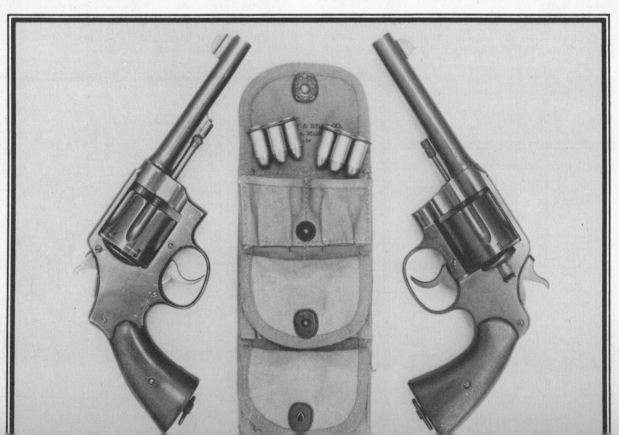

revolvers remained their handguns of choice. With the peace that followed WWI, demand for revolvers grew in the private sector. Police agencies of the United States were revolver-equipped organizations. The typical lawman of the Midwest or Southwest would pack nothing less than a Colt SAA or S&W .44 or .45. The M1917 Colt and S&W revolver became a top-choice police sidearm. Most state troopers preferred the big Colt New Service revolver in .45 Colt caliber.

The only interest in the then-new trend toward .38 Special revolvers came from the larger urban police agencies. In 1926, the New York City Police Department adopted the Colt .38 Special Army revolver. Colt renamed the Army Special to be the Official Police model. This Colt .38 Special OP revolver became the the most common police sidearm in the U.S. for the next thirty years.

The Colt Official Police .38 Special was an extremely fine revolver: rugged, reliable and accurate. Most important was the fine single-action trigger pull, coupled with the ease of thumb cocking; the OP became the favorite target arm of that era. This single-action firing technique was still the norm by which police officers trained. The bullseye target range was the only system used to prepare the police officer for lethal combat.

By the early 1930s, the lawless times brought on by prohibition were causing great concern in the law enforcement community and firearms training was taking on new meaning. A number of knowlegeable individuals were advocating the technique of firing the service revolver using the double-action mode. Trigger cocking was considered to be nearly impossible and anyone recommending this practice was considered to be a crackpot.

When the then-new FBI set out to establish a firearms

In the period between wars, Colt and Smith & Wesson brought the medium-framed, double-action revolver to the nation's police in this basic form. The Colt Official Police above; the S&W Military & Police model below.

training program, popular trick-shooting artist Ed McGivern was foremost in his recommendation that the new G-men be taught the skills of double-action revolver shooting. Many veterans of the First World War, particularly a number of English authors, recommended the concept that any skilled combat shooter be capable of firing his revolver quickly and accurately with the double-action trigger cocking mode. Often these men were the subject of a great deal of negative attitude from their Bisley shooting colleages in England.

A medium-frame S&W evolution: The top revolver is a pre-war M&P target model, the middle gun a World War II Victory model and the lower gun a contemporary M13 with round butt and three-inch barrel in .357 magnum.

Compare the shooting stance of this shooter with the one on other pages. This competitor is using the weak hand, simulating a disabling wound to the right arm. He is in a kneeling position, shooting at practical targets.

One of the most remarkable men of that era was William Ewart Fairbairn. Fairbairn was a veteran police inspector for the City of Shanghai, China. He had studied the problems of close-quarters battle with the handgun and had come up with a handgun training program that was certainly revolutionary by the standards of that time.

Fairbairn was brash enough to state to his colleagues in both England and America that target shooting was of no value in teaching an individual to use a pistol in combat. One can imagine the reaction to his published ideas at that time. As history would prove, his ideas and concepts were highly valid, but at the time of his announcement of these facts, Fairbairn was considered a man of unstable mind.

Between the years 1920 and 1939, much of the world remained at a slow pace regarding handgun utility. France fiddled about, trying to find a new service pistol to replace their M1892 Lebel revolver. Britain decided to replace the MK IV .455 revolver with a smaller frame .38 caliber Webley. The Brits reasoned that, if they were to load the .38 S&W cartridge with a 200-grain bullet traveling at 650 feet per second, they would have the stopping power of the .455, but with the lighter bulk and recoil of the .38.

Much of the rest of the military powers of the world were arming with whatever handgun they could afford. The Mauser Military of 1896 was most popular with many small nations and the war-lords of feudal empires. The M96 Mauser was popular in Russia in the last days of the Czar and later became a prize sidearm of the Bolsheviks. Vast numbers of the M96 Mauser pistols were sold in China. German arms merchants sold the M98 Mauser rifle and companion M96 Mauser pistol to many war-lord armies on the China mainland. The M96 Mauser was used as a police pistol well into the 1970s in much of China.

Above: The Radom or VIS pistol was made in Poland, first by native Poles and later by the occupying Germans. An exceptionally strong pistol, the gun was a German standard for some units.

Below: These are the revolvers used by Allied units in World War II. From top to bottom: The Colt Official Police, Smith & Wesson M&P and the Enfield. All are .38s of one sort or another. Many were traded for .45s.

World War II Eastern European service autos included the VIS and the Tokarev. Also called the TT-33, the latter gun used the 7.63 Soviet round, quite a bit like the 7.63 Mauser. The pistol was much like a Browning and was quite popular. It is an easy pistol to keep going in the course of battlefield use.

While the M96 was never a standard issue military pistol, it often found its way into many a conflict.

Like the Luger pistol, the Mauser M96 pistol was not a very good fighting tool. It was more an item of romance, a badge of rank — or just the only sidearm available from arms procurement agents.

In the mid-1930s, war clouds once again began to gather over Europe. The Japanese had begun their expansionism in the Pacific. Some changes in pistol design had started to surface in Europe. The French had adopted their M1935A and M1935S pistols.

Chambered for a weak .32 round similar to the Peterson round of U.S. development in the last days of the Great War, the M1935 pistols remain minor in their role as service pistols, the one good feature being the Charles Petter locking system that has gone on to become a popular pistol locking system of today.

The Polish Army adopted the VIS M1935 9mm pistol that used a Browning design. The VIS 9mm is a fine pistol, but shows influence of the Polish Cavalry in its small sights that clearly reflect the concept of pointed fire used by the horse-mounted trooper at close range. The Soviets adopted the TT-33 Tokarev pistol chambered for the 7.62 Soviet pistol cartridge that is similar to the M96 Mauser cartridge. The Tokarev is very much a John Browning design: however, a unique hammer group sub-assembly is used that also sports feed rails to insure positive, trouble-free feeding in this pistol.

The TT-33 is the classic example of a "Murphy-proof" service pistol.

The FN firm of Belgium commissioned John M. Browning to design the great Hi-Power military pistol in the late 1920s as part of the French Army pistol trials.

Browning began the project, but before it could be completed, he died while working at the FN plant. Dieudonne Joseph Saive of FN completed the design and development of the FN M1935 Hi-Power pistol.

While it gathered little notice outside of Belgium in the late 1930s, the P-35 was an exceptional pistol that featured a thirteen-round staggered box magazine and was chambered for the 9mm Parabellum.

Carl Walther of Germany had begun work on a 9mm

They came along at about the same time; each has a feature that made it unlike all earlier pistols. The P38 was the first successful battle pistol to use a double-action trigger system. The Hi-Power used a detachable box magazine with two columns of cartridges. Those features are standards for today's guns.

The damned old thing just keeps rolling along. This .45 is "stock," a World War II veteran unmodified in any way. It is a perfectly good fighting pistol just as you see it.

service pistol to meet German Army demands. His new Heeres pistol utilized the double-action trigger system of his earlier popular PP and PPK pocket pistols. This new service pistol, chambered for 9mm Parabellum, was adopted by the Wehrmacht in 1938.

When the Second World War broke out, despite much effort to regard the handgun as a weapon of minor military importance, the demand for fighting handguns was tremendous. Nearly every type of service pistol available was pressed into service. The English not only used their Enfields and Webleys, but also purchased vast stocks of American-made Smith & Wesson M&P .38 revolvers

Smith & Wesson continued to manufacture the Military & Police .38 S&W, plus the .38 Special version for military delivery until the end of the war. Colt was utilizing all of the company's production capacity to manufacture the M1911A1 pistol. The P-35 Browning 9mm pistol was manufactured under FN license in Canada by the firm of John Inglis.

The Germans utilized each form of service pistol captured and produced in occupied countries. The variety of Nazi service pistols was extreme, but wartime demands made this logistical nightmare a practical choice.

Regardless of the type or model of service pistol issued by either the Allies or Axis armies, little was done to improve practical pistol skills. The Germans did introduce the stylized silhouette target, but remained dedicated to shooting from a one-handed dueling stance at twenty-five meters. Bullseye target shooting was used as the primary means of teaching the new soldier combat handgun skill. While many nations were issuing service pistols with far greater combat effectiveness, the skills to use such a weapon were sadly lacking.

The British realized the condition of their forces and, after the dark days of Dunkirk, set about to train an elite force of commandos. Now was the time to call upon the close-quarters battle skills of Edward Fairbairn. Along with Captain Eric A. Sykes, he set up an excellent training facility in Scotland to prepare the then-new commando force. Fairbairn's school of combat pistol shooting finally got its place after much work and improvement from the back alleys of Shanghai.

In our own country, service pistol training was much the same as it had been in the first years of the century. The typical recruit was marched off to a pistol range, told to fire from a one-handed dueling stance at a bullseye target twenty-five yards downrange. Most often, this was the first time he had fired a pistol, let alone the M1911 .45 auto pistol. The new recruit usually would conclude the pistol was loud, recoiled terribly and was highly inaccurate. His attitude toward the pistol was that it was worthless

Even in the law enforcement community, the typical new police recruit was issued a service revolver and taken out to the local range, stone quarry or landfill. After firing a couple of cylinders of ammo, he was declared competent and sent on his way to defend himself and the community. Occasionally some forward-looking agency actually would require their police officers to go to the range once a year to fire at bullseye targets for qualification. Skill at arms rarely resulted.

While American service sidearm training was remote at best, the experience in Europe was even worse. Few individuals ever got close to a firing range. Most soldiers of the Axis armies in WWII were poorly skilled with the sidearm. Any skills learned were acquired in the field and combat is rarely a good place to learn correct firing skills. The battlefield will test combat skills superbly, but rarely teach them.

It should be of little surprise that so many men came home from the Second Great Hate with a low regard for the pistol as a viable weapon in combat. This is more a testimony to the inability of the military services to teach combat sidearm skills properly than the viability of the handgun as a close-quarters battle tool.

While Captain Fairbairn was busy teaching his close-quarters battle drill in England, an American Army officer was being tasked with the job of setting up a close-quarters battle school for the newly formed Office of Strategic Services (OSS). Lieutenant Rex Applegate deserves recogni-

Above: Shooting through a simulated window, this combat match shooter used his .45 for its intended purpose. It can be built into a good bullseye gun, but that wasn't what John Browning had in mind when he designed it.

erns did the rebirth of the single-action revolver come into being. While the late 1950s saw demand for this single-action, it was a small part of the sporting market.

American police agencies continued to train on the NRA bullseye target course. Some agencies began to take interest in the Practical Pistol Course (PPC) that was established in the mid-1930s as a training vehicle for the FBI. Military sidearms training throughout the world still consisted of the same techniques used in the 1920s. A new trend did develop in the early 1960s with the introduction of free-style combat pistol competition. Jeff Cooper, a former Marine with great insight regarding practical pistol use, set the stage for the "New Technique" of practical pistol shooting. While his views on practical pistol training were quite radical for the police and military of that time, Cooper's approach was judged the most effective means of improving practical pistol skills in this century.

In the early 1960s, Cooper's concepts were of some interest, but failed to catch on for another decade or two.

The top pistol is "stock" and so is the bottom one. In between are two examples of customized .45s. No pistol ever received such elaborate attention from so many of our best custom pistolsmiths. It comes in many variations.

tion as the man who gave America the first combat shooting school. Applegate served under Fairbairn and Sykes, then started his own version of the tactical service pistol course at the then-secret OSS training camp outside Washington D.C. Applegate called upon such noted American handgun pros as Cap Hardy of Los Angeles and Fitz Fitzgerald of Colt Firearms for many of his training ideas.

While only the intelligence agents of the OSS got any real taste of this practical pistol training, the methods of teaching it finally had made themselves known in the U.S.A. Few GIs ever derived any benefit from this advanced combat shooting technique. Later, the classic manual, "Kill Or Be Killed," was published in which Rex Applegate, retired as a colonel, offers in depth insight to the Fairbairn school of combat pistol shooting.

With the end of the Second World War, interest in fighting pistols and the means to use them was lost. Any interest in improving the service pistol remained minor. After all, vast stocks of service pistols were left over from the 1940-45 years and the world market was flooded with surplus service models.

Many of the European police forces were rearmed by the U.S. with the American standard police revolver, the Smith & Wesson .38 M&P. Once the Americans had gone home, the European cops soon traded these S&W revolvers for the first small .32 or .380 auto pistols they could get.

Target shooting became popular in both the United States and England; in fact, to many individuals, target shooting was the only socially acceptable reason for owning a handgun. American firms rushed to offer a line of target grade pistols and revolvers. The U.S. police standard was the S&W M&P .38 Special revolver and most civilian shooters favored the wheelgun as well. Only with the new interest in the Old West created by the TV West-

Left: The modern technique of combat shooting calls for teaching the shooter to react in all kinds of real-life circumstances — like stepping out of a phone booth. Above: Three generations of .45s: From the top: World War I M1911, World War II M1911A1, modern customized pistol with adjustable sights. There is a veritable cottage industry in the United States, all centered around making the .45 into a better gun.

The main factor that led to changes in combat pistol skills was the violent changes in our society that came in the late 1960s. The conflict in Southeast Asia created a variety of problems, both in the combat zone and here at home. Racial conflict, anti-war activist movements and hardcore criminal behavior began to take a toll on American law enforcement. Police officers found themselves to be targets and often the cop was too poorly trained and armed for such difficult encounters.

Slowly, the idea of improved combat pistol training began to gather interest. By the mid-1970s, most police agencies had begun instituting changes in firearms training to better prepare the police officer for violent encounters.

The pistols and revolvers used by policemen also began to change. The revolver remained the king of law enforcement duty sidearms, but the autoloading pistol was being used more often. This switch to the auto pistol was largely the result of Jeff Cooper's teachings. The .357 magnum revolver became the trendy weapon to carry. Lee Jurras of Super Vel fame was making history with his excellent high-performance hollow-point .38 Specal, .357 magnum, 9mm and .45 ACP pistol ammo. The prize police sidearm of the 1970s was a Smith & Wesson Combat magnum in blued steel or the highly sought M66 in stainless steel. In 1976, Jeff Cooper established the International Practical Shooting Confederation (IPSC) which became the shooting discipline destined to have a far reaching effect upon tactical sidearm training.

The auto pistol began to become much more popular with American police agencies. In 1968, the Illinois State Police adopted the S&W M39 9mm pistol. Other smaller police departments began to follow this example. The M1911 .45 ACP pistol had been well received in much of the Southwest due to Cooper's influence, but the pistol that really started things rolling was a model that copied design features from two of the more desirable pistols of the Second World War. Both the Walther P-38 and Browning P-35 pistols had captured interest among serious students of small arms. The double-action trigger of the Walther P-38, coupled with the large magazine capacity of the P-35 pistol, became the basis for Smith & Wesson experimenting with the early version of the M59 pistol. In 1973, S&W introduced the M59 pistol, providing the DA feature of the M39 pistol, and a fourteen-round staggered box magazine. The idea of giving the police officer a fifteen-shot 9mm pistol was an immediate success.

While American police organizations changed both their direction of sidearms and training in the late 1960s and '70s, most of Europe remained solidly behind the small .32 and .380 auto pistols that were primary sidearms of European policemen. With the rise of urban terrorist activity in much of Europe, the concern for police officers coming up against heavily armed terrorists was enough to cause European police agencies to take a hard look at their weapons and training.

The German Federal Police were among the first to select new sidearms. Test criteria were established and various manufacturers were asked to submit viable pistols. Each pistol was to be chambered for the much more powerful 9x19mm Parabellum cartridge. The final products were the Walther P-5, SIG P-6 and H&K P-7. Each pistol was of excellent design and function. These new German pistols represented the first real attempts at improving service pistols since before the Second World War.

Soon after the West German police pistol trials, the U.S. Army began to gather information for a new 9x19mm service pistol. The decision to replace the grand old M1911 .45 ACP had been made and a variety of manufacturers worldwide began to offer pistols for the M9 pistols trials. Many fine pistols were tested and a number quickly were found to be wanting. When the smoke had cleared — and politics served — the Beretta M92F became the new U.S. M9 service pistol. A number of excellent pistols were developed and marketed as a result of the M9 trials. The H&K P7M13 is one of the most advanced pistols offered for combat pistol work. The P7 remains the Porsche of

Above: This somewhat unusual pistol is the Heckler & Koch P7. It has a host of utterly unique features that set it off from its peers. Most important is the squeeze-cock system. Author Hackathorn's "Porsche of Pistols."

Left: The P7 comes in eight- and thirteen-shot versions. A lever on the frontstrap is the key to the system. As the shooter grasps the gun in firing position, he cocks the pistol. It becomes safe when he relaxes his grip.

The Beretta Model 92F becomes the M9 when it goes into uniform. It is the new service pistol, replacing the decades-old .45. The M9 has its work cut out for it.

Walther's advanced P5 was a fine pistol that came out of the pistol trials which the Germans conducted in the 1970s. It is very popular in Germany and Scandanavia.

combat pistols, even in a world of Volkswagen drivers. The SIG P266 is one of my favorite wondernine pistols. Smith & Wesson finally got the M59 pistol to its top form in the M459 military model pistol. The S&W M459 and its offspring remain the hard-core auto pistols of American law enforcement.

Along with the adoption of the Beretta M92 as the M9 service pistol, vast numbers of police agencies have also adopted the Beretta M92, often the result of low bid prices over any other factor. The Beretta M92 is a fine pistol and should remain popular for decades as result of the M9 military contract.

By the 1980s, the effect of Jeff Cooper's teaching had reached nearly every level of American law enforcement. U.S. military forces had begun to use the "New Technique" to train the modern soldier. Elite military units worldwide use or train with combat pistol techniques pioneered by Cooper in the 1960s. The new generation of "wondernine" pistols has become the rage, with the Austrian-made Glock 17 causing a real stir in the handgun market.

Many police agencies are using the Glock and, while it is too early to predict the real practical effect of the Glock pistol, one can assume the Glock will have a long-term effect on the approach to manufacturing a service pistol.

The Colt M1911 .45 ACP still remains popular and is favored by an ever-growing number of skilled combat shooters. The Browning P-35 Hi-Power 9mm remains the most commonly encountered service pistol in the world. Smith & Wesson finally has entered the .45 auto pistol

Not all of the modern wondernines answered roll call as this picture was taken, but the (top to bottom) Beretta, Sig-Sauer, Heckler & Koch and Glock were there. Not present: The excellent Smith & Wessons and the Ruger.

Below: Despite the automatic pistol hype, the revolver rides in more police holsters. This is a selection of fine double-action revolvers from Ruger and S&W. They are pictured with speedloaders that make them competitive.

market with the M645 DA service pistol.

Revolvers remain the dominant choice in U.S. law enforcement, with the heavier L-frame S&W 586/686 revolvers as the current favorite. Like the new Ruger GP100, the L-frame S&W offers an under-lug barrel and heavier frame to make use of .357 magnum ammo more controllable.

Trends for the remainder of this century appear obvious. Far better tactical firearms training will be the rule for both military and police. American police officers will continue the switch to the semi-auto pistol; probably the 9x19mm. Drug wars of the 1980s are going to become far more dangerous than the gangland wars of the 1920-1930s. Cops today are up against extremely violent, hostile criminals. The drug criminals are armed with highly sophisticated weapons that often are much better than those of the police agencies they face. Cops will demand the large capacity auto pistol and much better close-quarters tactical sidearm training.

The Soviets have standardized the Makarov pistol which is similar to the Walther PP and is chambered for an intermediate 9x18 round. While not impressive by our standards, it does reflect the Soviet approach to sidearms use.

The other armies of the world will continue to issue various 9x19mm Parabellum caliber pistols. The Colt M1911 .45 ACP will be issued for many years to come, be it soldier, street cop, or FBI agent. The sidearm they pack into the Twenty-first Century will be chambered for a cartridge that was designed in the first years of the 1900s.

---

*Anyone who was ever shot at has the same instinct —
he looks for cover. The modern technique teaches the
shooter how to use both cover and concealment. It does
so in such a way that he can return the fire — and hit.*

ABOUT THE AUTHOR

KEN HACKATHORN describes his military service in straightforward fashion: "I was a good soldier," he says. Then that mischievous Hackathorn sense of humor sneaks into his voice: "A good soldier, you understand, not a great soldier."

Humorous protestations to the contrary, Ken Hackathorn has been involved in some damned serious business in the past two decades and has gained valuable insight into what is practical and what is not. He's also developed the ability to teach others the necessary skills of gunhandling. Combining his knowledge of real, practical, workable technique with the ability to teach others, Hackathorn is one of the most sought-after instructors in the country. He is currently teaching a number of military and law enforcement personnel whose duties send them in harm's way.

Ken was a founding member of IPSC and finds himself somewhat dismayed at the direction that the organization currently follows. Although he was the first author of the Combat Weaponcraft column in *Soldier of Fortune* magazine, he doesn't often sit down at the typewriter. I am pleased I was able to persuade him to make this contribution to *Handguns '89.* — *WC*

CHAPTER 14
SPARKS LEATHER

Above: The man himself. Milt Sparks during his recent visit to author Clapp's California headquarters. Sparks produces some of the best holsters in the world. Left: Here's an example. The Summer Special fits between a shooter's pants and shirt, with the strap holding the holster in place. Holster won't collapse after the draw.

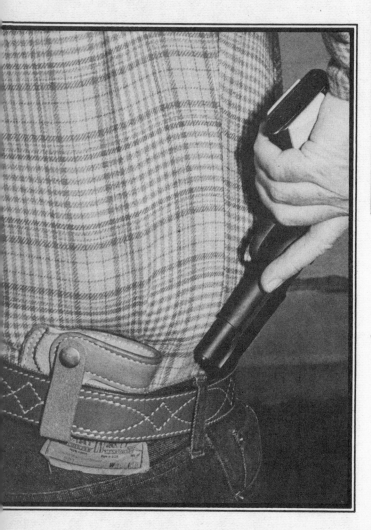

**Best-Bet Holsters
For Range And Field**

"**S**ECRET? HELL, there ain't no secret; just keep your hands movin'."

Milt Sparks was discoursing on the trade that has made him a name: the small, but growing business of custom holster production. Since he was full of good lunch and influenced by a spectacular view of the Pacific from the window of a Dana Point eatery, the gray-haired gent was a bit more expansive than usual. The moving hands commentary was a reflection on the fact that workers in the holster business have to stay right on what they are doing in order to produce enough to make it pay. There isn't any time to waste; this is handwork.

"Careful handwork is a necessary evil in the holster business, at least, if you want to make them right," Sparks said. We were in the midst of a luncheon conversation in California, a long ways from the Sparks plant in Idaho City, Idaho. I had recently visited the idyllic little mountain town in central Idaho and had come away with pic-

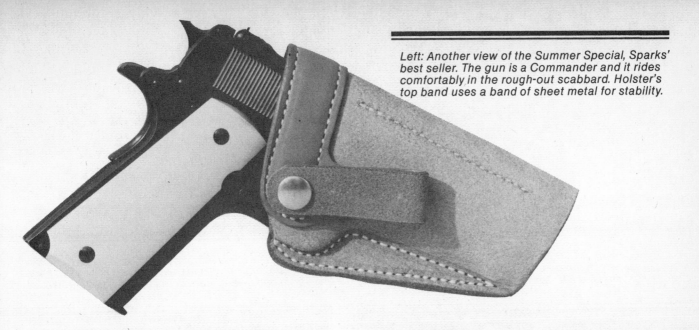

tures of a holster being made before my very eyes. I also learned a little more about how it is done and gained a vast respect for the fine products of this little shop.

Milt Sparks makes holsters for many kinds of handguns and many kinds of handgun carrying. There are the special rigs he turns out for the IPSC/speed shooters. He designs and makes some of the best police duty and concealed carry holsters you'll ever find. Even hunters and outdoor users of handguns can select an appropriate scabbard for that pet magnum.

The little shop in the tiny mountain town is the birthplace of holster ideas as well as holsters, themselves. With rare exceptions, the Sparks holster is a Sparks idea. There is not one of them that relies on tricks, gimmicks, unnecessary catches, studs or the like. All Sparks leather is completely functional. All is designed from the standpoint of simplicity and strength. His holsters last for years, because they are well designed and well made from the best of materials.

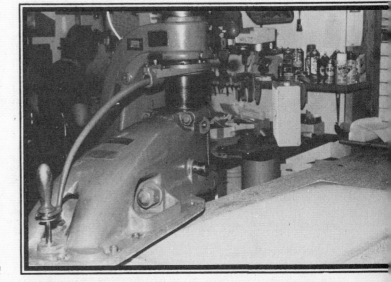

Below: If the need arises, the Sparks craftsmen can cut out a holster by hand. These are the patterns they use. Each will result in a holster that fits the handgun perfectly. This means hundreds of patterns kept on file.

Above: This massive press can punch out a holster in a second. The secret is having a "clicker," like the ones shown in the lower photo, made in advance. Sparks has these for the majority of his most requested holsters.

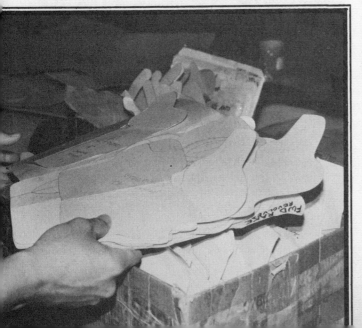

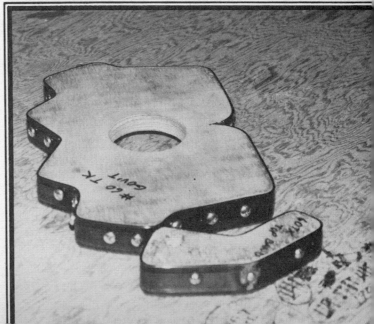

Leatherworker Cliff Harris started with this blanked-out piece of leather in making a 60TK Roadrunner for my S&W Model 645. We'll follow the holster from here.

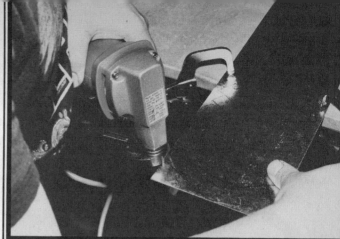

The 60TK has a reinforced top band. Cut from heavy-gauge galvanized metal, the band keeps the holster from collapsing. Harris cuts the steel with power saw.

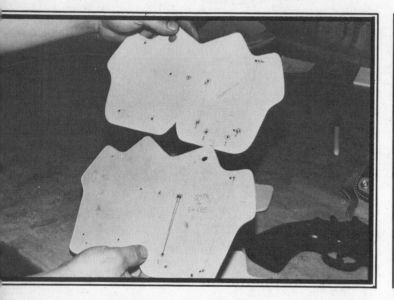

Harris has to have a stitching guide to work with, so he traces the pattern onto the holster while it's still a flat piece of leather. He'll follow the lines carefully.

Cliff marks the holster with the Sparks cartouche, or logo. It is done by hand on a block of granite with the leather moistened slightly — an accepted mark of quality.

The main ingredient is leather and Sparks picks the best available. This does not always mean the heaviest. Leather is available so thick that a weightlifter couldn't bend it into a holster. Obviously, the thicker the leather, the more it costs. Sparks uses the best quality he can get and a thickness that is commensurate with the use to which he will put it. Invariably, this means high-quality, thick cowhide. It's usually a little thicker than the competition's. He also uses a similar philosophy in selecting other components. The heavy thread and galvanized steel that go into a Sparks holster are first-quality.

The hardware is a similar story. Buckles, snaps and tension screws are used in many Sparks holsters. Tension screws across the welt of a number of Sparks holsters are the key to gun retention. Particularly in the case of the screws, they must be the best available. If a tension screw works loose, it could mean a gun loose in the holster and possibly a gun on the ground. That can't be tolerated. Therefore, Sparks uses the best he can get.

Despite the fact that Milt Sparks uses the best of raw materials, he does not sell holsters on the basis of what they're made of. He sells them because of their superior design. The best design is usually the simplest.

By way of proof of the latter credo, consider the Summer Special. This is the mainstay of the Sparks line, a bestseller since the first one was built. The Summer Special is an inside-the-waistband holster made for a wide variety of handguns, but most commonly found with an auto in place.

There's nothing new about a holster inside the waistband of a pair of trousers. The first one probably was invented by the first fellow who got his butt scratched after he pushed his flintlock down in his britches and had it fall through. Many modern makers produce designs of this sort, some of which are pretty good and some of which are, shall we say, strongly influenced by the Sparks model.

The Sparks Summer Special is different and better for several reasons. For one thing, the holster is made from a heavy grade of rough-out leather, with the rough side on the outside of the holster. The coarse texture of this leather tends to stabilize the holster in place between the trousers and the shirt. To really lock the little scabbard in one spot, there's a small loop of leather that encircles the belt and locks with a one-way snap fastener.

But that's not the whole story. Most holsters that ride inside the belt react to the pressure of the belt. When it is snugged up tightly enough to keep the shooter's trousers up and the gun is in place, there's no problem. But as soon as the gun is drawn, the holster collapses. For a law enforcement officer who has just drawn his gun in the process of making an arrest, this is a problem. Good tactics demand that he get the cuffs on quickly. That takes two hands and it means he has to re-holster his sidearm. It's tough to do when he has to unbuckle his belt to take the tension off the holster.

Sparks solves the problem nicely. The mouth of the Summer Special is reinforced with a band of galvanized steel sewn between the body of the holster and a top band. The steel makes the mouth of the holster rigid. It can't collapse and the gun is easy to return. The execution of the simple design is uncluttered and the Summer Special is an efficient holster.

If the Summer Special is uncluttered, the Mirage and Yaqui Slide are downright plain. These two designs might be called minimum holsters in that they use an absolute minimum of leather. The Yaqui Slide, in particular, is utter simplicity. It is nothing more than a carefully stitched and moulded pouch formed between two pieces of leather with both bottom and top completely open. Not much wider than the belt on which it rides, this holster cradles an automatic pistol, actually covering only a small portion of the gun. For some uses, this is an excellent design. The Yaqui Slide is frequently photographed on the hip of the father of modern pistolcraft, Jeff Cooper. There's no point mentioning what is in the holster — everyone knows.

None of the foregoing is to suggest that Sparks doesn't make more elaborate rigs, as he certainly does. His competition rigs are worn by a number of the top shooters in the IPSC ranks, including Colorado rancher Ross Seyfried, who took all the marbles in the internationals several years ago. Invariably, the more elaborate holsters that come out

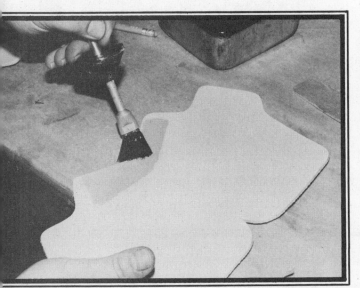

The band is both glued and stitched in place. If this is not done, the band would eventually work loose and cut its way out of the holster. Glue goes on the holster.

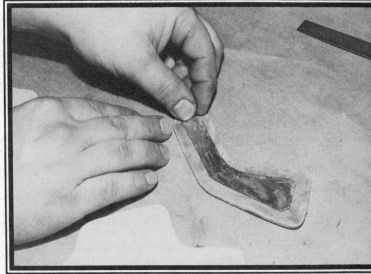

Glue also goes on the leather band and metal insert. When the glue gets a trifle tacky, Cliff will put it in place on the body of the holster. Bond is considerable.

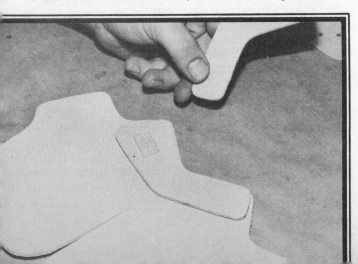

On the hard surface of his work table, Cliff presses the three pieces together. The strong glue takes effect in short order. In a few minutes, the band is firmly fixed.

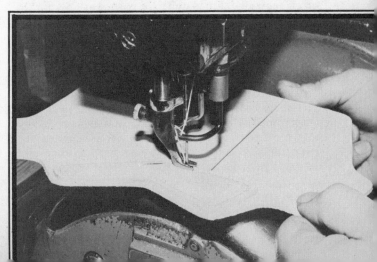

Harris adjourns to the other side of the Sparks factory, where they have several sewing machines. The top band is stitched firmly in place on the top edge of holster.

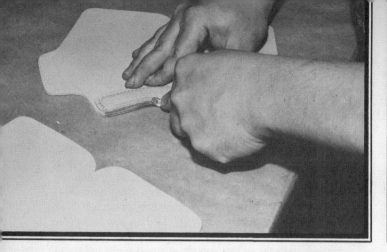

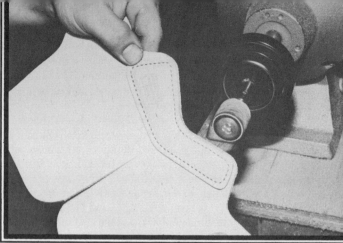

After the stitching is finished, Harris uses this special tool to even up the edges around the band. It is done with a firm stroke that comes with lots of experience.

The edge still isn't quite what the boss wants, so Cliff moves over to a power wheel and trues up the edge on the contoured edger. The result's a softly-rounded edge.

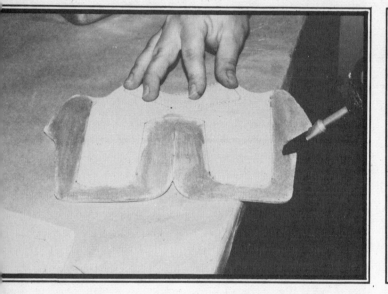

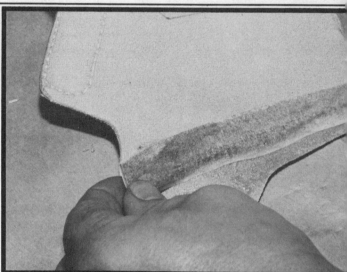

Getting ready to fold the leather over and make it into a holster, Harris applies the right amount of glue to the edges. The pattern lines guide this step of the process.

A sliver of leather is used to give the holster a welt. Harris is fitting it in place in this photo, with glue on both sides to insure it stays put during the stitching.

of the Sparks shop reflect the same design philosophy that produced the Summer Special and Yaqui Slide. They are clean, uncluttered and simple designs, flawlessly executed.

The competition and heavy-duty holsters from Sparks have businesslike names: Arbitrator, Gauntlet, Gold Label. All three work on the basis of an adjustable tension welt, which allows the slotted welt to be pushed against the bottom of the slide and set in that location with the provided screw. With one exception, there is not a single holster in the Sparks catalog that holds the handgun in place by the action of a safety strap across the gun. They all work by the tension welt and by a precise fit of the gun to the holster. Even the exception, the AZR Revolver Duty Holster, uses the tension welt.

Some might argue that a safety strap is a useful accessory, but when the holster is designed for persons who routinely carry guns with the reasonable expectation of firing them, the argument pales a bit. Professionals use Sparks holsters and they are familiar with gun handling.

While the slim little Sparks catalog shows a lot of holsters for automatic pistols, there are some for the wheelgun. One of the nicest is the HSR, designed by pistolcraft authority Ken Hackathorn. Like so many other Sparks rigs, the HSR uses a tension welt. It also has a covered trigger guard for safety and Milt will make it tilted several different ways, so that you can use it as a cross-draw.

The catalog photo shows the HSR in basket-stamped style, a feature that is available on most Sparks designs. Basket-stamping was developed as a means of hiding defects in less than perfect hides and evolved into a practical way for a working cop to get the most out of his leather, since the surface hides a lot of scratches and dings. In the Sparks shop, it is damned near an art form. Basket-stamping is done by a big stamping device in the major plants, but they do it by hand in Idaho City.

You'd think that basket-stamping would be easy — just follow the rows — but the people who think that are the ones who also regard gunstock checkering as child's play.

It's a bitch of a job and they do it well in the Sparks shop. They even guarantee that the angle of the stamping will be the same on each piece of a three-piece rig.

There are a number of excellent products in the catalog beyond the ones that I have already discussed. They include a first-rate rifle sling, shotgun shell carriers (including the late Mel Tappan's famous Cold Comfort) and even plain belts. One of them holds up my Levi's, as I write this. It is comfortable to wear, because it was cut on a contoured curve to avoid pinching and binding.

I have to comment on what I have come to believe is the design jewel in the Sparks catalog. That is the Model 60TK, the Roadrunner holster designed by Tony Kanaley of Milt Sparks' staff.

I don't carry a gun concealed every day, but there was a time when I did, as a deputy sheriff for the better part of two decades. If this holster had been available then, I am quite sure I would have used one. It is a high-riding concealment holster that just plain snuggles up against the body. The accompanying photos show leatherworker Cliff George

Above: Cliff bends the holster as shown. When the edges come together, the glue will start to take hold. Below: several sharp raps with a mallet fix the edges together.

The critical stitching process is performed on special Landis sewing machines. They are no longer made and command hefty prices. You can't do better for the job.

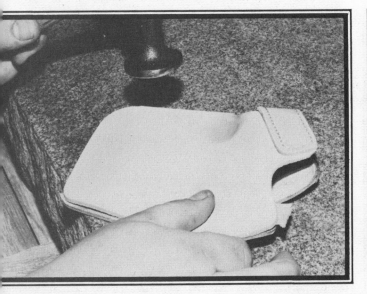

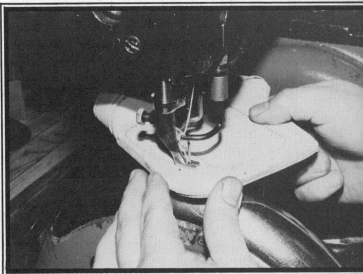

Having followed the sketched pattern carefully, Harris produced a neatly stitched holster. It is beginning to assume its final form — a functional Sparks Roadrunner.

The pattern used left a good bit of leather outside of the stitching and Cliff gets out a special semi-circular bladed knife to cut away the excess stock on the edges.

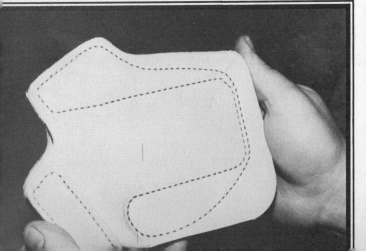

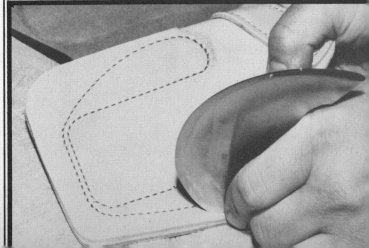

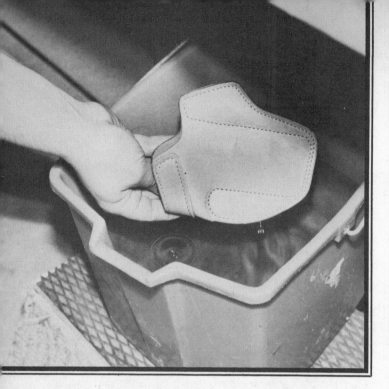

building one of the simple but effective scabbards.

The Roadrunner is perfectly in keeping with the Sparks doctrine of simplicity. It is made from two main pieces of leather, stitched to form a pocket for a particular gun. The design tilts the gun rather sharply forward, raking the muzzle to the rear in Sparks terminology. The abrupt tilt is necessary when a holster rides this high; if it wasn't used, the gun couldn't be drawn easily. And the Roadrunner carries the gun quite high. The ejection port of the S&W 645 is about even with the top edge of the waistbelt.

There are a pair of belt slots on the leading and trailing edges of the holster. A trouser belt goes down through a rear slot, then under a loop on the trousers and back up through the front slot. When the belt is buckled up, the holster is all but locked in place. There's just no way that it will move around. When the shooter reaches for his handgun, it's going to be right where it was the last time.

The actual pocket in which the gun rides is wet-moulded by hand to fit the model of the handgun to be carried. This means the gun won't be allowed to move within the holster, a condition that wears out holsters as well as guns. Every-

Below: The holster goes back to the power wheel for a cleanup on the edges. That's a necessity before hand-forming is done. Above: Dunk it in water before molding.

The wet holster is pushed over a steel rod in the first forming step. This rounds out the leading edge of the holster. Harris has to work fast on the moistened rig.

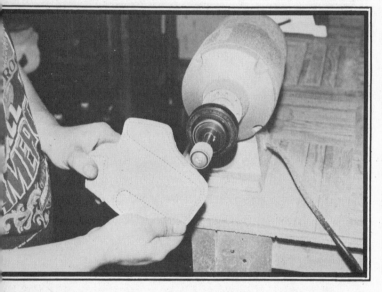

The hand molding process. The tool in use is simple. It is the tip of an elk antler. With fast, practiced strokes Harris is forming the holster to my individual handgun.

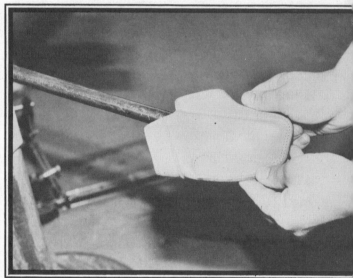

The more precise details of the holster are formed in with a tool made for clay sculptor's use. Harris also has taped the band around the pistol's trigger guard area.

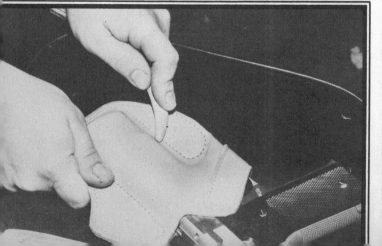

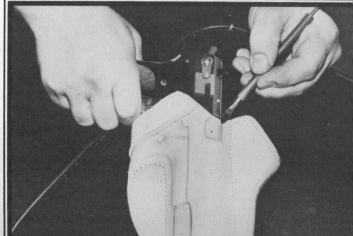

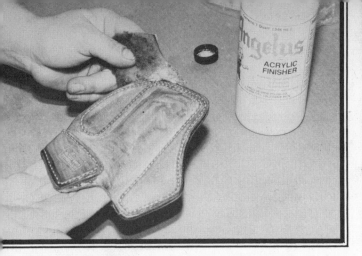

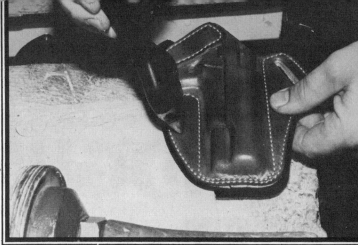

The finish is applied with a soft cloth. It darkens the leather slightly and protects against premature wearing out or drying. A special dark dressing is used on edges.

The very last step is cutting the belt slots. The cutter is actually a big punch that cuts the characteristic hole through which the trouser belt passes. Angle is critical.

thing thus far described is clever, but the final touch is even more so. Like the Summer Special, the Roadrunner has a steel reinforcing band in the top edge. This insures the holster won't collapse, helps retain the gun in place and, best of all, allows the front edge of the holster to be cut down to the point that a smooth fast draw can be accomplished. The Roadrunner's band goes around the rear of the holster.

I have been playing around with holsters for a long time and I have yet to find one that does what it is supposed to do quite this well. The Roadrunner is a small design masterpiece.

Milt Sparks will send along a copy of his brochure if you want to learn more about his products. The address is Milt Sparks, Dept. HG89, P.O. Box 187, Idaho City, Idaho 83631. You are going to get a big surprise when you see the price list. Despite the handwork, he doesn't ask any more than a comparable design from a mass-producer.

The real delight in dealing with the Idaho resident is the personal touch that goes into nearly everything he does. I ordered my first Summer Special for a Star PD many years ago. I got the holster in short order with a note to the effect that I hadn't asked for sight rails in the holster, but Milt felt they belonged, so he included them. If I wanted to send the difference in price, it was okay, but not necessary.

I sent the difference. The rails were necessary and I wanted to stay on the good side of a holster maker who had the intelligence to know it and the integrity to back his convictions. This kind of business practice is the norm for a man who runs an operation where he combines technical knowledge, innovation and the best of materials. That is most of the reason why Sparks holsters are found so often where they are appreciated so deeply — on the hips of people who really *use* their handguns.

That's most of the reason, but not all. The rest is simple: You just keep your hands moving.

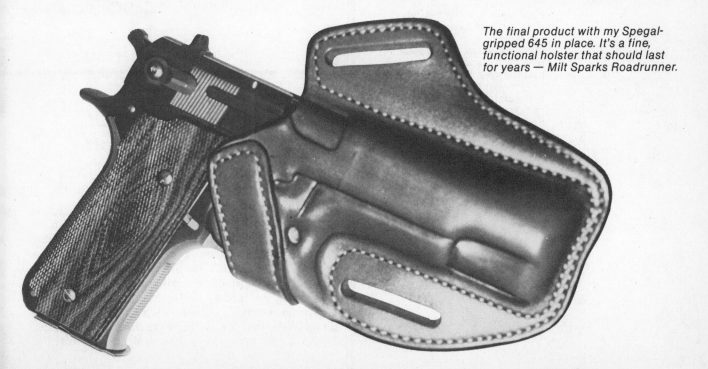

The final product with my Spegal-gripped 645 in place. It's a fine, functional holster that should last for years — Milt Sparks Roadrunner.

CHAPTER 15

HANDGUN TEST TECHNIQUE

If my shooting partner Stan Waugh holds carefully, then squeezes with patience and a delicate touch, he will be rewarded with hits close to the point of aim. This is a worthwhile goal of training, but this isn't a logical way to find out what the pistol and the ammo will really do.

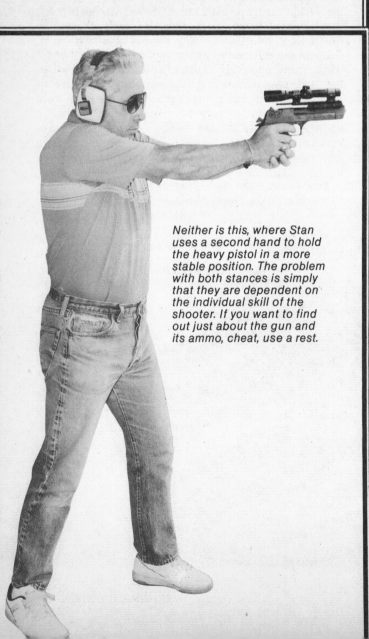

Neither is this, where Stan uses a second hand to hold the heavy pistol in a more stable position. The problem with both stances is simply that they are dependent on the individual skill of the shooter. If you want to find out just about the gun and its ammo, cheat, use a rest.

Making The Most Of Your Time And Effort

THE POSTMAN was only half welcome on that day so long ago. He brought me a letter from the NRA with a wallet-sized card proclaiming me a Master in Outdoor Pistol. I had worked like the devil in local matches in the San Francisco area to reach that level of competence and it was nice to have the effort recognized. But it had a downside. I was now in the big leagues and I couldn't expect to win as much — if at all. All things considered, it was simply the effect of competition. By developing my bullseye skills to a certain level, I had

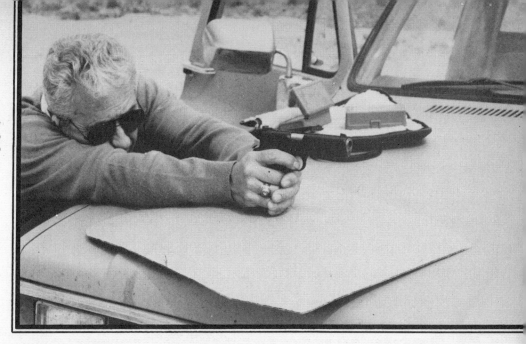

In this shot, Stan is holding his newly-barreled Gold Cup across the hood of a pickup truck belonging to Irv Stone.

earned the right to compete seriously. I had no cause to complain.

What does my personal handgun skill have to do with a chapter on handgun test technique? Not much, and I mention it for a single reason. Despite my dubious skill in those days, part of which remains on tap, my ability to shoot a score with a handgun has no direct bearing on the potential of any handgun and ammunition combination. Accuracy of any ammunition in a particular firearm can be established empirically. When a shooter does so, he can be assured that a poor score in a match is really his fault.

This chapter deals with the ways and means of determining handgun and ammunition accuracy. In its simplest form, testing does involve some elements of marksmanship. But if the test procedure relies heavily on the ability of the shooter to hold and squeeze, the results will have to be interpreted through the imprecise screen of individual ability.

The bullseye shooter wants to find out what is the best possible handload to use for the local matches and for match practice. Beyond that, he wants to know which of the several brands and types of handgun ammunition will perform best when he gets to a big match. The silhouette shooter uses handloads almost exclusively and he wants to know the same things, but he also wants to find out whether his loads have enough whump to take down the distant ram.

Similar situations exist with every other kind of competition shooter — IPSC, bowling pin, PPC and others. Usually, the first consideration is accuracy, followed by terminal performance. Even the handgun hunters want to know how well their loads shoot. They trust in the combination of bullet construction and velocity to do the job in living tissue. Finally, those who choose ammunition for defensive purposes want the best they can get.

Having been fortunate enough in the past few years to have had access to lots of different guns and ammunition for the purpose of journalistic review, I believe I have learned a good bit about the ways and means of wringing them out. Throughout the learning process, I have been deeply concerned with obtaining definitive results. In cer-

tain aspects of the evaluation process, I know what works and what doesn't.

But in one aspect of ammo/handgun testing, I don't think that any of us know much. That's in the field of terminal ballistics. Gunwriters are fond of shooting blocks of colored ice, bleach jugs of water, chunks of clay, duxseal or jello, boxes of wet sand or sawdust, even soggy newsprint or last year's phone book. Good photography can produce some pretty spectacular photos from some of these targets. Even a sectioned block of clay with a gaping teardrop-shaped cavity can be pretty impressive.

The problem with all of these things is that they aren't relative to any real use of the gun. They are contrived to be spectacular and using the data obtained from such testing is far from objective. Only in the case of the type of research done by men like Massad Ayoob and Evan Marshall, who have access to the autopsy rooms, do you begin to have an idea how defensive handgun ammunition performs. And, I'll bet that both of them would agree that the results must be interpreted most carefully and in the light of the circumstances of the particular shooting.

I am somewhat less strongly convinced that energy figures are meaningful. To some degree, the calculated kinetic energy of a given round of ammunition, as fired from a particular gun, seems to make sense. But when you look at it a little more deeply, it becomes obvious that such a calculation puts the premium on velocity. Shooters tend to look at this and select ammunition that goes the fastest. That is not necessarily the best choice, since the circumstances of its use aren't always taken into consideration. More often than not, when ammo is evaluated, the most accurate load is seldom the fastest.

Terminal ballistics is an inexact science, despite the laboratory work of the white-coat boys. The only sensible course of action is to select ammunition for its terminal effect on the basis of what it has done in the past under similar circumstances. Unfortunately, this kind of information is not always easy to come by.

We can, however, determine a great deal about how our guns and ammunition will really perform. By means of several relatively inexpensive test devices, today's shooter

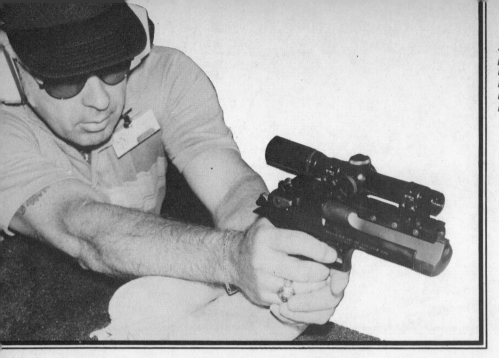

Shooting from the braced sitting position has some advantages, as long as the shooter is careful in his technique. In this photo, Stan is using sandbags to steady his hold, a technique that works well.

can come up with a pretty solid evaluation of his handgun and/or his handgun ammunition. Much of this will be in terms of accuracy.

On a recent test outing, myself and my shooting friend, Stan Waugh, loaded and fired about seven hundred rounds of 10mm handloads. We shot the loads in a pair of 10mm handguns at twenty-five yards and measured the velocity of every single shot. We shot a ten-shot group with each load in each gun and measured the size of the groups. It was a damned good day's work.

Take someone like Bill Blankenship, who has won the National Pistol championship so many times he's lost count (not really). Bill is still capable of shooting that same 10mm test series the way he shot for years. That's one-handed and standing. For a while, he'll do pretty well — certainly far better than either Stan and I could do. But the results we obtained are far more valid than Blankenship's, because every single shot we fired was from a Ransom Rest.

The point is simply this: If you want definitive results in determining accuracy, you must eliminate as many variables as possible. One distinct variable is the ability of a shooter to consistently hold and squeeze in the offhand

position. For a few shots, you can get a pretty good idea. But in the long run, you'll want to eliminate the swaying movement by bracing the hand and arm in some fashion.

I prefer to use the Ransom Rest whenever possible, but there are times when I can't, because the inserts for a particular handgun aren't available. On those occasions, I plunk my butt down on a stool behind a concrete shooting bench. Even here, there are techniques that produce better results than others.

A shooter working from the bench with a handgun needs a sturdy bench. He can't get by with one that wobbles and weaves around. The bench also should be large enough in terms of surface area that he isn't cramped for space. While some of our local shooters use relatively low benches, I prefer a shooting bench that is high enough to minimize bending over. The more you're forced to bend, the more your head and shoulders will be in an awkward position in relation to the sights. Shooting this way can be extremely fatiguing and results borne of fatigue are suspect.

Actually, one of the better platforms for testing pistols is over the hood of a full-sized pickup truck. The curve of the fender is comfortable to lean against in a standing position and the expanse of hood gives you plenty of room. For

Another view of the sandbags on the shooting bench. It is possible to get a steady hold and produce some positive results shooting in this way. The wrist and part of the hand are virtually immobile.

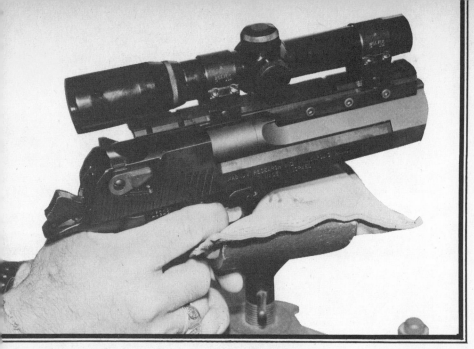

This position adds a rifle-type rest to the equation and results will be better yet. This view has the shooter positioning the gun with the trigger guard on rest. For most handguns, this is best.

shooters who must do their testing on established ranges with hard-nosed rangemasters, this is probably not possible, but it works just fine in desert and plains regions.

The test shooter's hands and forearms should be braced solidly, as he grasps the handgun to be tested. Carpeting, folded towels, hard foam rubber sections are all good choices, but the best is the simple sand or shot bags. Several canvas bags, filled with sand, shot or even fired primers from the reloading shop form a good base for the shooter's hands. They can be punched into necessary shapes to accommodate any handgun. Best of all, they are stable.

The gun needs to be rested in some support. Holding it by hand on a bench is a pretty stable position, but not as stable as if the gun sits on something fairly firm and immobile. A couple of sections of wood, a rifle shooter's bench rest or other surface is okay, just as long as it's the correct height to hold a handgun with the hands rested in the sandbags and the gun aligned on the target.

With one notable exception, the gun's frame or receiver should be in contact with the rest. Leave the barrel free by setting revolvers and most autos on the rest at a point just forward of the trigger guard. The surface of the rest should be lightly padded to prevent marring the pistol. The not-

able exception to the rule of resting the pistol on the frame is the Contender. The Thompson/Center single-shot usually shoots better with a positive upwards pressure on the forend.

The shooter who does all of the things we've described so far will be startled at how stable his position actually is. So much so in fact, that he might be inclined to think that he can't miss. That's a mistake, because what benching a handgun as discussed actually accomplishes is to remove the natural wobble of holding the gun at arm's length with one or two hands.

The shooter still has to align his sights carefully, then squeeze the trigger and follow through so as to not disturb the lay of the gun. If he doesn't do these things with absolute consistency, then his results still will be somewhat questionable. It's easier to shoot good groups from the bench, but it is still not easy. Most of the difficulty lies in reacting consistently to each shot fired. The bench shooter must be certain that he grips the handgun with the same pressure from shot to shot, as well as resisting the recoil in the same way each time. This is the bullseye shooter's follow-through and it may be even more important for the bench.

It is possible to have all of these things done for you. For

For this heavy automatic, there's not much difference between the position shown and the one above, but bracing on the frame is most often the best way to bench test a handgun. Leave the barrel free.

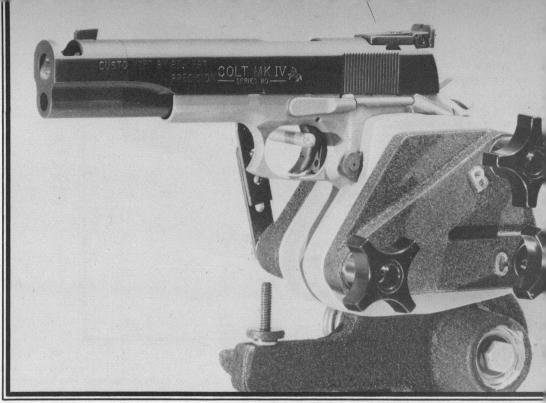

The best way to find out what your handgun is doing is to use a Ransom Rest. The cast aluminum robot will hold your pistol in a consistent grasp and align it on the target with monotonous regularity. It is worthwhile.

a small fee, Chuck Ransom will arrange to have your handgun aimed, fired and re-aimed to the same exact spot. He'll do it as many times as you like for the same price. And each and every time, you can rely on Chuck to do it with utter consistency.

Facetiousness aside, serious shooters need to take a long look at the Ransom Rest. One of them will cost a little less than a quality handgun and it will last forever. Best of all, Ransom's machine rest lets you find out what a particular gun and ammo combination really will do. Correct-

ly operated, the Ransom Rest holds, aligns, fires and re-fires a handgun hundreds of times. It does it the same exact way each and every time. You can depend on a group fired from a Ransom-Rested handgun to be indicative of what that particular gun and ammo combination will do.

The rest removes human error from the test equation. It is a device, cast from aluminum, consisting of two main parts. They are a base, which the user bolts down to an immobile surface, and the rocker arm, which fits onto a shaft on the base. Bolted into place with a firm friction fit and augmented with a massive spring, the rocker arm is free to move through an upward arc and in no other direction.

At the downrange end of the rocker arm, there's an arrangement which allows a handgun to be attached. Clamped in a sandwich of rubber-faced blocks which mate to each individual gun, the handgun thus becomes a rigid part of the rocker arm. The shooter needs a separate set of inserts for each handgun to be tested. One set will often suffice for many different guns (such as all N-frame Smith & Wessons). The handgun goes into the inserts with its grips removed. The rubbery material from which Ransom molds the inserts is the only surface on the rest which contacts the gun and thus it cannot be marred.

To use the reset, a shooter clamps his gun in place and tightens it down via three nuts on the left side of the rocker arm. He then pushes the arm down until it contacts the base of the rest. He pulls the pistol's trigger via a lever on the right side of the arm. Since it's held in a grip that covers no more of the gun than would a shooter's hand, the pistol can be loaded and fired without removing it from the rest.

The Ransom Rest requires a different set of rubber-faced inserts for each pistol to be tested. The more a shooter uses the rest, the more he becomes fond of it. The library of inserts tends to grow at a rapid rate.

When it fires, the arm recoils in an upward arc. The shooter pushes it back down to the adjustable index position and fires another shot. He can do so with complete confidence that the gun will be pointing at the same spot on the target.

A properly mounted and operated Ransom Rest mechanically aims a handgun at the same spot on the target shot after shot after shot. It does so with a minimum of attention from the shooter and is reliable to an extreme degree. Even the hardest-kicking magnums don't particularly trouble the rest. Mechanical aiming totally eliminates the imponderables of human eyesight, steady hold, sight alignment and trigger control. They just don't matter when the gun is cradled in the rubbery grip of Chuck Ransom's delightful invention.

Lots of serious shooters are intent on their sport to the extent that they are willing to pop for a Ransom Rest to do their test holding and squeezing. They should be aware that there are more advantages to the rest than mechanical aiming.

After a shot is fired, the rest performs with more consistency than most human arms. The inserts are faced with that material, which responds to grip pressure and the torque of recoil in exactly the same away every time. So does the arm, recoiling up in response to recoil. In the human hand and arm, gun movement begins before the bullet has left the muzzle. In the mechanical hand and arm of the Ransom Rest, the same thing happens. The difference is that the Ransom Rest is one hundred percent consistent in its response. The amount of movement will therefore be the same from one shot to the next and it will have the same effect on accuracy.

There is another subtle advantage to the Ransom Rest which escapes some of its critics. If the shooter has the rest do the tough part, aiming and firing, then the shooter is free to do something else. He can and should watch the developing group on the target. This can tell him some interesting things about how his gun and ammunition perform.

There are a few other items of equipment that comple-

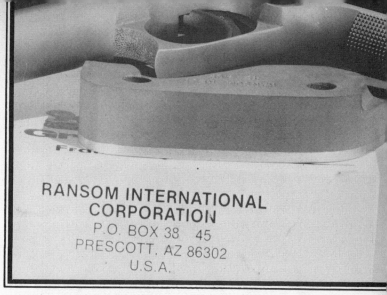

A customized Colt Government Model atop the insert and the shipping box. This particular pistol was quite accurate, as the author determined in a long shooting session. The Ransom Rest performs for hours at a time.

ment the rest on a range trip. Normal ear and eye protection is essential, but if I am going to do much in the way of looking over the rest, I like to wear a full face shield. Particularly in the case of revolvers, there's a fair amount of unburned powder and particles of lead flying around. Getting tabbed in the kisser with a few of these is unpleasant if you are over the rest.

Other stuff is also handy. A good set of screwdrivers for different grip screws, Allen wrenches for the various things to be adjusted on the rest, cleaning gear and even such things as a long brass drift for the inevitable primer load are all handy; so is a spotting scope, if you are shooting at distances beyond twenty-five yards. The Ransom Rest works just as well for shooting at one hundred yards as it does at twenty-five, but you'll need a scope to see what's going on. My best choice here is one of the Simmons line. They have

The Colt Delta 10mm being readied for testing. In the case of Government Models with grip safeties, it is a good idea to tape the gun as shown. The safeties can often move enough to work as they were designed to do.

Working up over the Ransom Rest can put the shooter in a spot to get tabbed with flying particles of debris when the gun is fired. If you do it enough, you'll come to appreciate face shields like this one from Brownell's.

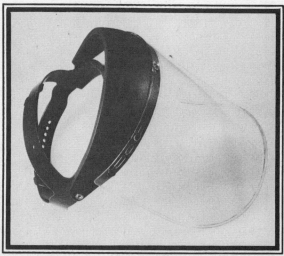

A good scope is essential if you are testing at longer ranges. Author's favorite is one of the Simmons line, because they have a small "finder" scope integral to, and parallel with, the main scope. It's a handy feature.

a coaxially mounted 2.5x finder scope which speeds up alignment on target enormously.

Chronographs. There are lots of them on the market these days and some of them must be good. Long ago, I began to use the Oehler and I have no reason to change. Their Model 33, particularly with the Sky Screen IIIs, is simple and easy to use. More important, it is accurate and reliable.

A little ways back, I mentioned watching the target to find out certain things. This can be quite informative, assuming that a test shooter has gone to the trouble and expense of equipping himself with machine rest, chronograph and related paraphernalia. He now needs a little more information to get the most from it.

Over the past few years, I have fired a great many automatics in the Ransom Rest. Sometimes I was shooting a new kind of ammunition and other times a variety of ammunition in a new kind of handgun. With rare exceptions, autos have a little known and maddening quirk. They

Below: There is an extended discussion of the automatic syndrome in the adjacent text, but this pair of photos gives graphic evidence of the effect of shooting with the slide locked back at the end of each five rounds. On this gun, the first shot from each magazine is high.

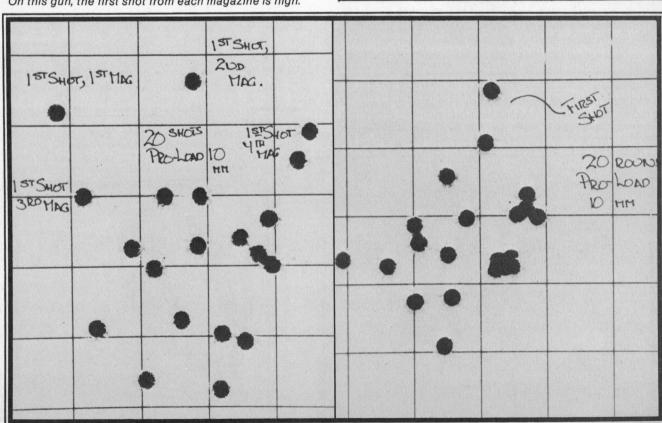

shoot the first round from the magazine to a different point on that target than all the other rounds.

It isn't particularly obvious, until you have a gun and ammo combination that is pretty decent to begin with. Good Ransom Rest technique calls for a few shots to settle the gun in the inserts and to foul the barrel. After that, the shooter can start shooting for record. In the case of an automatic pistol, you insert a magazine into the pistol, run the slide forward to chamber the first round and fire the shot. Assuming that you have the rest more or less centered on the target, you'll get an obvious bullet hole.

As you fire successive shots, a group will form. The size of the group will vary with the accuracy potential of the gun-ammo combination. But more often than not, that first shot will be farther from the center of the group formed by the other shots in the series. I can't honestly say that the tendency to throw away the first shot is universal, because I own a couple of autos that shot one-hole groups right out of the box.

Most autos aren't that accurate and the overwhelming majority display this quirk. There's no particular brand that does it to any greater degree. I have seen it happen with Brownings, Colts, Rugers, CZ75s, S&Ws and others. I theorize that it happens because of slide velocity. If the slide closes under the pressure of the recoil spring alone, the barrel and other parts settle into contact with one another. The actual position of the parts and the cartridge in the chamber is different when the slide is returning to battery after a shot has been fired, because they are moving at a different speed.

This is a theory which I can't prove completely, but one I

GROUP SIZE BY CHAMBER	GROUP SIZE, EXCLUDING ONE CHAMBER PER GROUP
Chamber #1: 2.131 inches	w/o Chamber #1: 3.130 inches
Chamber #2: 1.345 inches	w/o Chamber #2: 2.903 inches
Chamber #3: 1.615 inches	w/o Chamber #3: 2.658 inches
Chamber #4: 1.558 inches	w/o Chamber #4: 2.002 inches
Chamber #5: 1.133 inches	w/o Chamber #5: 2.527 inches
Chamber #6: 1.128 inches	w/o Chamber #6: 2.577 inches
5-shot groups. #1 is worst and #6 is best.	10-shot group w/o #1 is worst and w/o #4 is best.

have discussed with a number of leading pistolsmiths. Most of them agree, but the most insightful comment that I received was from Jim Clark, who has been building superb handguns for many years. He also uses the Ransom Rest extensively. Clark said the phenomenon exists, but that it disappears as the gun breaks in. It may take several thousand rounds before it is not a factor, but it will disappear eventually.

To keep the "automatic syndrome," as I have termed it, from skewing the test results, I have developed a procedure which minimizes the distortion. If a test series is to consist of twenty shots (as it should), I feed the first shot manually, then never allow the magazine to run dry. As the last round from the first magazine of five is *fed*, I stop shooting long enough to load another magazine of five. Continuing in this fashion will insure that each shot will be fired with more shots below it. Therefore, the siide will never lock back and need to be manually released.

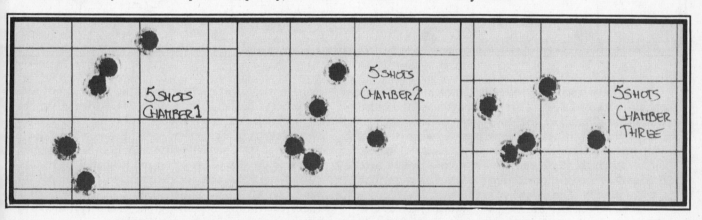

The author fired these groups with a Smith & Wesson Model 25-5 in a Ransom Rest. Each chamber was numbered, then five shots fired from it. The result is a fairly good picture of how each will perform. In this way, a shooter can determine which chamber to use if he wants to make his revolver work as a single-shot. It will not tell him which one to exclude if he wants to use the six-shooter as a five-shooter.

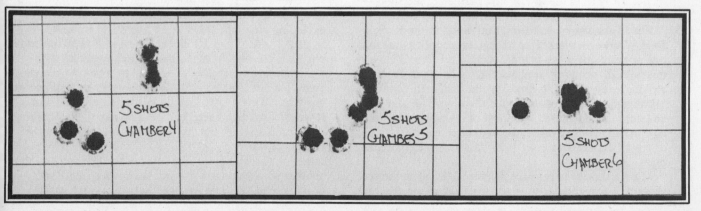

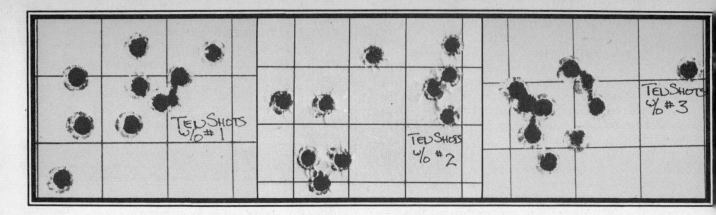

These groups were fired from the same revolver as used on the previous page and with the same ammunition. These are ten-shot groups and they systematically omit one chamber from each group. In effect, this evaluates each potential five-shooter in succession. You'd think the worst chamber, as determined earlier, would cause the other five to shoot the best group when the worst one was omitted. No way!

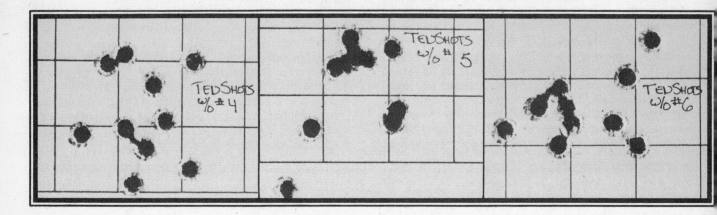

If you have trouble accepting this, look at the accompanying photos of a pair of twenty-shot groups fired with a Colt Delta 10mm. The first group resulted from firing four consecutive magazines of five and marking where the first shot out of each one landed. This particular pistol likes to throw them high, as you can see. The second twenty were fired as described in the preceding paragraph, never letting the gun run dry. The difference is graphic.

Had it not been for the Ransom Rest, which enabled me to watch the group develop as I fired, I doubt that I would have discovered this curious situation. Some guns have the problem to an astonishing degree. I fired a Colt .38 Super not long ago that would throw the first shot as much as five inches away from the rest of a magazine of nine shots — which went into as little as two inches.

Revolvers also benefit from evaluation in the Ransom Rest. Many observers of the handgun scene are aware that one or more chambers in a production revolver often are misaligned, resulting in shots fired from that chamber striking away from shots fired from the rest. In this context, misalignment is a gross oversimplification. The maverick chamber can be caused by a host of maladies, including alignment, but also cylinder throat dimensional differences, crane alignment and even such things as a bent center pin.

Many shooters believe the solution is to make the six-shooter a five-shooter by finding and marking the bad

chamber, then using it last, if at all. I tried this recently with a new S&W Model 25-5 revolver which I knew had one chamber that persisted in shooting away from the others. I marked each of the chambers, arbitrarily numbering them one through six. Then I fired five shots from each chamber, measured the size of the group and tabulated the results.

From the table, you could conclude that chamber #1 was by far the worst. In theory, that means excluding it would result in an exceptional group. In theory, I should be rich, because I work so hard. When I went back and carefully fired the revolver once again, theory came up hard against measurable fact.

In this part of the test, I fired ten-shot groups with the same Winchester Silvertip ammunition. Each of six groups of ten shots excluded one chamber. When I started by excluding chamber #1, I fired two shots from #2, two from #3, etc. Then I followed the same procedure for chamber #2 and, in succession, the other four.

Tabulating the results was startling. The best ten-shot group included the so-called bad chamber as well as the one that had previously fired the best single-chamber group. It would seem that each chamber and barrel combination constitutes a "gun" and that whichever one often is the best is not necessarily going to agree with the point of impact on target of its neighbors. The information is useful to the shooter who wants to use his revolver as a single-shot — or a five-shooter. The Ransom Rest makes it happen.

Section Four

CUSTOM HANDGUNS

IT REMAINS A MYSTERY WHERE THE FIRST CUSTOM HANDGUN WAS BUILT, BUT IT COULD HAVE BEEN WHEN A SOLDIER OF YEARS PAST WENT TO A BLACKSMITH AND ASKED TO HAVE HIS MATCHLOCK SHORTENED FOR EASIER CARRYING. HANDGUNNERS ALWAYS HAVE INDULGED A FONDNESS FOR PERSONAL ALTERATIONS, SO MUCH SO THAT PRESENT-DAY PISTOLSMITHS MAKE A LIVING BY TAKING PERFECTLY GOOD HANDGUNS AND CHANGING THEM TO THE OWNER'S NEEDS. PISTOLSMITHING IS COMING IN TO ITS OWN AS AN ESTABLISHED FACET OF GUNSMITHING.

OUR COVERAGE BEGINS WITH SINGLE-ACTION SPECIALIST GEORGE DILEO BUILDING UP A SPECIAL REVOLVER FROM SCRATCH; A REVOLVER THAT COMMEMORATES THE FIRST EDITION OF THIS BOOK.

THEN WE LOOK AT THE WORK OF AN OLD MASTER, GEORGE MATTHEWS, WHO HAS MADE NICE REVOLVERS NICER FOR HALF A CENTURY. IRV STONE, OF BAR-STO BARREL FAME, GETS HIS TIME IN THE LIMELIGHT AS WE EXAMINE HIS JUSTLY FAMOUS BARRELS. ONE OF THE BEST OF THE NEW BREED OF PISTOLSMITHS IS WAYNE NOVAK, WHO BUILDS BUSINESS GUNS FOR PEOPLE WHO MUST BE ARMED IN THE COURSE OF LAWFUL BUSINESS. FOR SOME PISTOLEROS, A PAIR OF CUSTOM GRIPS WILL SUFFICE, SO WE LOOK AT CRAIG SPEGAL'S. FINALLY, WE CHECK OUT GRIPS FOR AN OLD FAVORITE, THE .45 AUTO.

HANDGUNS 89

CHAPTER 16
GEORGE DiLEO

Building The Handguns '89 Special

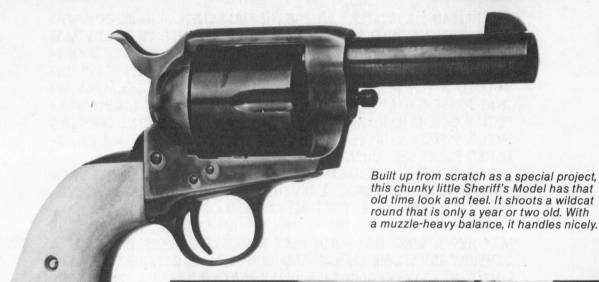

Built up from scratch as a special project, this chunky little Sheriff's Model has that old time look and feel. It shoots a wildcat round that is only a year or two old. With a muzzle-heavy balance, it handles nicely.

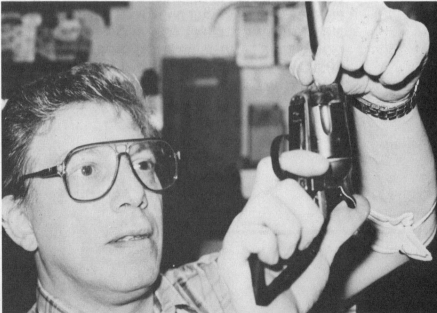

George DiLeo hard at work on the special gun. He had to be careful to get the mix of old and new parts to go together properly. Here, he is trying that unusual base pin for a proper fit in the revolver. Hand work did it.

Would you believe a revolver came out of this pile of old and new parts? Even on the original Colts, parts were not totally interchangeable. A challenge to DiLeo's skill and knowledge, the project produced a working revolver.

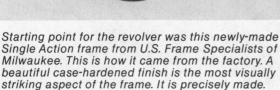

Starting point for the revolver was this newly-made Single Action frame from U.S. Frame Specialists of Milwaukee. This is how it came from the factory. A beautiful case-hardened finish is the most visually striking aspect of the frame. It is precisely made.

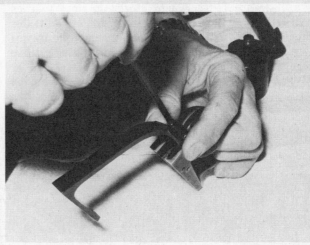

Above: If everything on the gun is to fit properly, there will be a lot of cut-and-try work. Luckily, a brand new Colt-made backstrap fit the USFS frame. Only a small amount of fitting was needed to mate the two for a proper fit. Trigger guard was harder.

"I GUESS it was the Saturday matinees that did it," George DiLeo commented distractedly. He was in the process of figuring out why the hammer of the gun you see on these pages didn't fit. Although he's always courteous, George was busy and didn't really have a whole lot of time to respond to my question about why he spent so much time fooling with Single-Actions.

His remark was nonetheless accurate. For George DiLeo and so many more of us, our affection for the old thumbuster is a reflection of all those Saturday afternoons spent in darkened theaters, watching our celluloid heroes. Long after the Colt Single-Action had any importance in the real world of competition or defensive handgunning, it lived on in the fanciful world of Hollywood. We are shooters in love with our own frontier beginnings and will never turn away from a love affair with those graceful contours of hammer and butt.

For this reason, George DiLeo spends a good bit of his working life cleaning, tuning and modifying Colt Single-Action revolvers and their many clones. Sure he does all the other bread-and-butter work characteristic of a one-man gun shop, but he likes to work on SAAs whenever the opportunity presents itself. George watched his childhood movies in the theaters of New Jersey, a long way from the West. I watched mine in Southern California moviehouses, much closer to where they were made. We share a common bond of affection for the old guns.

When this first edition of the DBI handgun book came my way as a writer, I thought it might be a good idea to build up a handgun from scratch. The idea was to show just how much the American craftsmen can do in the way of full custom work. In discussing the project with my friend, George DiLeo, he insisted that the gun should be a single-action. He also insisted on doing the majority of the work himself.

The idea was to produce a special SAA to commemorate the first edition of Handguns, the DBI annual. The gun would be a tasteful blend of traditional and modern features, rendered in an attractive package. As an aficionado of the custom handgun, I wanted the chance to show off what good custom work can look like.

If you wanted to build a .45 automatic from scratch, it would be pretty easy to get a frame. The 1911 is the most copied pistol ever made and there are several plants making receivers for them. In the case of the SAA, there is no choice except to buy a used Colt frame or work from one of the modern Italian replicas. Then we discovered a little firm called United States Frame Specialists.

The Milwaukee firm is headed up by a SAA lover named Jeff Peskie. His product is an investment cast copy of the Colt Single-Action that is so close to the original that Sam Colt would be scratching his head over it. Not content to produce just the simple frame, Peskie went on to make the backstrap and trigger guard. One of the nicest touches on the USFS product is the loading gate. Peskie fits this critical part to absolute perfection before any of his frames leave the factory. On the SAA, the loading gate fit is like pregnancy — either it is or it isn't. Peskie's is.

When he heard about the project, Jeff offered to build a

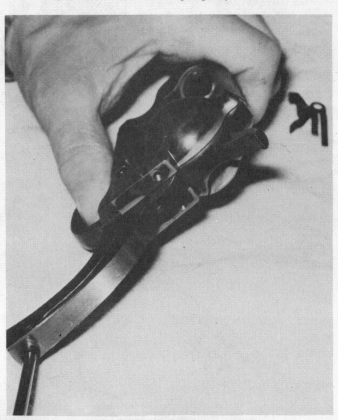

This part of fitting a trigger guard wasn't particularly difficult, but Geroge had a hard time getting the trigger guard to match the backstrap. It had to be done in order to get a smooth junction of the two parts in the front of the grip where the little finger grasps the butt.

Almost a gun. At this point, the little revolver begins to take shape. Everything is together, but fitting the internal parts for a clean trigger pull is yet to be done. Note that the trigger guard and backstrap are fitted to each other at the front corner, with no unsightly step.

The barrel was a wreck on the outside, with buggered threads and crummy looking nicks and dings. The muzzle crown was really bad. However, the bore was perfect and the threads could be chased. DiLeo cut the barrel back to 3½ inches in his lathe as shown here. Then he put a new crown on the muzzle, approximating the contour of the original. Polished, the barrel looked new.

In this shot, DiLeo fits up a front sight. Getting the sight precisely located on the barrel is a problem. It was a little easier to fit a new sight because the barrel was a .38 and thick enough to cut a fairly deep front sight slot. Fitting the front sight came out just fine.

frame any way that we wanted it — and there is considerable variety there. Original SAAs came in a great many variations: with or without the black powder frame screw, adjustable sights or fixed, ejectorless sheriff's model or regular, and with two different types of barrel thread. USFS makes all of these variations. After due deliberation, George and I chose a sheriff's, or storekeeper's, model with the old-style barrel thread. We ordered it color case-hardened.

There is no more intensely debated topic among SAA purists than the quality of pure Colt case hardening. The process by which Colt puts that smoky, swirly blend of gray, blue, green and purple on the frame is widely respected. Further, most authorities believe that it cannot be duplicated on investment cast steel. Maybe it can't, but those who believe that need to look closely at the frame of this revolver. In all candor, I cannot tell the difference.

With the frame on hand, George DiLeo started to assemble the necessary array of parts to make a gun. It turned out to be an incredible array of new and old stuff. I provided a brand-new second-generation cylinder from my goodie box. The matching barrel was a battered relic with a distorted crown from George's. The trigger guard came from

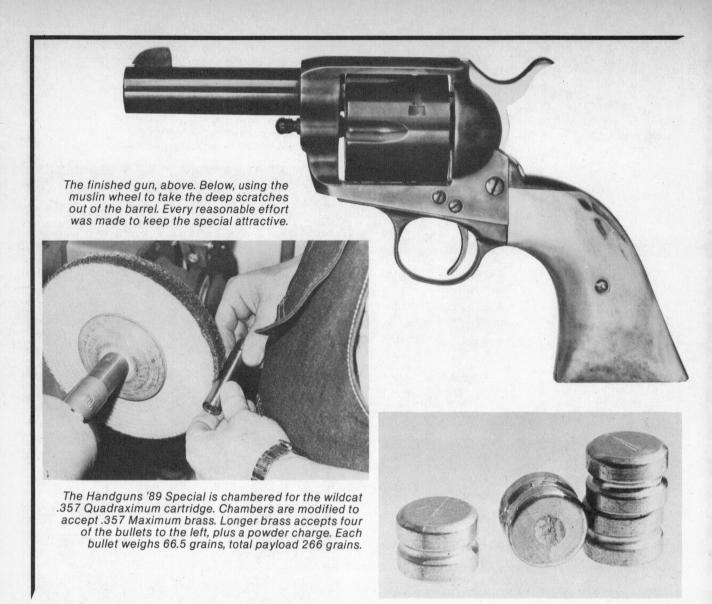

The finished gun, above. Below, using the muslin wheel to take the deep scratches out of the barrel. Every reasonable effort was made to keep the special attractive.

The Handguns '89 Special is chambered for the wildcat .357 Quadraximum cartridge. Chambers are modified to accept .357 Maximum brass. Longer brass accepts four of the bullets to the left, plus a powder charge. Each bullet weighs 66.5 grains, total payload 266 grains.

a rusty old parts gun that George had bought many years ago. I bought a new backstrap from Gary Thiry Parts.

The rest of the project went pretty much like that. The hammer was an old one; the trigger was brand new. The problem is simply that the basic gun was made over so many years that parts are not truly interchangeable. Since George is a SAA specialist, he had a wide variety of new and used parts on hand; because he is a SAA specialist, he knows how to fit them to one another and make a working handgun. It was not, however, the easiest single-action project that he tied into. On more than one occasion, I heard unprintable exclamations from the back room.

But in the fullness of time, a graceful single-action began to take shape. The gun was a sheriff's model, without ejector rod or housing for same. The barrel was made from a defunct .38 Special barrel, cut back to the uncommon length of 3½ inches. George made a special front sight and fitted it in place.

The SAA is a handgun with a grip shape that has been termed universal. It is an exceptionally attractive butt, one that I did not choose to alter, even though George has done several guns up with a tempting bird's-head pattern. We

could have used a number of materials for the grips, but I chose stag. The basic slabs came from India via Art Jewel and we looked through a few before we found the pair that I wanted..

Most stag grips have the coarse texture of the original material on the surface. But if you polish it off, you will be rewarded with some of the prettiest natural material you'll ever see. It is a pleasing blend of gray and black speckles on a field of creamy light yellowish white. In spots you may find a bit of black or dark brown. George fitted these grips to the frame of the revolver with meticulous care. They match the backstrap and trigger guard to perfection.

He wanted the Handguns '89 Special to be special, so the caliber was different. This gun is chambered for one of my own wildcat designs. I call it the .357 Quadraximum and it is a powerhouse close-range defensive cartridge.

The cartridge was not possible until the advent of the .357 Maximum. This extra-length .357 round is loaded into brass that is as long or longer than the cylinders of typical .357 magnum revolvers. For the wildcat, George used a special reamer to alter the six chambers of a .357 magnum cylinder to accept .357 Maximum brass. The brass runs clear to the front face of the cylinder and beyond, requiring a simple trimming operation. In effect, this produces strong brass the length of the cylinder.

The cartridge was not feasible until Dean Grennell designed a bullet mould for Hensley & Gibbs designated the #333. This bullet is a little lead cylinder, a full wadcutter weighing about 66.5 grains, depending on the alloy used. Quadraximum handloading puts *four* of the little bullets atop a charge of slow-burning powder. Finished off with a Redding profile crimp die, the long cartridges slip easily into the modified chambers. There is no wasted space in the chamber and the full payload weighs 266 grains. It leaves the muzzle of the gun at about 900 fps.

The effect on the target is awesome. Each pull of the trigger slams four .38 caliber slugs into the target. Each of them is fully stabilized in flight. The pattern produced widens as the range increases, but it will stay inside the torso dimensions of a man out to twenty-five yards. The cumulative effect of the four hits is going to be greater than the effect of four individual hits. The Quadraximum delivers four hits simultaneously in a small area. It is a powerful defensive proposition.

The revolver is further unique in the clever way that George handled the problem of no ejector rod. Sheriff's models don't have them and that leaves the shooter to punch out the empties with a nail or stick. On a miniature lathe, George crafted a special base pin for the gun that is hollow and female-threaded on its forward end. Into this hollow pin, a long rod fits perfectly. It's held in place by a

Right: Craftsman Danny Herrera made a presentation case for the gun. He operates a small shop in Walnut, California and specializes in fancy boxes for various types of guns and knives. His handiwork is exceptional.

Left: The presentation case. Note the exceptional grain in the French walnut, ivory panel and around the keyhole. The revolver nestled into the precise French fitting of the velvet interior. The cloth is a dark red-maroon and it contrasts beautifully with the case-hardened frame.

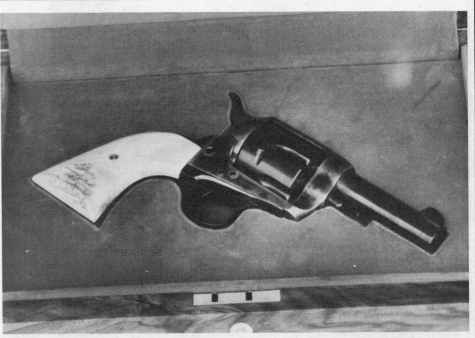

section of threads that match with the female threading in the base pin. In use, the shooter unscrews his ejector rod from its place in the base pin and pokes out the empties with it, then he slides the pin back into place and tightens it down with the screw feature. It works and it is slick.

The gun as you see it here is about 98% completed. Deadlines didn't allow us to get the barrel up to final polish and have an appropriate inscription engraved thereon. It is an attractive and well finished handgun completely functional and practical, a tribute to a fine American craftsman who did the work.

That is almost the end of the story, but not quite. We were discussing the little revolver one day at George's shop (appropriately called the Gunsight) when Danny Herrera ambled in and got into the conversation.

Herrera is a garrulous, talented hispanic gent with an interesting background. A native of East Los Angeles, where he attended schools through high school, Danny went away to college in the redwoods country of northern

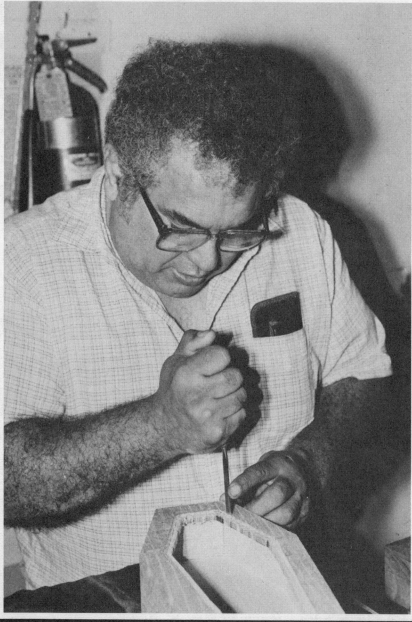

Herrera at work in his shop. He's making a coffin-shaped box for a ghoulish customer with a sense of humor. The octagonal box, above, has precisely-mated corners and strikingly handsome inlays. It is an example of fine wood working.

The Handguns '89 Special is not the fanciest handgun you will ever see, but it is an example of what custom pistolsmiths can do with a minimum of materials. The stag grips suit the author's tastes perfectly. It is a quick-handling little belly-buster of a gun. Made by craftsman George DiLeo of Fullerton, California, the revolver uses the author's wildcat cartridge. DiLeo has altered many .357 magnums to .357 Quadraximum.

California at Humboldt State. He returned and taught woodshop for a time in the Los Angeles area. He currently operates a small business in Walnut where he turns out an unusual product.

Danny Herrera makes boxes; not just orange crates, you understand, but fine, closely fitted presentation cases. While he laughs at the prestigious term "cases," preferring to call them boxes, he is turning out some of the finest custom cases you could possibly find.

Naturally, we roped him into doing up the Handguns '89 Special in a fancy presentation setting. After due consideration, we all agreed on an unusual case. Made of beautiful French walnut, the case is fitted with a French-style interior. This particular box has the gun setting at an angle, instead of parallel to the edges. The interior space is thus better alloted and the box looks a lot better.

The rest of the box is a delight to examine. The corners are carefully mitered and joined with a spline of hardwood. Top corners are beveled and the interior is a lush maroon velvet. I can't tell what the hinges are like; they're recessed completely out of sight. Danny was reluctant to do up the box in such a simple and straightforward style. He can do far more elaborate shapes, like octagons and coffins, often inlaying the tops with all sorts of flashy panels of contrasting wood.

I am completely satisfied with the lush grain of the box's walnut material and the flawless craftsmanship that went into it. Among boxes, this one is a lily that needs no gilding.

The gun that it contains is a one-of-a-kind special which shows off the craft of the pistolsmith in a positive light. It may not be as elaborate as one of the fancy pin guns, but the basic shape of the SAA is timeless and requires no alteration. George DiLeo's modifications merely bring the gun in line with modern ballistics and some clever innovations.

Just before finishing this chapter, I picked up the Handguns '89 Special and rolled it around in my hand for a moment. It has all of the familiar feel. It even balances about like my Colt Single Action .44 with a longer barrel, because the .357 cylinder and barrel are heavy. In so doing, I am reminded why the SAA is such a treasured handgun to me — and George DiLeo.

It's because of all those Saturday matinees.

CHAPTER 17
GEORGE MATTHEWS:

Forty-Five Years of Rebuilding Revolvers

Here's a late 1940s-era Matthews Combat Special. Built on a WWII Victory Model Smith & Wesson, the little .38 has most of the practical custom touches that are the hallmark of George Matthews' work.

"BACK IN those days, the boys just couldn't get a decent .38 to carry in civvies," George Matthews reflected. "It was right after the war was over and S&W and Colt hadn't even started to tool up for post-war stuff. The only guns they were making were M&Ps and Official Police Models — and they didn't come with short barrels. The Cobras and Chiefs Special were a long ways off. I had a lot of requests for carry guns over there in my old L.A. shop." He smiled at the recollection.

Where good guns are concerned, George Matthews has plenty of pleasant memories. He earned his first money working on a firearm sometime in '42 or '43 and after World War II service, he opened a gun shop. The shop has moved from the original location in the garage behind his Los Angeles home to its present site in Downey, California. While he has done nearly everything in the way of gunsmithing, from custom rifle stocks and metalwork to rebuilding exotic shotguns, he prefers to work on handguns.

When he talks about the boys who couldn't find a decent .38, he's talking about hundreds of Los Angeles PD

officers who made their way to that first little garage shop. Usually, they brought in a pre-war M&P Smith, sometimes a Victory Model or a Colt OP. What they wanted was a gun modified for civilian-clothes carry. LAPD mandated that an officer was to go armed at all times and a six-inch holster gun just didn't get it. The detectives brought a lot of business to the 62nd and Vermont address, too.

A week or so later, they got back a much-modified revolver they usually put into the holster and carried. But what they didn't realize was that they were using an American original. George Matthews' revolvers are unique —

unquestionably design masterpieces which never received the attention they richly deserve. They represent custom pistolsmithing at its best. The lack of recognition doesn't upset Matthews particularly. He never intended the guns to be anything but using handguns for a couple of generations of friendly cops that came to see him.

While the first few years of custom work centered on the policeman's carry gun, the basics of rebuilding revolvers carried over into the production of some fine specimens for use in the field by sportsmen. The essence of either kind of revolver is the combination of modifications that are truly practical as well as aesthetically pleasing.

When he worked up the first of the combat specials for LAPD, using a S&W M&P, the obvious first thing to do was shorten a barrel. That's not particularly difficult, although many gunsmiths have screwed it up. Matthews quickly realized the hard part was putting some kind of ramp-style sight on the barrel. Being an avid shooter, he knew the value of adjustable sights, so he developed a feature that turned out to be the hallmark of his work: the characteristic Matthews ventilated rib.

The rib was inspired in part by the fancy ones S&W mounted on the pre-war .357 magnums, but even more by the target ribs built by the King Gunsight Company of San Francisco. Matthews' ribs differ in that they are wider, grooved for a glare-free sighting plane. But they also differ in that they appear to have grown in place, right out of the steel of the revolver's barrel and frame. Rather than an obvious addition, the Matthews ribs seem part of the gun.

Machined out of a solid bar of tool steel, each rib is made for a particular gun to which it will be fitted. Each rib incorporates a rear sight fully adjustable for both windage and elevation. Even without the graceful ventilated rib, the sight itself is a design marvel. The rear sight blade is totally

Some gunsmiths of the 1930s and 1940s cut away the entire front of the trigger guard, but Matthews preferred to modify a carrying gun as seen here. By thinning the trigger guard on the strong side, he made the revolver almost as fast to use.

Another view of that modified trigger guard suggests the ease with which a shooter's finger might glide into firing position.

Matthews builds this special rear sight as part of the one-piece rib. Also note the shape of the hammer spur. It's a low-snag contour, but one that is fully functional as well as exceptionally attractive. Nice!

protected from possible damage by a sturdy housing. The housing contains the click-adjusting mechanism and is shaped to avoid snags on clothing or holster. Matthews mills a recess into the top strap of the revolver to fit the machined rib and attaches it to the gun with the slickest solder job that you'll ever see.

With a graceful ramp and base towards the muzzle, the end result is a graceful, but functional sighting system for a combat handgun. It's also damned pleasing to the eye; as much as any fancy quarter rib on a Rigby custom rifle for African work. Good looks aside, the sight is exceptionally practical with full adjustments for zero and a proper sight picture.

While the rib is the keystone of a Matthews revolver, it is not the entire story. George also developed several ways to modify the hammer shape in order to make it better looking, as well as more useful. His most common hammer spur modification ended up as sort of a modified "humpback" hammer. The original humpbacks were offered by the S&W factory in the 1930s and many are found on the pre-war .357 magnums.

Matthews would take an original hammer, cut off the spur, then weld up the area where a new spur would grow. Then it was time for the files. With a variety of files and a lot of patience, he would sculpt a new hammer spur shape completely out of the weld metal. Invariably, the result was clean and symmetrical. It was also functional, since the gunsmith radiused away the edges that tend to snag on

clothing. Not surprisingly, the total effect is most pleasing to the eye, particularly in light of neatly executed checkering as a finishing touch.

On customer request, Matthews would perform other special modifications. One of the most popular was the trigger guard window. Other 'smiths of that era completely removed the front face of the trigger guard. This was done to ease the movement of the trigger finger onto the trigger for fast double-action shooting. George never did this, simply because he considered the modification to be unsafe. It's obvious that a trigger with no protection to the front could conceivably catch on the lip of a holster and fire. The gun so modified is fragile and the trigger guard can be bent inwards in a scuffle, jamming the trigger and rendering the revolver inoperable. Instead, Matthews preferred to slim the trigger guard's forward face on one side, allowing the trigger finger to slide easily into place. It is a far more sensible modification and he is not the only pistolsmith to do it.

In the course of looking at all of the fancy cosmetic touches he has performed over the years, it's easy to overlook the interior things — like the trigger jobs. I have handled an S&W Model 10 with two-inch barrel which received the full Matthews treatment over thirty-five years ago. There aren't a whole lot of edges left on that gun; they've been worn away by carrying in pocket or holster. Two generations of deputies of the Orange County Sheriff's Department have carried that revolver nearly every day

The old King Gunsight Company of San Francisco used to put a lot of these ribs on target guns. The front sight area has a chrome mirror angled to reflect light on a front sight post, a workable system.

While the King rib inspired Matthews in a number of ways, he wanted to create a rib for essentially combat guns. This S&W Model 58 has a barrel five inches long. The rib looks like it grew out of the gun.

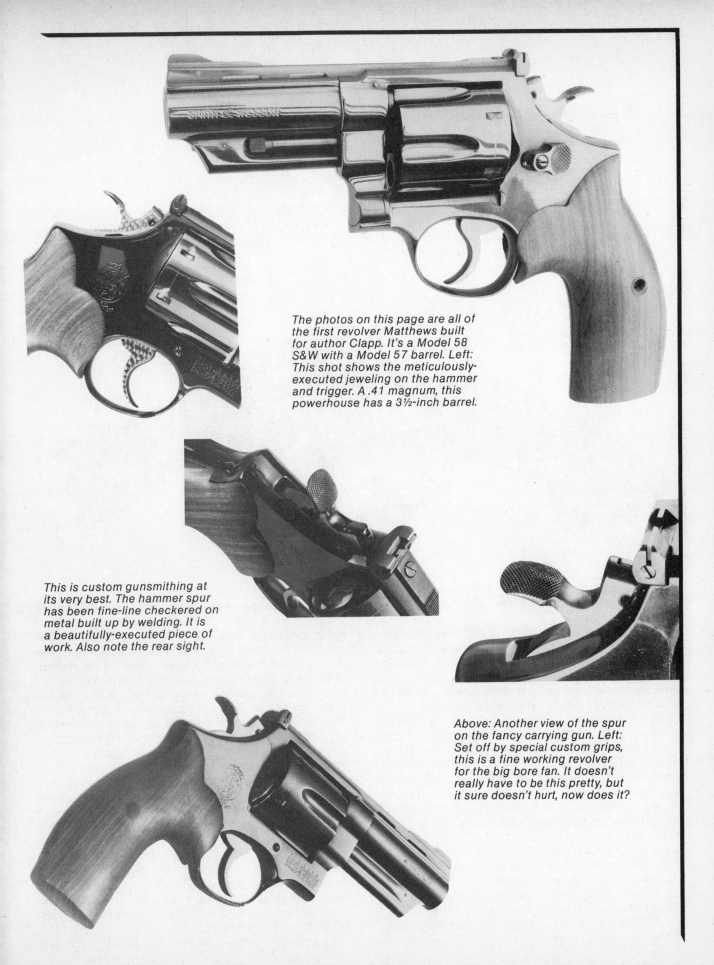

The photos on this page are all of the first revolver Matthews built for author Clapp. It's a Model 58 S&W with a Model 57 barrel. Left: This shot shows the meticulously-executed jeweling on the hammer and trigger. A .41 magnum, this powerhouse has a 3½-inch barrel.

This is custom gunsmithing at its very best. The hammer spur has been fine-line checkered on metal built up by welding. It is a beautifully-executed piece of work. Also note the rear sight.

Above: Another view of the spur on the fancy carrying gun. Left: Set off by special custom grips, this is a fine working revolver for the big bore fan. It doesn't really have to be this pretty, but it sure doesn't hurt, now does it?

Rugers also respond when Matthews goes to work on them. This revolver started out as a plain .41 magnum Blackhawk. It has been re-barreled with a 1:14 tube from Douglas. It also has a stainless steel...

...grip frame and hammer. The action is a delight to handle and the racy rib on the top of the frame and barrel is both pleasing in appearance and functional in use. Here's a regal single-action revolver.

since it left the shop. To the best of my knowledge, the gun never has been back and the double-action pull defies my ability to describe it.

As time passed, Matthews moved his business to Downey, branching out into all phases of custom gunsmithing. Presently, his son, Steve, is working with him. Everyone has his personal interests and Steve's eyes light up when someone comes through the front door with a Model 12 Winchester that needs his attention.

George Matthews' handgun work hasn't been exclusively on revolvers or even combat-type revolvers. He has worked his magic on autos for every phase of pistol shooting from bullseye to IPSC. In the days when revolvers in certain calibers were hard to get, George laboriously built the necessary tooling to rebore revolver cylinders to larger calibers. In the process of so doing, he usually corrected the inevitable misalignments in the factory cylinder. I own a Highway Patrolman that he buzzed out to .44 Special. It is one of the most accurate wheelguns in my battery.

Over the years that I have done business with Matthews, I have acquired a number of handguns on which he has performed varying degrees of work. Some of them have just a little touch here and there, like my late father's K-38 which got a cockeyed hammer for fast single-action cocking. Others are totally rebuilt, sometimes from guns that were

just a step away from being stripped for parts.

The first gun Matthews built up for me has an interesting history. It is a Model 58 S&W .41 magnum, the fixed-sight M&P-style gun introduced in 1964 for police service. This particular revolver lived its early life in the holster of some unknown San Francisco policeman, until his department ill-advisedly abandoned the use of the best police revolver ever built. I bought the revolver from a police surplus dealer in 1972 for sixty-five bucks. It was in pretty decent shape inside, but the finish showed signs of hard holster use in a seacoast city. I took the revolver to George Matthews, along with a four-inch Model 57 barrel from a gun show bargain table.

I got back the works. He completely rebuilt the action of the revolver, smoothing it out considerably. The hammer and trigger flats were meticulously jeweled and the rest of the gun polished to a mirror finish and reblued. Per my request, he rounded the butt and cut the window into the right side of the trigger guard. The fancy rib went on the Model 57 barrel, cut back to the end of the underlug for a total length of 3¼ inches. On this particular revolver, the single most pleasing cosmetic touch is the incredible checkering job on the wide hammer spur. To say I was pleased would be an understatement.

In the early Seventies, Smith & Wesson did not make a

Another Smith & Wesson Model 58. A .45 Colt by virtue of a Model 25-2 barrel and a re-bored .41 cylinder, the gun is designed to be a heavyweight holster gun. Author specified the five-inch barrel length, which is the best possible using size for the big, beefy N-frame wheelguns.

revolver for the .45 Colt cartridge. I just had to have one, so I bought another Model 58, this one brand new. Along with a Model 25-2 barrel from the S&W parts department, the revolver went to the Downey shop. George rebored the .41 magnum cylinder to .45 Colt, did his usual magic on the action and installed the .45 barrel. This time, we agreed on a five-inch barrel length and he installed his rib on the barrel cut to what has become my favorite length. He also rounded the butt.

These two views of the .45 Colt conversion show the racy lines and fancy cosmetics of a beautiful revolver. Re-boring the cylinder was necessary when Smith & Wesson wasn't making guns in .45 Colt. It's a tricky job.

There's no revolver in the S&W line at the present time that can compete with the 58 as a starting point for fancy N-frames. It looks better all dolled-up, but plain-Jane M&P style N-frames need to be brought back.

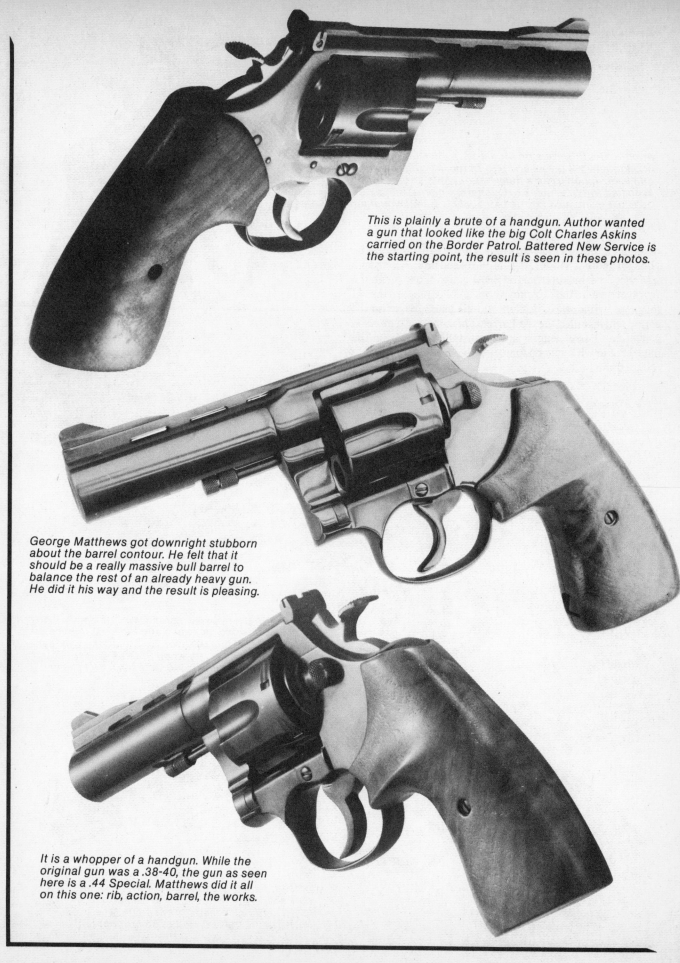

This is plainly a brute of a handgun. Author wanted a gun that looked like the big Colt Charles Askins carried on the Border Patrol. Battered New Service is the starting point, the result is seen in these photos.

George Matthews got downright stubborn about the barrel contour. He felt that it should be a really massive bull barrel to balance the rest of an already heavy gun. He did it his way and the result is pleasing.

It is a whopper of a handgun. While the original gun was a .38-40, the gun as seen here is a .44 Special. Matthews did it all on this one: rib, action, barrel, the works.

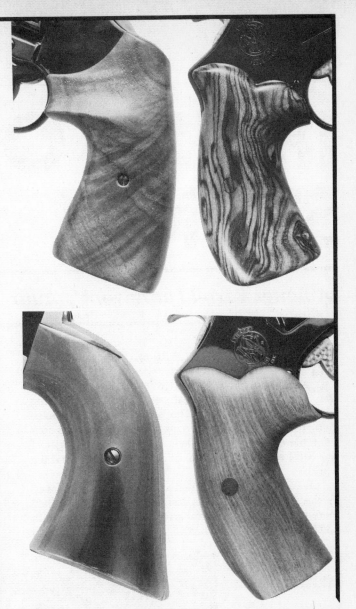

Matthews doesn't make grips, so the author turned to other craftsmen for these. Upper left: Herrett's Jordan Trooper Stock in presentation walnut on the New Service Colt; lower left: Art Jewel gray buffalo horn grips on the Ruger single-action; lower right: Lignum vitae grips on an S&W, custom from the late Dick Tracey; and upper right, bocote custom from the incomparable Craig Spegal.

The lignum vitae grips on the first gun, the .41 magnum, were made by Dick Tracey, but he had tragically passed away. It took me a number of years of looking to find another gripmaker whose work suited me, but I eventually became acquainted with Craig Spegal. Craig used a piece of fancy bocote for the grips, carving them to my general specifications. The big S&W is an easy gun to handle, even with stiff loads, and the precision rebored cylinder makes it accurate.

My growing collection of Matthews custom handguns had no single-actions, so I found a good used Ruger Blackhawk in .41 magnum. After a discussion with Matthews on the type of handloads I was planning to use in the gun, he suggested re-barreling with a Douglas blank, using the 1:14 twist. His judgment turned out to be correct; the Ruger shoots beautifully with the original cylinder and the new barrel. Cosmetically, the Ruger had the full-length rib added, plus a stainless steel frame, hammer and trigger. The stainless surfaces were lightly bead-blasted, contrasting beautifully with the polished blue steel of the rest of the gun. The grips are from Art Jewel, shiny gray buffalo horn against the soft gray of the grip frame. It's a handsome, elegant single-action that shoots like a house afire.

So far, no Colts in the collection, a situation that had to be rectified. When I stumbled on a big New Service, I knew it was a gun for the Matthews touch. The gun was just about ready for the parts bin, with a bulged barrel and several broken internal parts. It was a long-barreled .38-40, but definitely not shootable. Since I had a brand-new .44 Special cylinder for the New Service in my goodie box and Douglas was producing barrel stock with a .429-inch groove diameter, I bought the gun and headed for Downey.

This time, we agreed to make a bull-barrel shooter. With a heavy four-inch tube and the usual rib, the resulting revolver is heavy, but it balances quite well. Matthews had to do more inside this gun than any of the others. The entire action required overhaul and replacement of several parts. The hammer has been rebuilt with a wide spur for easy cocking. It turned out to be one of the better old-style Colt action jobs that I have ever seen.

The stocks are interesting, too. To the best of my knowledge, Steve Herrett never cataloged the Jordan Trooper stock for Colt New Service frames. Jordan's style makes a big stock for the smaller K-frame Smith and they are massive on the big New Service. I found a pair of them in the back of a dusty showcase in Bucky O'Neil's Sporting Goods in Prescott, Arizona. Made from select walnut, they have found a home on my Matthews New Service.

It isn't all fancy at the Matthews shop. They do all of the normal gunsmithing work of installing scopes and recoil pads, replacing broken parts, even cleaning up old guns for clients who need an heirloom handled with care. But whenever possible, George Matthews finds some way to make the job look just a little better. I have asked him to cut down several of my favorite N-frame S&Ws to what I consider the best barrel length for these guns — five inches. To do so requires a new front sight. The one that George puts on does no more for the gun than the original — but it sure looks better.

Making guns look better, as well as shoot better, has preoccupied this Californian for a long time. Well into his fifth decade of service to shooters, George is still in the shop five days every week. There won't be any more of the Matthews ventilated ribs, because they take about four working days to do and aren't economically feasible. Still, he stands ready to make your gun look — and shoot — better.

Out of the Southern California area, George Matthews is not well known. Mostly that's because he's too busy working to do much promoting — and he's a lot better workman than promoter. That he has never received the attention he deserves is a certainty.

It is equally certain that George Matthews is one of the best gunsmiths America has ever produced.

CHAPTER 18

IRVING O. STONE

A Better Barrel For Anyone's Auto

"**A** HUNDRED YEARS ago, they used to do it that way, but we know better now," Irv Stone commented whimsically. He was at the workbench in his California desert shop, talking about his favorite subject. That's how to make an automatic pistol more accurate, a matter in which he has considerable experience. Irv Stone is the owner-manager of Bar-Sto Precision and his barrels are famous around the world.

"Oversized barrel links used to be the way we tightened up the sloppiness that was designed into the .45. When there were no replacement barrels available, a gunsmith had to use that kind of technique to get the barrel to index in

the same relationship to the slide every time," Stone added.

Shooting partner Stan Waugh and I were in 29 Palms to visit with Stone and watch as he installed a fancy stainless steel barrel in Stan's ailing Gold Cup. I had been there on other occasions and I've had barrels installed in several handguns. There are a number of comments I could make about Bar-Sto barrels, but the so-called bottom line is simply this: In my experience, a Bar-Sto barrel *always* improves the accuracy of a handgun. The amount of improvement varies, but when the pistol goes into the Ransom Rest, under controlled conditions, there is a measurable increase in accuracy.

Even though the degree of improvement varies from one

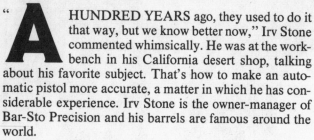

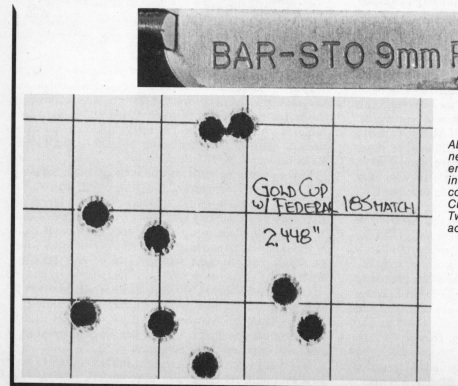

Gold Cup
w/ Federal 185 Match

2.448"

Above: The Bar-Sto trademark is neatly pantographed into the breech end of each barrel — a Browning P35 in 9mmP. Left: This is the best we could get out of Stan Waugh's Gold Cup as it came from the factory. Two and a half inches just isn't an acceptable level of performance.

Above: The slide of the ailing Gold Cup all set up in the special fixture Stone uses to measure the slide's dimensions prior to fitting the new barrel. The idea is to determine just how far from true the slide was made. After taking measurements in certain critical areas, it is easy to cut an oversized barrel down to fit the gun.

Bar-Sto'ed pistol to the next, it is assuredly obvious. After a good bit of testing in about a dozen handguns, I can state that the groups tighten up by an average of forty percent. That is true with all calibers of barrels and all models of handguns for which Stone makes barrels. The improvement is less dramatic in pistols that were accurate to begin with and far more dramatic in guns like Colt .38 Supers which once used a questionable system of headspacing.

Stone's main product is a stainless steel barrel for the Colt .45. The one fitted to Stan Waugh's pistol is the top-of-the-line match variety, which Stone, himself, fits to individual pistols. The .45 barrel is also available in a drop-in form and remains the best-seller in his catalog. So much so, in fact, that a great many people overlook the other barrels that come out of the desert shop.

Bar-Sto barrels are made for lots of other guns. In the popular 9mmP caliber, you can order a barrel for your Smith & Wesson (any one of the several models), Beretta, Browning, Colt, CZ-75 and copies thereof. There are others, like the Sig-Sauer 226, in the final stages of development. Stone also offers a .38 Super barrel for the Colt and, on special order, for the Browning. One of his lesser-known models is a .38 Special for the S&W Model 52. You might even be able to talk him into a special barrel for the old .38/45 wildcat.

One of the hot sellers right now is a Bar-Sto barrel for either of two new automatic pistol cartridges, the 10mm Auto or the .41 Action Express. They're available for Colt pistols only. We used barrels for each in developing the data reported to you in Chapter Nine of this book.

The .41 Action Express already has spawned a spin-off round called the 9mm Action Express, which is the parent .41 necked down to form a stubby little bottle-necked cartridge. It's still in the wildcat stages, but we may see this one on dealer's shelves in factory form at an early date. The cartridge has enough capacity to move typical 9mmP bullets to some impressive velocities. Stone can fit your Colt with a barrel.

During the course of our visit to the Bar-Sto shop, we saw prototypes of another model and caliber barrel. It's also for a Colt, but an unusual one. How about a match barrel for the Colt .380 Government Model? The pistol is a natural for the Bar-Sto touch, it has essentially the same locking system as its big brother, the M1911A1 .45. We may be shooting the world's most accurate .380 in the next year or so.

The barrels are made one hundred percent in Stone's own shop. There's enough business to keep a half-dozen good machinists busy the year around. Stone himself is everywhere in the shop, constantly checking and supervising to insure high quality. He's also spending a fair amount of his time making sure his son learns all that he can about the barrel business.

With a background in producing precision components for the aerospace industry, Stone approaches barrel making very systematically. After examining a new pistol for which he'll be making a barrel, he'll identify the spots in the design where he can improve the accuracy potential of the barrel. The bores of all barrels of the same caliber are alike. They are broach-rifled with broaches cut to Stone's own specifications. The broach goes through a tube that has been honed to diameter with a tolerance of .0002-inch.

The inside of Bar-Sto barrels are all alike, regardless of what gun they'll go into. Part of the key to their accuracy lies with the rifling itself, but another part is the means by which the barrel fits into the pistol. Most Bar-Sto barrels are of the Colt-Browning tilting barrel type. To be accurate, the barrel must return to the same position relative to the slide every time that the pistol is fired.

Irv Stone makes sure that happens by subtly re-designing each barrel. In some cases, he leaves extra material on the barrel so the gunsmith can hand-fit it to the other parts and get a precise lockup. On other guns, he improves cam angles and matching flats to be sure the fit of major parts is consistently firm.

This is what prompted the comment about long links "...a hundred years ago." Stone explained what the barrel link on the bottom of a Colt barrel is actually for. It's function is to unlock the barrel when a shot has been fired. In the absence of barrels with oversized lugs, fitted precisely to the slide stop, gunsmiths made longer links that served to force the barrel up into positive contact with the top of the slide. It works to a degree, but it will wear out eventually.

Stone does it a better way. He manufactures the barrel with oversized lugs and hood, then precisely fits them to the individual pistol. A procedure like this is too expensive and time-consuming for the original maker to use, but Stone makes it pay. The pistol thus fitted is remarkably consistent in the shot-to-shot relationship of the barrel and slide.

We watched as Stone fitted up Stan's barrel. In the course of the conversation, Stone also described the procedure he went through in designing and producing a barrel for the Sig-Sauer 226 pistol. He had three different prototype barrels on hand and we tried them all in a later range session.

The first barrel was externally a duplicate of the factory barrel, but internally had Stone's favored 1:16 rifling.

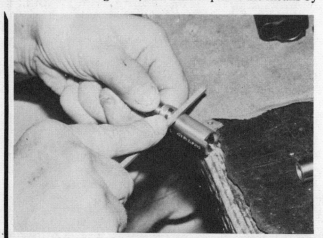

Below: For each barrel, Stone charts the deviations from true, inherent in the slide. The barrel hood is cut to fit the slide so that the barrel will return to the same position from shot to shot. Left: Stone is seen here in the act of breaking the edge of the locking lug to insure that the pistol will function correctly each time.

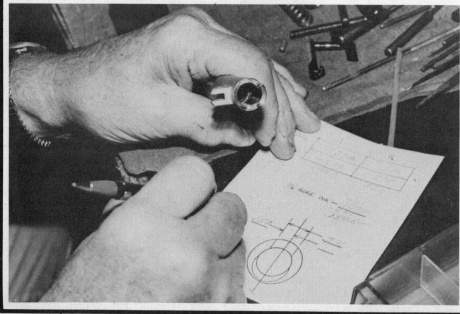

Above: Use a tool whenever possible, says Stone. Here he is using a specially contoured grinding wheel to cut the barrel locking lug to fit. This is probably the most critical part of the fitting process on Colt 1911s. Right: The effort is worthwhile. Here's another group from the Gold Cup with the same ammo. It is about 31% better.

With two different kinds of quality Federal ammo, the pistol shot groups better than the original. In an effort to improve the system, Stone built a second barrel, but modified the lockup to index a flat on the barrel top against the flat upper surface of the slide's ceiling. This produced groups better than the first one, but groups then tended toward the vertical stringing characteristic of inconsistent locking. In a third effort, Stone moved the position and angle of the cams on the barrel lug, as well as changed the top locking points. The latter barrel shoots beautifully, with just a hint of vertical stringing. Knowing Stone as I do, I expect there will be a fourth version soon.

In the same range session, we tried Stan's Gold Cup. Five different kinds of ammunition were on hand for the test, including a pair of the handloads that Waugh assembles for his own use. We first tried the ammo through the pistol with original barrel and bushing in place. This confirmed the need for the original trip to the desert — this Gold Cup was not shooting well. The best group measured 2.448 inches for ten shots. It was with 185-grain Federal JHP Match.

We then went back and fired the same five loads with the Bar-Sto barrel and bushing installed. The results were dramatic; more so than the average. All five loads performed substantially better. The typical group shrank from the four-inch-plus mark to under two. The *least* decrease in group size was with the same Federal Match stuff, which shot the smallest ten-shot group at 1.682 inches. The improvement on that one was thirty-one percent and the improvement with all loads averaged fifty-six percent.

Cutting your handgun's groups in half is a reasonable goal and one that is fairy simple. Just install a Bar-Sto barrel. Lest there be confusion on the matter, Stone does not claim that every pistol will respond as did Stan Waugh's. In my experience, a change like this is not the norm, but I do believe that Bar-Sto barrels tighten groups by about forty percent.

Nevertheless, Stone does claim he can improve the performance of any gun. I have plenty of test targets that say he's dead right.

CHAPTER 19

WAYNE NOVAK:

"Just Basic Badass Businessguns"

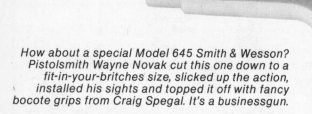

How about a special Model 645 Smith & Wesson? Pistolsmith Wayne Novak cut this one down to a fit-in-your-britches size, slicked up the action, installed his sights and topped it off with fancy bocote grips from Craig Spegal. It's a businessgun.

WHAT A DAY!'' exclaimed a shaken Jack Mitchell. He had just settled into a chair in a restaurant down the street from the school where he was enrolled. It was the first day of orientation in The Colorado School of Trades gunsmithing course. Mitchell, fresh from the Army and a stint in the publishing business, had spent a day in the company of machinists and toolmakers who talked knowingly of mills and millimeters. With absolutely zero mechanical background, he was confused completely and was questioning the wisdom of his choice of new occupation.

He turned to his companion, the only other person in the class who seemed as confused as he and who already had confessed to experience as a produce buyer for a Chicago supermarket chain.

"Did you have any idea what those crazy people were talking about?" Mitchell asked.

Wayne Novak paused in the act of eating and answered his new friend's nervous question, "None whatsoever."

Mitchell has gone on to become a gun writer and advertising executive. He's authored several DBI titles on combat handgunning and gunsmithing. He must have learned something in the months that followed that first encounter with the other fellow.

Novak? It would seem the bearded Chicagoan also must have paid attention in class. In the intervening years, Wayne Novak has worked at his trade diligently and currently enjoys a reputation as one of the nation's leading pistolsmiths. His handguns have appeared in several national magazines and, perhaps more significantly, in the holsters of people who must carry a pistol in the course of their daily work.

That's the Novak specialty: business guns; handguns modified in a number of ways that make them more effective as fighting tools. Most commonly in the Novak shop, the guns on the workbenches are automatics. His personal preferences run to autos, but he has done a fair amount of revolver work, too.

At the present time, Novak works in a small West Virginia shop with two assistants. When he left the Colorado school, he worked for the legendary Armand Swensen. In the early Seventies, you couldn't pick up a gun magazine without seeing another Swensen gun pictured. The California-based elder gunsmith earned a deserved reputation for high-quality work, including such innovations as the ambidextrous safety and the trademark squared trigger guard. Novak acknowledges the value of his time in the Swensen shop.

But Novak had ideas of his own. The main idea that is making Novak famous in the pistol world came from his own experience as a combat pistol shooter. In the course of a match, the only thing a shooter sees is the target and the pistol's sights. Gunhandling comes from a practiced feel, but the shooter must look at what's ahead of him. In the actual act of firing, he's focused on sight alignment.

There are lots of sights that serve a shooter admirably in aligning his gun in the aiming area. Various large, easy-to-see handgun sights have been mounted successfully on the combat handguns. The square one-eighth-inch rear sight notch, mated to a front ramp sight, is nearly universal. You can get it in a Bo-Mar, Micro, Millett or other quality sight.

But when the gun is subjected to hard use on the range or, worse yet, in the rough and tumble of law enforcement, the sights have to be modified. We've all seen the fine Bo-Mar buried deeply in the slide of a Colt and the "Melted Micro" is a fact of life. None of these modifications really remove the possibility of a sharp edge hanging up on a holster mouth, coat lining or even a human hand. The ideal sight should perform its aiming function, but shouldn't make handling the gun a hazard. Novak's combat sight does just that.

The innovative unit comes with a front sight correctly matched in width to provide a clear sight picture when viewed through the rear sight. Novak's front sights are fitted into a small dovetail milled for the purpose. They are locked into the dovetail with a tight-fitting Allen screw. Novak puts several different degrees of rearward slope to his front sights, but the rear-facing plane is usually sharply serrated. It's a highly visible unit.

All of the photos on this page show Novak's superb rear sight. Above: The sight from above and to the rear. Note how the notch is recessed and nearly always in shadow. This can be a big advantage. This one is mounted on a worked-over S&W 669, one of today's better carry guns.

Above: The Novak sight in profile. The sloping angle of the sight as it rises from the top surface of the slide is one key to its success. Below: Looking straight down on the sight, as mounted on a Model 459. The hex-head Allen screw locks the windage adjustment firmly in place.

It's the rear sight that is the jewel of the system. As a pure sight, the Novak rear sight is not materially different from many others. It is a simple square notch approximately one-eighth-inch in width. The main visible difference in the sight as it is viewed by the shooter from the rear is that the notch is a milled recess. This additional relief of the metal on the rear of the sight produces a desirable effect. Simply stated, it puts the rear sight notch in shadow and that means a shooter can expect his rear sight to appear pretty much the same in most light conditions. A flat-faced rear sight usually is blackened deliberately for the same general purpose.

If you can agree that Novak's sight is as good as any and better than most, you can move on to the other major advantage. The combat pistol is a gun made to be handled fast in crisis circumstances. There's little need on such a pistol for extraneous edges and corners. Such protuberances tend to hang up on clothing, belts and even holster edges. Worse yet, they can scratch, cut and irritate the hand when the gun is being used rapidly. It's been said that a combat handgun should feel like a well used bar of soap.

The rear sight is a particularly critical area on a combat auto. Autos sometimes jam and modern weaponcraft calls for a sweeping motion of the hand across the slide as part of a clearance drill. If there's a big, sharp-edged rear sight in the way, the drill could result in a distracting, if minor injury. In an emergency situation, like a life-or-death gunfight, it's best that a man's attention stay focused on the matter at hand.

Novak's sight doesn't stick up in the way and there are no sharp corners. In profile, the Novak sight does not have a step where the body of the sight rises from the uppermost surface of the slide. A backward sweep of the hand across this surface will merely cam the hand up and away. Even right and left edges of the sight get the bevel treatment. From the rear, the sight angles forward slightly. It's easy for a shooter to strike the rear of a slide that hasn't quite returned to battery. A sharp blow with the heel of the hand usually will get it done and without the distracting pain that would result from tapping something like a Bo-Mar.

Most shooters have the same reaction to the Novak sight before the considerable practical advantages of the unit are pointed out to them. It looks good, with clean lines that

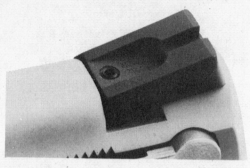

This shot shows why the sight shape makes sense in better handling. Imagine the effect of sweeping the hand across the slide's top surface to clear a jam. The sight won't interfere with the movement.

In this view, notice the bevels cut on both sides of the sight. It is obvious that the sight, while it is large, fits into the lines of the gun. Looks good.

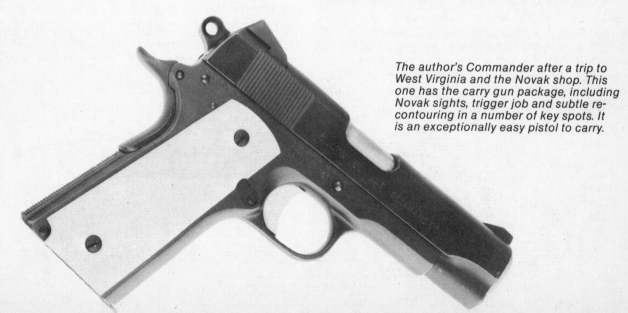

The author's Commander after a trip to West Virginia and the Novak shop. This one has the carry gun package, including Novak sights, trigger job and subtle recontouring in a number of key spots. It is an exceptionally easy pistol to carry.

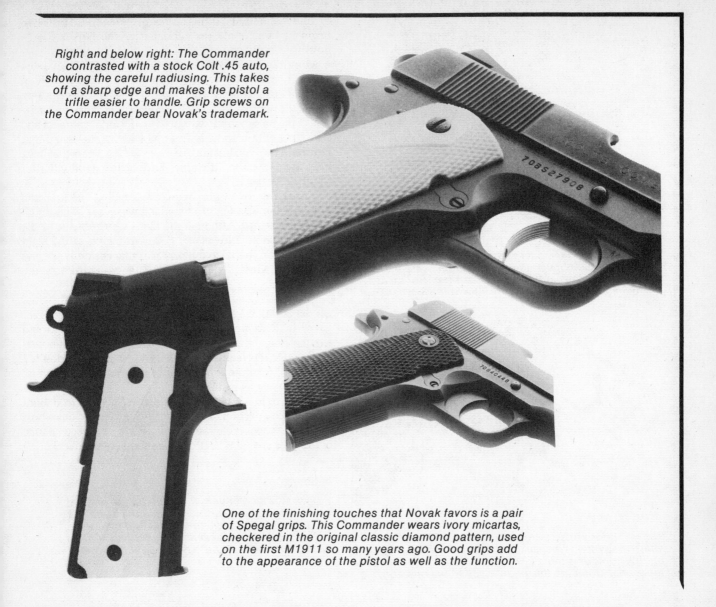

Right and below right: The Commander contrasted with a stock Colt .45 auto, showing the careful radiusing. This takes off a sharp edge and makes the pistol a trifle easier to handle. Grip screws on the Commander bear Novak's trademark.

One of the finishing touches that Novak favors is a pair of Spegal grips. This Commander wears ivory micartas, checkered in the original classic diamond pattern, used on the first M1911 so many years ago. Good grips add to the appearance of the pistol as well as the function.

flow evenly from the gun. And that feature gives us a bit of insight into the nature of this custom pistolsmith: Wayne Novak likes to make things practical, but attractive.

One of my pet pistols is a Novak .45 Colt Commander. The gun never was much of a shooter until Irv Stone insisted on installing one of his barrels in the gun. After a quick look at the machine rest results, I saw that this was not a pistol to be kept in the safe. This was a potential carryin' gun. I sent the gun to Novak for sights and a general slicking up.

I got back a real jewel. The trigger is a clean-breaking 3½ to four pounds, with no creep or overtravel. There's little else to say about this trigger, except that it is perfect for the job at hand. Wayne got the pistol with a Bar-Sto barrel in place, so there was no need to ramp the barrel. He did use an original Commander hammer and aluminum trigger, replacing the parts that were in the gun when he got it.

The grips are a pair of Craig Spegal's ivory micarta type, checkered in the traditional and attractive diamond pattern. This was a light carry gun package, so Novak did not checker the front of the grip. But he did perform several

subtle little contour changes that reflect a practical viewpoint in modifying a pistol for defensive purposes. Most of them also are attractive.

All of the edges and corners on the Commander have been softly radiused. It is done quite subtly and makes the pistol look even better than the original. Some of the contours of the mass-produced pistol needed to be trued up and straightened. All of them are now easier on the hand when the gun is used. The ejection port is lowered and relieved just a little. And the finish is a soft, ultra-light matte blue, one of the more attractive finishes I have seen.

Naturally, Novak installed a set of his sights. At my request, Novak made this set with bars of encapsulated Tritium, the glow-in-the-dark material that works so well in low-light shooting situations. The bar in the front sight is vertical, while the one in the rear is horizontal, just below the rear sight notch. The bar/bar effect produces an inverted "T" and an easy shooting sight.

Overall effects of the modifications performed on the Commander are most noticable when the gun is handled

Above: The original Model 669 has the hooked trigger guard that is so popular these days. I don't care for it or the sharp edges of the receiver and frame area. At my request, Novak modified the little Smith & Wesson.

Above: The modified pistol looks like this. The trigger guard area retains a small portion of the checkering, but the contour is more eye-appealing as well as more functional. Compare this photograph to the one above.

carefully and fired. At this point, an experienced pistolero begins to appreciate the subtleties of the Novak touch, however lightly applied.

More extensive modification of any of the popular autos is a daily chore in Novak's shop. You can see what happens (in the accompanying photos), when Novak ties into one of the popular little S&W Model 669s. This is a variation of the basic 9mmP Model 459/659 auto, compact and carryable with a short barrel and slide, a shortened butt housing a twelve-shot magazine. In the few years that have been available, the little nines have been a good seller for Smith & Wesson.

Novak improved this one considerably. The first and arguably the best feature he added was a set of his small carry-gun sights. Although the factory sight is one of the better available, Novak's is better. It increases the sight radius a little, but also makes the sights easier to see and shoot with. Most of all, the pistol is far easier to carry and use with the snag-free sights in place.

The shooting public demanded a feature on the original Model 669 that I strongly oppose. It is the hooked trigger guard that became popular a number of years ago and which seems unwilling to die. There are lots of shooters who prefer the feature, but there are more who don't. I don't care for it and asked Novak to remove it when he worked over this pistol.

He did so in a way that might please shooters from both sides of the question. The sharp corner is gone, but a portion of the checkering remains. There is a reduced chance of the edge snagging, but there's enough of the checkering

Below: Modified 669 on the left, with the original gun on the right. The differences don't seem to be extreme until you pick up the gun and start using it. The combination of sights, trigger and contour changes makes this auto better to handle and shoot.

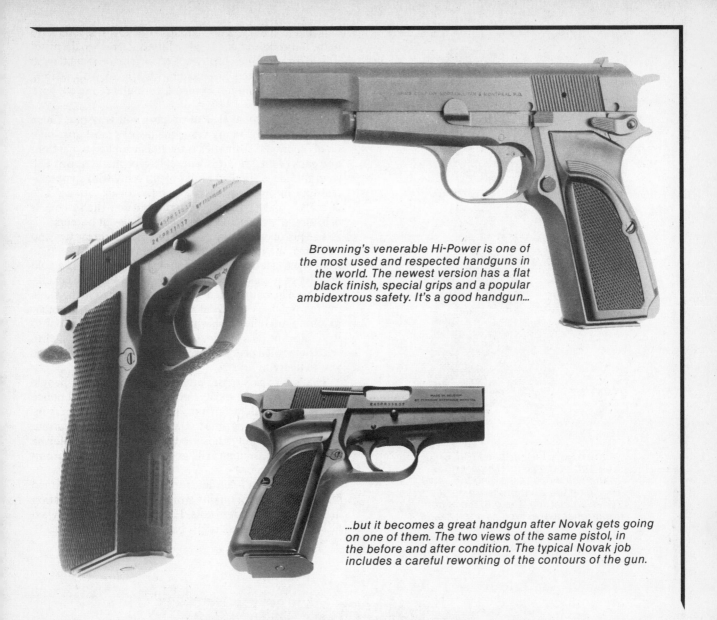

Browning's venerable Hi-Power is one of the most used and respected handguns in the world. The newest version has a flat black finish, special grips and a popular ambidextrous safety. It's a good handgun...

...but it becomes a great handgun after Novak gets going on one of them. The two views of the same pistol, in the before and after condition. The typical Novak job includes a careful reworking of the contours of the gun.

left to use in the intended finger-forward firing position. The resulting contour is much like the original Model 39 pistols.

In the process of rounding off the trigger guard, Novak altered some other contours on the pistol. At my request, he went a little farther than he usually does and the receiver of the pistol has some markedly softened edges. He refinished the receiver of the pistol with a pleasant silvery-colored anodizing. It looks and feels considerably better.

The final touches are internal. I have no idea what Novak does to the insides of Smith & Wesson autos, but they came back from West Virginia a lot better than when they left Massachusetts. I have handled about a half dozen of his S&W autos, both 9mmPs and .45s, and they are universally superior in a world full of DA automatics. This little 669 mini-gun has a smooth, easy-to-control trigger that is a delight to use. The single-action trigger is similarly creditable.

Both of the pistols we have discussed thus far spent brief periods of time on Novak's workbench. In other words, he did not pull out all the stops and do a complete reworking of the pistols. For the next pistol, he assuredly did. Not surprisingly, it's his own gun.

Novak is a real fan of the Browning Hi-Power and owns an extensive collection of them. His personal preference in carry guns is a suitably modified P-35. For the purposes of illustrating a full re-build in the Novak shop, Wayne bought a new dull-finished Hi-Power and sent it to me to photograph in the before state. I returned it to him and waited until he could do the work and send it back. In time, the pistol came back to me with all of the work done.

It is a beautiful piece of gunsmithing. The most noticeable alteration is the extended grip tang. Hi-Power shooters, including Novak, have been complaining about hammer bite since 1935. On this gun, which Novak built as his own personal piece, hammer bite is impossible. The pistol's tang extends back over the web of the hand in such a way that the hammer could not possibly reach it. It is a drastic modification, but an ergonomically sound one.

Ergonomics — or making it handle better — is really what it is all about in the Novak shop. Look at the junction of the trigger guard and the butt of the pistol, the area

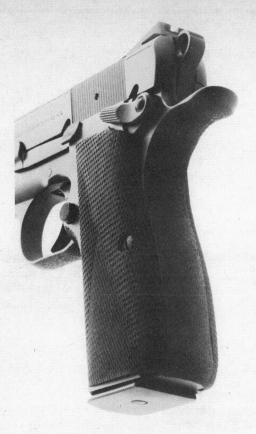

adjacent to the magazine catch. Note how it is altered to allow the middle finger to ride a little higher when the pistol is held for shooting purposes. The difference is subtle and is best appreciated by grasping the pistol with a firing grasp. A small amount of metal, carefully removed, pays big dividends.

Novak's personal Hi-Power has a soft gray-blue finish over all surfaces. In my view, the pistol's most attractive bit of functional cosmetics is the finish applied to the front and back of the grip. It is a crackle-type matte finish. The steel surface is stippled or dimpled evenly with some special tool in order to leave a slightly rough surface. The effect is to make an easy-to-handle, but non-slip surface. It is beautifully done and even has straight-cut borders.

The pistol carries the excellent Novak sight system and this time Wayne indulged a preference of his own. The front sight, neatly dovetailed into the slide, carries a gold bead for easy sight acquisition in dim light shooting circumstances. The entire top of the slide is finished in the same matted finish as the front and rear of the grip. Another touch is a soft blue finish which has a dull functional look to it. Craig Spegal's meticulously checkered black Delrin grips finish off a pistol that is about as fine a businessgun as you're likely to find.

That's Novak's trade: producing pistols for the people who need them the most. Federal, state and local police officers often order from him, as do lots of military personnel. Novak still finds time to shoot a great deal. His current passion is the legally registered submachine gun, which he shoots with consumate skill, good enough to be the current national champion.

But that doesn't detract from the business that earned him a reputation for quality work and technical innovation in sights and combat pistols. He's only half kidding when he says: "My business is just basic badass businessguns."

Above: Note the surface finish on the butt of the pistol. The previous page has a photo showing the same finish on the front of the frame. It's an even matting. The surface is both non-reflective as well as non-skid.

Overall view of Novak's personal Hi-Power, shows extended tang, combat sights, Spegal Delrin grips and flat blue finish.

CHAPTER 20

CRAIG SPEGAL

Handsome Grips For Better Shooting

This little Chiefs Special is a lot easier to shoot after the Boot Grips were installed. It's a subtle design, making a small revolver controllable. Best of all, the beautifully-crafted grips are easy to conceal. The design is Spegal's own inspiration.

"I JUST LIKE the wood," Craig Spegal remarked quietly, "and I like to give shooters a better grip to shoot with." The craftsman was looking out over the green Oregon meadows that surround his rural home. As a visitor from the crowded cities of Southern California, I was impressed with the quiet beauty of the place where Spegal lives and works. His wife sees to expanses of flowers all around the house and the tiny, cluttered shop where the craftsman turns out flawless grips for handguns. It's an easy place for a guy to like.

In the world of custom gunsmiths, we pay great and deserved deference to the stockmakers. Spegal doesn't make rifle stocks, but probably could. He makes handgun grips, one pair at a time, and sells them through the mail and at local matches. A rifle stock is a vastly more complicated operation that usually has an effect on the accuracy of the weapon. Handgun grips may be less critical and certainly are less appreciated.

But a properly fitting pair of handgun grips contributes markedly to the shooter's ability to hit his mark. This is true to a greater degree with revolvers than with autos. In the case of either handgun type, nicely fitted and finished grips add to the aesthetics.

Spegal is rapidly becoming a leader in the field of custom grips. His work has been featured on the cover of national magazines and in DBI books. Custom pistolsmith Wayne Novak uses lots of Spegal grips on the fancy pistols that leave his shop. There aren't many people doing this kind of work and I contend it is a somewhat overlooked skill in the gunsmithing trade.

I watched as Spegal produced a pair of grips for a favorite handgun, the Smith & Wesson Model 645. At the beginning of the cycle, the Oregonian laid out a selection of pre-cut grip blanks and let me choose my own.

There were lots to choose from: bocote, cocobolo, rosewood, myrtle and a number of others. Spegal explained that he spends a fair amount of time choosing the material in hardwood specialty yards, then matching it up in pairs at home. His shop invariably houses a wide selection of different woods, most of it in first-rate exhibition grade. After due consideration, I picked out the flashy piece of bocote shown here. It has a pair of natural diamonds peering through the mottled yellow-brown-black grain of the wood.

Spegal went through a series of steps to shape the grips, most of which involved the use of power tools. With the grips mounted on an aluminum holding plate, he did the majority of the shaping. Even when it came time to make the rounded final contour of the grips, he took off a lot of stock by careful manipulation of the grips on the bandsaw. He brought out the router to cut the involved contour in the top inside edge of the grips. This is where the gun's involved drawbar lockwork is housed. To speed up the process, he used a template which was pre-cut for that purpose.

Naturally, the final shaping was done by hand as was the final sanding. Since the grips would be fully checkered, Spegal didn't have to get the finish down to the 0000 stage. The checkering operation itself was a delight to watch.

Although Spegal uses the MMC power checkering tool, he handles it as deftly as an artist does a brush. The initial lines are cut by hand, but after that, it's full power. At one point, Spegal offered me the tool and I did a line or two, but quickly surrendered it lest the grips be ruined with my ham-handed efforts.

The finish is sprayed on after the grips are checkered. Two to three coats of a special catalyzed varnish are applied with drying time between coats. The end result is a beautifully made set of grips for my pistol; nice and thin, as I prefer. The checkering does not hide the exotic grain of the wood. The pistol is rendered more handsome.

As I got ready to put the gun away, Spegal noticed the original nylon grips that came on the S&W. He dryly commented on what he was able to do with them, so I handed them over. Several weeks later, the mail brought me a package with my original grips. Craig had sanded them smooth and checkered them completely from top to bottom. They are vastly better than in the original configuration, considerably thinner and easier to grip.

So far, we have dealt only with Spegal's auto grips. Automatics don't leave a lot of room for exotic contours, except for some of the bullseye target guns. Revolvers are a

Below: Spegal is downright handy with that band saw. In the lower of the two photos he's cutting the shape of the 645 grips. The blanks are mounted back to back on a special plate. Upper photo: Radiusing with the saw.

Wearing a dust mask, Spegal sands the contour down to the gentle curve they'll wear in their final form. A lot of experience goes into the careful shaping of each pair of grips. The result is well worth the time and effort.

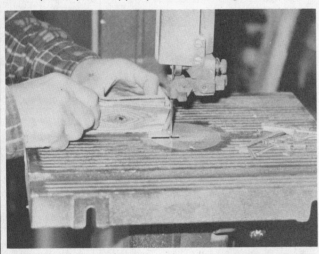

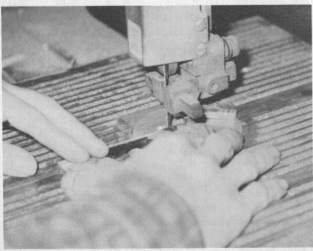

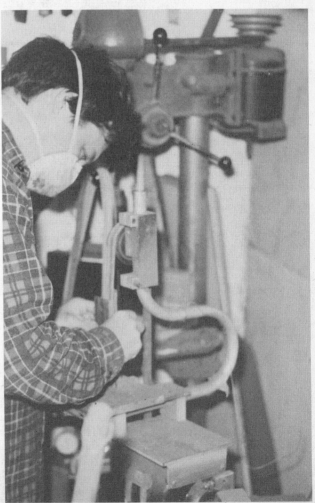

The left grip of the Smith & Wesson 645 covers some essential parts of the gun's mechanism. In order to make the grips fit, Spegal uses this...

...special template to hold the grip while he runs it against the cutter in his router. The relieved contour which results is a perfect fit on the gun.

The sanded, contoured grip needs to be checkered before it is finished. Spegal begins by placing a strip of masking tape across the grip at the...

...correct angle. Then he cuts the first, master line by hand with the tool shown. A second line is cut in the same way at an intersecting angle.

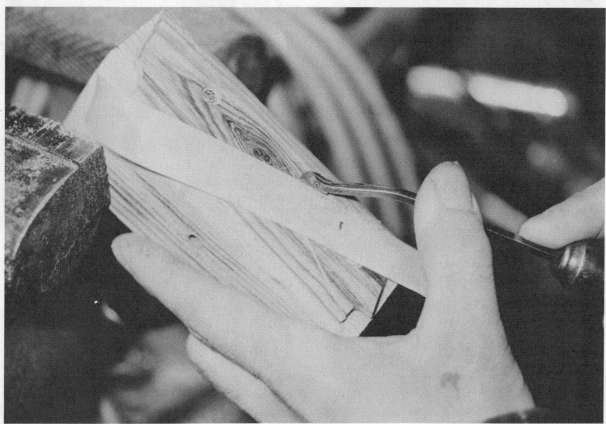

different story and Spegal makes a single, distinctive style.

He is particularly pleased with a model he calls the Boot Grip. When he showed me a pair on a favorite personal gun, I was turned off immediately. The Boot Grip style has a couple of things I do not like in a revolver grip. For one thing, it is too short, with no wood extending below the butt of the Chiefs Special. Second, and worse, it had a finger groove. Finger grooves on revolvers tend to confuse the hand in an emergency draw-and-shoot situation. I picked up the offered revolver with concealed reluctance.

Boy, was I ever wrong! In the hand, the grip feels right. It is obvious that Spegal understands the human hand as well as handgun shooting. The Boot Grip fills the hand well by virtue of a hefty amount of wood on either side of the frame. But the key to the effective shape is the finger grip I didn't care for.

Spegal's design is intended to be used on a concealment gun and that means that the grip must be held to minimum proportions. Rather than attempt to fill the hand with wood below the butt, Spegal makes the grip even with the bottom of the frame. That's a relatively short butt, but it's controllable because of the finger groove. The groove — in fact, the entire grip — is shaped to route the middle finger into a position of control on the gun. It's damned near impossible to pick up this little revolver and not have the longest and strongest finger slide right into position. The second finger drops into place on the bottom front of the grip and the pinkie flaps in space.

Actually, it doesn't. The little finger folds away where Colt Single Action shooters have been sticking it for years — under the butt. In this location on Spegal's Boot Grip, the little finger completes a tight, controllable grasp of the revolver. It is a delightfully effective addition to a hard-to-shoot handgun.

Spegal told me his grips have been selling so well lately that he is focusing on the Colt Government Model and Smith & Wesson autos, plus Boot Grips for J frames. On the big Colt, Spegal puts grips of various woods and even Delrin. The latter material, a synthetic, makes effective grips for autos. It is almost indestructible and checkers well. Spegal checkers them with meticulous care, using the current pattern or the original diamond type.

If Craig Spegal has any problem with his business, it's the lack of another pair of hands. It's a one-man shop and there's no plan to take on more help. For that reason, you might have to wait a bit for your order. He has a brochure that describes the product line. Write Spegal Grips, P.O. Box 1334, Hillsboro, OR 97123.

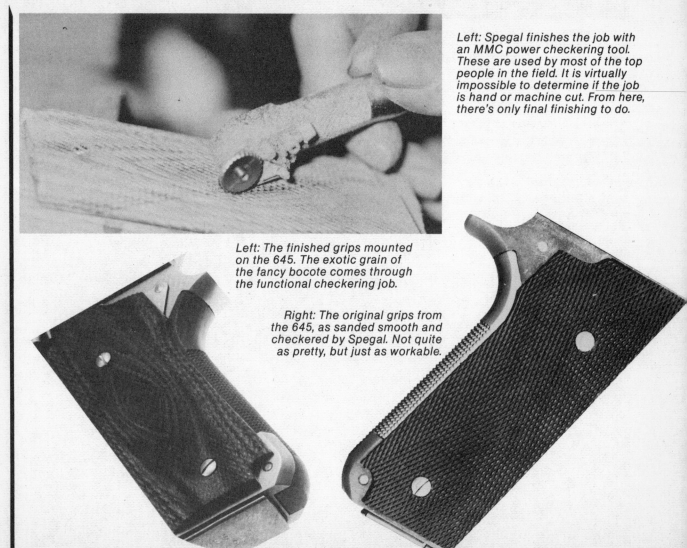

Left: Spegal finishes the job with an MMC power checkering tool. These are used by most of the top people in the field. It is virtually impossible to determine if the job is hand or machine cut. From here, there's only final finishing to do.

Left: The finished grips mounted on the 645. The exotic grain of the fancy bocote comes through the functional checkering job.

Right: The original grips from the 645, as sanded smooth and checkered by Spegal. Not quite as pretty, but just as workable.

CHAPTER 21

GRIPS FOR THE .45

An Incredible Variety From Which To Choose

At the top of the page, we have the pistol and grips in the original form. Then there are the adjustable stocks called Nationals by Herrett's. The ivory grips, below...

...were carved by some unknown Asian artisan. Sid Bell did the pewter grips with Marine emblems — still does. Others are contoured, high-polished bocote, by Ruswood

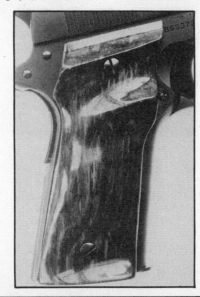

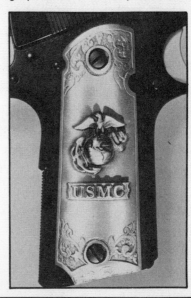

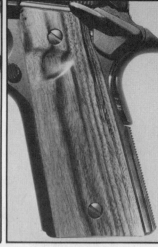

THE LEGENDARY John Browning submitted a new automatic pistol and the U.S. Government adopted it. It was 1911 and the pistol was the famous .45 auto, whose story is well known to American pistol shooters. Doubtless, some thought was given to the grips on the gun, but it probably was not a major consideration. Colt offered several other Browning-designed autos in those days and they sported grip plates of checkered walnut. Not surprisingly, the new .45 left the plant with what we regard today as a classic design.

They were plain plates of varnished walnut, slightly domed in cross-section and checkered with a distinctive pattern using a truncated diamond contour around the holes for the grip screws. The inside or back edge of the grips was dead flat, relieved by a pair of counterbored holes that fit over the grip screw bushings. It is a simple and functional design, one that's fairly easy to replicate. Over the years, the material and checkering pattern of the grips changed a bit on production versions of the pistol, but the basic shape remained the same. The expanse of flat surface of the pistol's grips leaves room for ornamentation.

In the late Sixties, I paid less than a hundred bucks for a battered GI .45 to re-build into a hardball match gun. It was ugly as hell and the ugliest thing about it was the so-called custom grips. Some nameless serviceman had made a pair of grips out of extra-thick slabs of clear plastic. On the inside of one piece of the clear material, he had glued a pin-up picture of a leggy blonde, while the other side sported an ace of spades. The custom grips went into the trash and the gun went on to other work.

Over the many years of the existence of the grand old gun and continuing to the prsent, lots of shooters have

Pachmayr sells thousands of pairs of their wraparound rubber models. Wallinsky makes these with thumb relief.

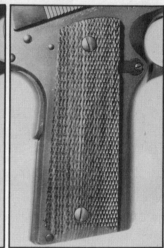

Herrett's stock — left: Fancy walnut finished up plain and pretty. Right: Plain walnut, with plain checkering.

More Herrett's — left: The Shooting Star model has a memory ledge for the thumb. This pair is fancy walnut.

The center pair of Herrett's stocks are walnut, done up in the skipline pattern. Right: Checkered Shooting Stars

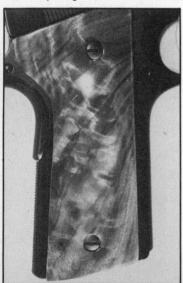

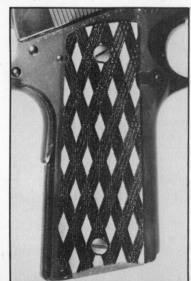

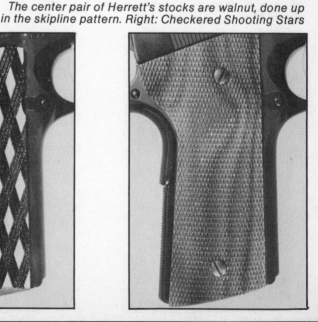

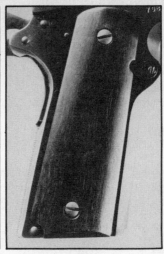
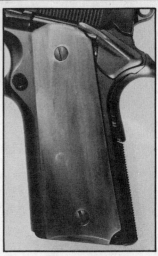

All of the grips on this page are from India, by way of Art Jewel Grips. Above, left to right: Sambar Stag...

...Black buffalo horn, plain East Indian Ebony and light grey colored buffalo horn. Natural materials are lovely.

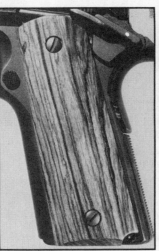
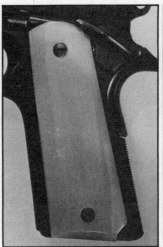
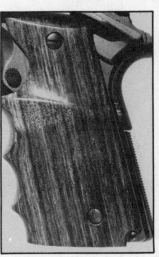

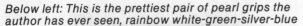

The white grips are milky ivory, hard to photograph. A panel of dark Zebrawood is next, then white-green...

Below left: This is the prettiest pair of pearl grips the author has ever seen, rainbow white-green-silver-blue

...buffalo horn. The last pair is Indian Rosewood. They are made in a way that shoots much better than it looks.

Below right. When you get a thick piece of stag, it is possible to polish off the grain, leaving this effect.

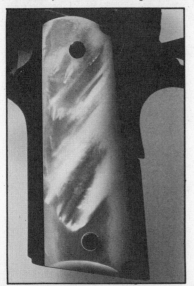

indulged their individual preferences for an ornamented sidearm by putting new grips on their .45s. Since America's favorite pistol is currently as popular as ever and an unprecedented number of makers are offering grips made from a host of materials, it's appropriate to review what's available. The *Hanguns '89* reader can make his own judgment as to what is stylish and what isn't.

I visualized such a review as an interesting commentary on the custom handgun scene at the basic level of customizing. I was unprepared for the size of the field. Once I got into the variety of .45 grips on the market, I was astonished by the incredible number of people who are offering better and prettier handles for old Slabsides.

This too-brief chapter is, therefore, a quick look at what a consumer can get to dress up or improve the handling (or both) of his Colt .45 auto. At the outset, you have to understand I've just scratched the surface. Lots of makers not mentioned here are doing similar things. There's a bewildering array of grips out there — most of them are worthy of your attention.

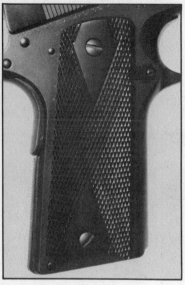 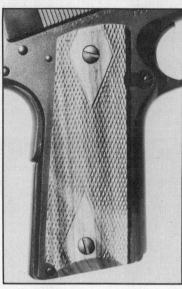 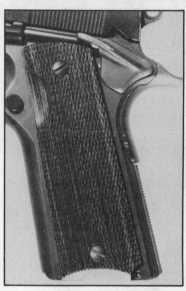

Brownell's sells these grips from Ahrend. The left two both have traditional checkering, ebony and morodillo.

Another Ahrend style is called the Combat and features a relief cut for the thumb, working the magazine catch.

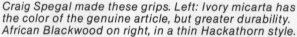

Craig Spegal made these grips. Left: Ivory micarta has the color of the genuine article, but greater durability. African Blackwood on right, in a thin Hackathorn style.

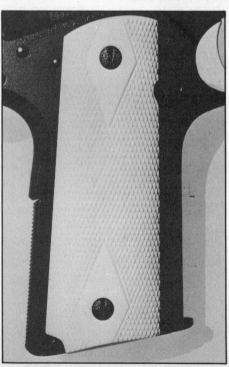 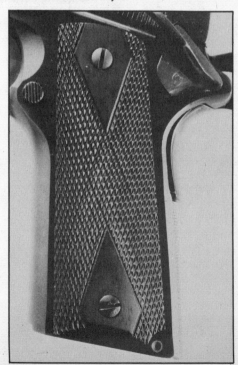

Section Five

YESTERDAY'S HANDGUNS

THERE ARE ADVANTAGES TO LOOKING BACK, EVEN IN AN ANNUAL ON THE YEAR'S HANDGUNS AND THEIR USE. TIME SPENT IN RETROSPECTION TENDS TO PLACE THINGS IN PERSPECTIVE. SHOOTERS COME TO UNDERSTAND THAT WHAT'S TOUTED AS NEW MAY BE OLD HAT. BY EXAMINING WHAT HAS GONE BEFORE, WE GAIN A BETTER APPRECIATION OF WHAT WE NOW ENJOY AND WHAT WE CAN EXPECT IN THE FUTURE.

ONE OF THE BETTER REVOLVERS TO LEAVE THE COLT FACTORY WAS THE NEW SERVICE, A HANDGUN THAT SELDOM DRAWS COMMENTARY IN THE FIREARMS PRESS. THIS IS IN SPITE OF THE FACT THAT OVER A THIRD OF A MILLION OF THE GUNS CAME OUT OF THE HARTFORD PLANT AND WENT TO PEOPLE ALL OVER THE WORLD WHO PUT THEM TO HARD USE.

GUN COLLECTING AUTHORITY CHUCK KARWAN GIVES THE OLD GUN ITS DUE IN A LENGTHY TREATMENT OF THE HISTORY OF THE COLT NEW SERVICE. YOU'LL FIND HIS COVERAGE DETAILED AND THOROUGH, WITH INSIGHT INTO THE ACTUAL USE OF THE BIG REVOLVER. A MODERNIZED NEW SERVICE MIGHT FIND A MARKET TODAY.

WE ARE WELL INTO THE MAGNUM ERA, WITH A NEW MAGNUM HANDGUN AND CARTRIDGE POPPING UP EVERY MONTH OR SO. OUR FINAL CHAPTER COMMENTS ON THE DAYS OF YORE, WHEN THE MAGNUM ERA BEGAN.

HANDGUNS 89

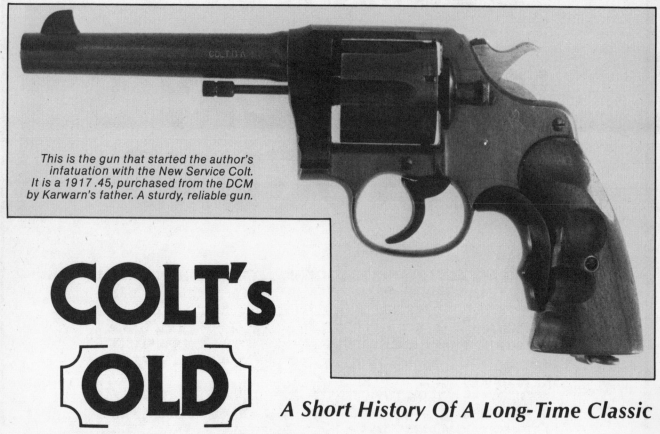
This is the gun that started the author's infatuation with the New Service Colt. It is a 1917 .45, purchased from the DCM by Karwarn's father. A sturdy, reliable gun.

COLT's ⟨OLD⟩ NEW SERVICE

A Short History Of A Long-Time Classic

I guess it was inevitable that I grow up interested in Colt New Service revolvers. My late father claimed that when I was a baby, I once cried terribly because I was cutting teeth. He tried everything to get me to shut up, all to no avail. Out of desperation, he unloaded the old M1917 New Service .45 that he kept as a house gun and tossed it in the crib with me. He may have done it because he didn't want to be tempted to shoot me to get me to stop wailing. He said that I shut right up and immediately started gnawing on the old Colt's barrel. Now, I can't say for sure that I cut my teeth on a Colt New Service, but one of my earliest memories is my dad giving me the same old M1917 as a mere toddler. It was unloaded, of course, and he challenged me to pull the trigger. I now realize he was testing to find out if he needed to lock it up or hide it from me. Today, that old Colt is one of my most prized possessions and it still is on duty, loaded as a house gun.

The Colt New Service revolver series holds a number of distinctions. These include the fact that it is the largest Colt cartridge revolver ever produced. Furthermore, it was the last large framed double-action Colt produced and it has a very interesting and colorful history of use by some of the world's foremost police and military services. It is, in my opinion, far more historically significant than the more famous and more sought-after Colt Single Action Army (SAA) revolver. The Colt SAA was made obsolescent by the top-break Webley revolvers within a few years of its introduction, but the Colt New Service is about as good a defensive handgun today ninety years after its introduction, as just about any revolver. When chambered for a major caliber, it is a far better fighting handgun than the ones carried by the vast majority of today's police officers.

The New Service was first cataloged by Colt in 1898. Colt had been tremendously successful with its swingout cylinder .38s introduced in 1889. It was only natural to come up with a swingout cylinder revolver capable of handling the larger .44 and .45 caliber cartridges. Throughout its production life, from 1898 to the early years of World War II, it was made in two basic configurations, a service model with fixed sights and a target model with a flat-topped frame and adjustable sights. However, there have been many subvariations in these two broad categories, not to mention a constant evolution of improvements to the basic design. Before I get into the various subvariations, let me walk you through the evolution of the New Service to put things into perspective.

THE OLD MODEL

The term Old Model New Service is collector's terminology for the early production New Services from serial number 1 to about 21,000. These early guns have substantial differences from all the New Services that would come later. The most obvious difference is the narrow trigger guard and the different frame contour on the rounded topstrap. The first 10,000 or so had a firing pin that was machined integrally with the hammer instead of

Right: A New Service is right at home in the GI flapped holster of the World War I era. Plain walnut grips were used on the 1917 .45 version.

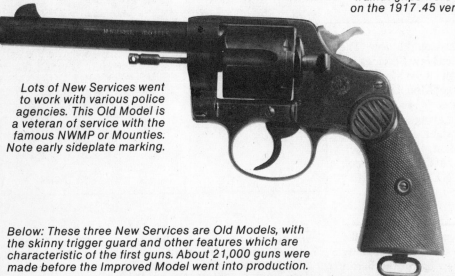

Lots of New Services went to work with various police agencies. This Old Model is a veteran of service with the famous NWMP or Mounties. Note early sideplate marking.

Below: These three New Services are Old Models, with the skinny trigger guard and other features which are characteristic of the first guns. About 21,000 guns were made before the Improved Model went into production.

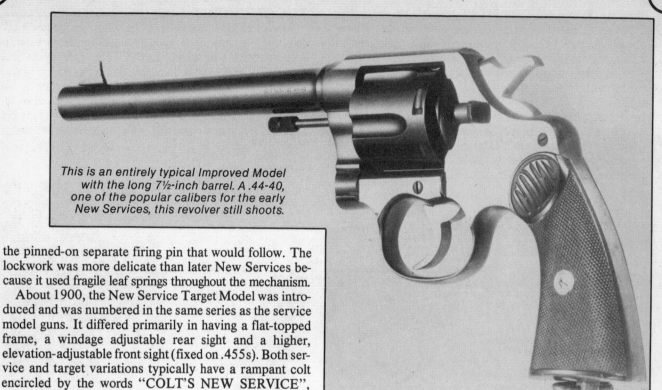

This is an entirely typical Improved Model with the long 7½-inch barrel. A .44-40, one of the popular calibers for the early New Services, this revolver still shoots.

the pinned-on separate firing pin that would follow. The lockwork was more delicate than later New Services because it used fragile leaf springs throughout the mechanism.

About 1900, the New Service Target Model was introduced and was numbered in the same series as the service model guns. It differed primarily in having a flat-topped frame, a windage adjustable rear sight and a higher, elevation-adjustable front sight (fixed on .455s). Both service and target variations typically have a rampant colt encircled by the words "COLT'S NEW SERVICE", stamped onto their sideplates.

IMPROVED MODEL OF 1909

This, too, is a term developed by collectors. Some use the date 1905 instead, because that is the patent date of many of the improvements and 1905 shows up on the barrel

Below: These three guns are all Improved Models, with the modified lockwork and positive safety lock. These show variations in barrel length and grips. The shape of the trigger guard is different from the Old Models. Also, note the different barrel contour on bottom gun.

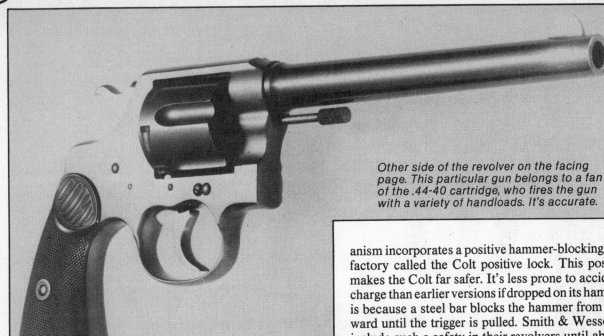

Other side of the revolver on the facing page. This particular gun belongs to a fan of the .44-40 cartridge, who fires the gun with a variety of handloads. It's accurate.

markings of the improved model group. This group begins with about serial number 23,000 and goes up to about serial number 328,000. The vast majority of New Services fit into this category, if you count the large number of military contract models.

Externally, the obvious difference is that the trigger guard is the same width as the frame and the front and rear of the rounded topstrap have a changed contour. Also, the rampant colt on the sideplate appears without the legend "COLT'S NEW SERVICE." On some, a stylized C surrounds the rampant colt. Internally, the Improved Model has even more changes. The bolt spring and hammer strut springs are the coil variety, instead of flat springs as found on the "Old Model." The rebound lever is made in one piece eliminating the separate fly. Most importantly, the mech-

Here are a pair of New Service barrels posed to show the change in barrel contour. The top gun has a shape first seen on military guns, but eventually used for all.

anism incorporates a positive hammer-blocking safety the factory called the Colt positive lock. This positive lock makes the Colt far safer. It's less prone to accidental discharge than earlier versions if dropped on its hammer. This is because a steel bar blocks the hammer from going forward until the trigger is pulled. Smith & Wesson did not include such a safety in their revolvers until about 1926, giving Colt a considerable safety advantage until that time.

Target Models made in the improved series have all the same cosmetic and mechanism changes as the service guns, keeping the flat-topped frame.

When the Army ordered the M1917 version of the improved service model during World War II, they specifically requested that the revolver barrel have a shoulder on it where it meets the frame. Prior to this, all New Service barrels had a straight-tapered outside contour. In fact, they were virtually identical to the SAA barrel, right down to the threads, except for the markings and the lack of an ejector rod housing stud. The addition of this shoulder on the barrel not only makes for a much more secure barrel fit, but it also improves the looks of the New Service. As a result, Colt decided to keep this barrel shoulder on future New Service production after the M1917 production ended in 1919.

Some collectors make up a sub-category for the post-1919 improved series, referring to it as the "Improved Model, 1919-1928." Logically, that would make the earlier Improved Models the "Improved Model, 1909-1917." Personally, I prefer to think of all the 1909 to 1928 New Services as "Improved Models" with the M1909 military, M1917 military, and post-1919 types as sub-variations. I do this because this group all share the same frame shape and internal mechanism. However, the other approach is good and possibly more explicit and concise.

The post-1919 Improved Models with the barrel shoulder and tapered barrels were produced in both service and target varieties and, other than the barrel shoulder, are largely identical to the Pre-World War I Improved Models. However, as a group, they are particularly desirable because production was quite limited. Typical yearly production of New Services in the Post-World War I period until the frame was changed in 1928 averaged only about 2000 pieces per year. Consequently, I estimate that the post-1919 Improved Models only make up some 14,000 pieces total.

A pair of Improved Models in two barrel lengths. The top gun is a 5½-inch .45 Colt, which may be the most common New Service. The lower revolver is a 4½-inch .44-40. That chambering was more popular in the early years of New Service production than in later times.

TRANSITION MODEL

If you have been following closely so far, you may have noticed that there is about a 2000-gun gap between the Old Model New Service (serial numbers 1 to 21,000) and the Improved Model New Services (serial numbers 23,000 to 328,000). This group constitutes what collectors call the "Transition Model."

Colt was never a company to scrap parts for obsolete models. Witness their use of percussion revolver parts in their early cartridge revolver production and their conversion of obsolete M1878 double-action cylinders for use on Colt SAAs, creating the "long flute" variation. So rather than waste the 2000 or so obsolete frames on hand, Colt remachined them to take the improved model lock work with its positive hammer blocking safety. The result was a New Service that is externally an Old Model and internally an Improved Model. Called the Transition Model, this variation, with serial numbers from about 21,000 to 23,000, is quite desirable because of its low production. There were only a handful of Target Models included in this group and they constitute one of the rarest of the New Service variations.

Externally, the Transition Models appear to be identical to the Old Models. However, one only needs to cock the hammer and peer inside to see the hammer block to identify this variation. Though rarely encountered, a few Old Models were returned to Colt for work and at that time were upgraded by the factory to take the Improved Model parts with the positive safety. I suspect this was done not from any liability or safety concerns, but simply because no more Old Model parts were available to make the repair.

THE LATE MODEL NEW SERVICE

Around 1928 and at about serial number 328,000, Colt made a significant change in the shape of the New Service revolver frame. This was part of a program to modernize the entire Colt line. Similar changes were also made to the Official Police and Police Positive revolvers. These changes were made over a period of time as the older frames and barrels were used up.

The features of the Late Model New Service that distinguish it from earlier New Services are largely cosmetic, though the improved sights are certainly functional. On the service guns, the topstrap was changed from the rounded, almost single-action shape with its "U" notch rear sight to a flattened shape with beveled corners. The rear sight notch was milled to a more prominent square notch that's

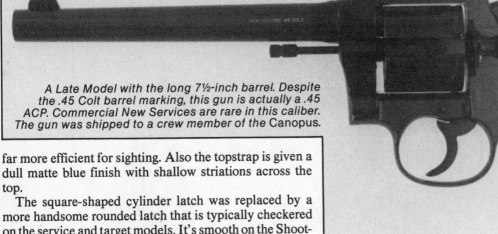

A Late Model with the long 7½-inch barrel. Despite the .45 Colt barrel marking, this gun is actually a .45 ACP. Commercial New Services are rare in this caliber. The gun was shipped to a crew member of the Canopus.

far more efficient for sighting. Also the topstrap is given a dull matte blue finish with shallow striations across the top.

The square-shaped cylinder latch was replaced by a more handsome rounded latch that is typically checkered on the service and target models. It's smooth on the Shooting Master variation. A 1926 patent date was added to the barrel markings.

Typically, the service front sights are thicker and without the prominent taper of the earlier service front sights. On the Late Model Target New Services, changes came slower because of the limited production. But as a group, they exhibit the same external changes as the service guns, while retaining the flat-topped frame. The frame's top was given a matte blue finish. The sights were most often the square post front with a square notch rear Patridge pattern, but many combinations of beads and other sight options were available. Throughout this period, the New Service Target Model was almost completely a special order gun and each was built to the customer's specifications. It was also during this period that the round butt became standard on certain subvariations and an option on others.

One group of guns produced during the Late Model period and serial range constitutes an aberration. In the early 1920s, with the Depression in full swing, Colt decided to use up a significant quantity of surplus M1917 parts left over from its large military contracts of World War I. These were assembled and sold as new commercial guns. Called the Civilian M1917 by collectors, this model has the rounded top frame and square cylinder latch of the Improved Model, in spite of being produced in the serial range of the Late Model.

The vast majority of these guns are .45 ACPs and have the barrel marking "COLT MODEL 1917 .45 AUTO CTGE." Interestingly, they do not have the lanyard swivel common to both the M1917 and most civilian service model New Services. A few in this group have been observed with barrels and cylinders in other calibers including .44-40 for sure and possibly .38-40. Since the Director of Civilian Marksmanship was selling surplus M1917s for $15.00, it is not surprising that these commercial M1917s were slow sellers at a half-again higher price. Regardless, this New Service variation, previously largely ignored, is now recognized as a desirable variation. Total production is believed to be about 1000.

During the Late Model production period, Colt introduced a variation of the service version that collectors call the .38/.357 Model. It differs from the other Late Model service guns in a couple of significant ways. First, the

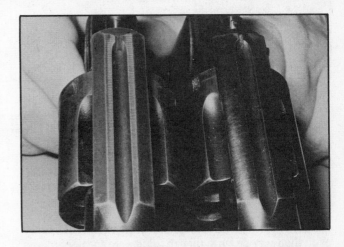

These photos show differences in Late Model topstrap contour and all earlier guns. Above: The flat, serrated Late Model on the left, Improved Model on the right. Below: Rear sight differences, with the square notch of the Late Model on right, round Old Model on left.

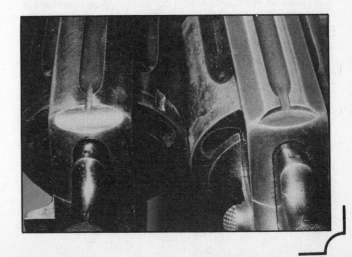

These are unusual guns from the Depression years. Both are what collectors call 1917 Civilian. Made from left-over parts, the guns were sold in the 1930s. Most were in .45 ACP, but some were .44-40s. They're in the Late Model period, but have earlier features. Colt did not want to waste parts.

While the overwhelming majority of New Service Colts were blue, there are some nickel-plated. This .45 Colt sports a pair of exotic fossilized mastodon ivory grips.

chamberings were limited to .38 Special and, a bit later, .357 magnum. Instead of the normal standard barrel lengths of 4½, 5½, and 7½ inches of the other service guns, this group had barrels of 4, 5, and 6 inches. Typically, they do not have the lanyard swivel found on the standard military or civilian service guns, though some were special ordered with this feature. The round butt configuration was standard on the .38/.357 Model.

This model put the New Service into the magnum era, but it was never very popular. Such a large-framed gun in the little .38 Special cartridge does not make a whole lot of sense. While a New Service .357 does have a lot of merit, most .357 users of the period went for Smith & Wesson revolvers because they had introduced and promoted the cartridge. Also, the Smith & Wesson .357 was a deluxe gun with adjustable sights that could be used in a holster. The service variety of New Service .357s lacked the fine finish and adjustable sights, while the target grade Shooting Master .357 had sights that were not readily adaptable to holster use.

A significant number of .38/.357 Models were on hand when the British Purchasing Commission was looking for guns in 1940 and consequently they will often turn up with British proof marks, a Parkerized finish, and sometimes even rechambered to take the British .380 (.38 S&W) cartridge. Collectors call these "Battle of Britain Colts."

The Shooting Master was a variation of the New Service Target that was introduced in the Late Model period. It will be covered in more detail in the section on target models.

It would appear from looking at the Colt factory assembly and shipping records that, for all intents and purposes, production of New Service frames and parts ended in 1941 or early 1942. The exact highest serial number is not known but it is believed to be under 357,000. Many of these parts and frames were assembled and shipped later, even into the post-WWII period. The last shipments seem to be

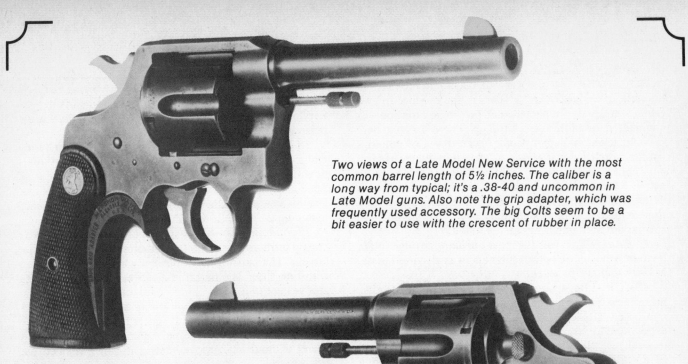

Two views of a Late Model New Service with the most common barrel length of 5½ inches. The caliber is a long way from typical; it's a .38-40 and uncommon in Late Model guns. Also note the grip adapter, which was frequently used accessory. The big Colts seem to be a bit easier to use with the crescent of rubber in place.

a few guns sent in 1954 to Winchester and Remington, ostensibly for ammunition testing.

A significant number of the highest serial number guns constitute one of the mysteries surrounding the New Service. In 1941, there was a series of shipments of New Service frames to Springfield Armory. Shipment size varies, but was usually 200 with at least one on November 3 being 400 and another in March of 731. The total number of frames shipped to Springfield Armory amounts to nearly 2000. Why was the U.S. government buying New Service frames at that late date? No one seems to know, nor does anyone know what happened to them.

A few individual frames have shown up assembled with commercial parts, but these could be lunch-box guns. The simple fact is that almost all of these frames and serial numbers are currently unaccounted for. Springfield Armory did make M1917 .45 barrels. For example, in 1931 they report: "5,099 Barrels for Colt Revolver, cal. .45, M1917" produced.

Possibly they intended to use barrels and spare M1917 parts on hand to assemble revolvers. Such an assembly program was carried out at Springfield for the M1903 rifle using spare replacement receivers and parts built at Rock Island Arsenal and Springfield Armory. If such an assembly program was intended for M1917 revolvers, it evidently never came about. Certainly it would have made a hybrid M1917 with a Late Model frame. There is even a chance that those frames are still languishing in our massive government spare parts inventory waiting for someone to call up the right Federal Stock Number. Who knows?

There you have it; the evolution of the Colt New Service revolver, starting with the Old Model going to the Transition Model, then the Improved Model, and finally to the Late Model, all made in both service and target varieties. There are many sub-variations such as the various military contracts, the Shooting Masters, the Fitz Specials, etc., but these will be covered in more detail under separate headings.

Below: This shot shows the variation in butt contour. The left-hand gun, a Marine Corps Model, has the butt which is shorter from front to back. The other revolver has a deeper butt. Most shooters find the round butt version a good bit easier to shoot. Walnut grips on both.

The New Service revolver was chambered for eleven different cartridges over the years it was produced. Two others were made on special order. No single variation was chambered for all thirteen cartridges. There is a great deal of confusion among some people because the Colt catalogs list far more than just eleven or even thirteen cartridges. This confusion is brought about by listing cartridges such as .38 Short Colt, .38 Long Colt, .38-44 (a special high pressure .38 Special loading), and others that can safely be fired in a .38 Special. The actual eleven standard and two special order chamberings are as follows:

.45 Colt — This was the most popular cartridge in the civilian New Service production and was also used in the M1909 military production.

.45 ACP — Because of the large M1917 military order, more New Services were made in this chambering than any other. However, in civilian production it is rarely encountered. Civilian New Services, special ordered in this caliber, will often have the barrel marking of "NEW SERVICE .45 COLT" rather than a special marking denoting .45 ACP.

.455 Eley — In the WWI period, England, Canada, and possibly other British Commonwealth countries, bought large quantities of New Services in this chambering. This one is therefore one of the most common chamberings encountered. There were also many commercial sales, including Target Models for Commonwealth Shooters, personal service guns for officers, and many to the Canadian Mounties. They're rarely encountered in any post-WWI production.

.450 Eley — A very few of the Old Models were made for sale in England in this chambering. Since this caliber was already obsolete in England, further orders were few to non-existent.

.476 Eley — Much the same as was said for the .450 holds also for the .476. Interestingly, in spite of its name, the chambers of the .476 are identical to the .455, except being bored through with no shoulder and it is believed that the barrels were also .455.

.44-40 — This cartridge was a natural for the New Service, since it was still popular for use in Winchester carbines, too. Later in the life of the New Service, interest in this chambering dropped off.

.44 S&W Russian — Often considered the most accurate of the 19th Century revolver cartridges, this was the original chambering for the Target Model intended for the U.S. market. Few service models were so chambered, since most shooters preferred the more powerful .45 Colt or .44-40. Depending on vintage, barrel markings may read ".44 S&W CTG." or ".44 RUSSIAN CTG."

.44 S&W Special — Officially adopted by Colt in 1913, this cartridge replaced the .44 Russian chambering, as that round could also be fired in the .44 Special chamber.

.38-40 — This chambering was popular in the early days of the New Service because of the same reason as the .44-40; it was in wide use in Winchester carbines. It is rarely encountered in the Late Model series.

.357 Magnum — Colt called this chambering just .357. Introduced about 1936, it found a good home in the New Service, but never reached significant popularity for the reasons outlined earlier.

.38 Special — Except in a target gun, this chambering makes no sense in a brute like the New Service. That's particularly true once the .357 became available, since .38 Special could be fired in the same revolver. In spite of that fact, many were bought by various agencies and individuals, including the U.S. Border Patrol.

.45 Smoothbore — This special order chambering was bought primarily by exhibition shooters for shooting aerial targets. The cartridge was basically the .45 Colt loaded with fine shot. The barrel is a .45 barrel without rifling grooves cut in it.

.44 Smoothbore — Everything said about the .45 Smoothbore holds for the .44, except that the cartridge is a .44-40 loaded with fine shot. Again the barrel is a .44 barrel without any grooves cut in it, not a reamed out rifled barrel.

Special Note on New Services with factory original smoothbore barrels: Normally handguns with smoothbore barrels would legally be classified as sawed-off shotguns under the National Firearms Act (NFA) and require registration and the payment of a $200 transfer tax on acquisition. However, the BATF will designate such guns as "Curios & Relics relieved of NFA status" on petition, if you include proof that the New Service was originally made with a smoothbore barrel. Normally, this is done with a factory letter. Once the specific gun is taken off NFA status, it can be bought and sold just like any other New Service. Original New Service smoothbore revolvers are extremely rare and valuable. I strongly suggest that this action be taken for all such guns.

See the nearby table for a breakdown on what chamberings were made in the various New Service variations. Realize that because of Colt's willingness to fulfill special orders other possibilities exist. Until a Shooting Master surfaced in .455, nobody had any suspicion that such a gun existed.

Besides the thirteen chamberings listed, a number of prototypes exist. At least one New Service was made experimentally at the factory in .22 Hornet with an extra-long cylinder. One prototype Shooting Master was made in .22 Long Rifle with an extra-short cylinder.

Probably the most interesting is #340905. Factory records indicate it had a four-inch barrel and was chambered in .41 Colt with the barrel roll-marked "COMMANDER .41 COLT." It was shipped October 8, 1943, to Colt representative Joseph Lorch in Washington, D.C. Undoubtedly this gun was meant to be used to register the name "Commander" as a Colt trademark. It is hard to believe that the very first Colt Commander was really a New Service chambered for .41 Colt! At least one other New Service prototype was chambered for an experimental .41 Special cartridge that is comparable to the present day .41 magnum mid-velocity loading.

COLT NEW SERVICE

Variation Barrel Lengths Inches	Approximate serial range	.45 Colt	.45 ACP	.455 Eley	.450 Eley	.476 Eley	.44-40	.44 S&W Russian	.44 S&W Special	.38-40	.357 Magnum	.38 Special	.45 Smoothbore	.44 Smoothbore
Old Model — Service 4½, 5½, 7½	1 – 21,000			1	1								1	1
Old Model — Target 7½	4,5000 – 21,000			3		3								
Transition Model 4½, 5½, 7½	21,000 – 23,000	3	3			3	3	3						
Improved Model — Service 4½, 5½, 7½	23,000 – 328,000		7			3							1	1
Improved Model — Target 7½	23,000 – 328,000						2	3			4			
M1909 Army 5½	30,000 – 49,500													
M1909 Navy 5½	23,000 – 53,100	3												
M1909 USMC 5½	23,101 – 26,300	3												
M1917 Army 5½	150,000 – 305,000													
M1917 Commercial 5½	335,000 – 340,000		3				1							
Late Model — Service 4½, 5½, 6, 7½	328,000 to end (6)		2	8					3					
Late Model — .38/.357 4, 5, 6	333,000 to end										3			
Late Model — Target 6, 7½	328,000 – 342,000		3				2							
Shooting Master 6	330,000 – 348,000	3	3	4					1			3		
Fitz Special 2	305,000 to end	1												
Prototypes	scattered or special	.22 LR Shooting Master, .22 Hornet, .41 Special Commander .41 Colt												

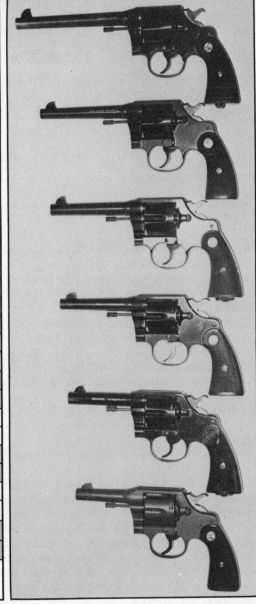

1 **Extremely rare**
2 **Special order, several known**
3 **Uncommon to rare**
4 **Special order, one known**
5 **Factory record just says .38, could be .38 Special instead**
6 **Highest number known to date is 356,914**
7 **Normally only found in M1917 production**
8 **Cataloged but none known**

Karwan's research into the New Service story produced the table above. Footnotes offer insight into the wide diversity of variations. The photo above shows the New Service barrel lengths: From the top; 7½, 6, 5½, 5 4½ and 4, all standard in one or more models.

The first U.S. Military New Service revolvers were the 1909 Military Models. The revolver, as seen to the left, is an Improved Model with a 5½-inch barrel. These guns use a special loading of the .45 Colt round, made with a larger-diameter rim for positive extraction.

MILITARY PRODUCTION

Of all the New Service production, more than half was to fulfill various military orders. The first military production New Services were the U.S. M1909 revolvers. These were a direct result of the failure of the Army's .38 Long Colt revolvers in action in the Philippines. Because of complaints from the troops in the Philippines about the lack of stopping power of the .38 revolvers and the subsequent famous Thompson-LaGarde tests, the Army decided it needed to initiate action to find a new service handgun.

It was specified that it be not less than .45 caliber, firing a bullet of not less than 230 grains at 800 feet per second or more. An ordnance board convened in 1907 to test and evaluate nine different handguns and to make recommendations as to the best course of action. Among the nine handguns tested were an early Colt .45 automatic and a Colt New Service .45 revolver. In their report the board states there was a "well recognized and urgent necessity for a caliber not less than .45 for active service." Service tests of the promising automatic pistols would take considerable time. Since "a satisfactory caliber .45 revolver can be obtained" they made the following recommendation: "That sufficient Colt double-action revolvers, calibers .45, be issued to arm the troops in the Philippines as soon as practicable."

Other recommendations also were made that led to procurement of test lots of .45 automatics. Eventually, this led to the adoption of the venerable M1911. The Chief of Ordnance disapproved the revolver recommendation because of lack of revolvers on hand, lack of funds to procure them, and the opinion that use of revolvers would only be temporary because they would be superseded by automatic pistols. The last statement proved to be quite prophetic. Regardless, sufficient pressure was brought from the field in the Philippines that eventually funds were obtained to purchase the Colt revolvers in 1909 as recommended by the 1907 board. This was the Model 1909 U.S. Army revolver.

The M1909 Army was basically an Improved Model New Service with a 5½-inch barrel. They have a bright blue finish, plain walnut grips, and are chambered for the .45 Colt cartridge. Because the narrow rim of the standard .45 Colt cartridge will sometimes slip under the ejector star on ejection, tying up the revolver, the Army made special .45 ammunition for the M1909 that had larger rims. Interestingly, this same ammunition cannot be used in Colt Single Actions except by loading it into every other chamber, since the rims will overlap in the smaller SAA cylinder.

Lots of 1909 and 1917 Military Models rode the half-flapped holsters of the early 20th century. The lanyard ring in the butt was on the majority of all New Service revolvers. It was a standard feature on Military Models.

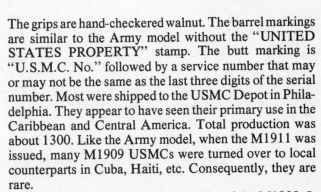

The M1909 Army revolvers are marked "COLT D.A. .45" on the left side of the barrel, "UNITED STATES PROPERTY" on the bottom of the barrel and "U.S. ARMY MODEL 1909 No." with the serial number on the butt. Somewhere between 13,000 and 18,000 were produced, with all but a few hundred sent directly to the Philippines. As a result, it was never general issue anywhere else in the Army. When the M1911 eventually reached the Philippines several years later, most of the M1909s were evidently turned over to the Philippine Constabulary. This accounts for the scarcity of this model.

The Marines desired to procure some of the new Colts for themselves. Naturally, being Marines, their version had to be different. The M1909 USMC has a rounded butt similar to the later Shooting Master and .38/.357 Models.

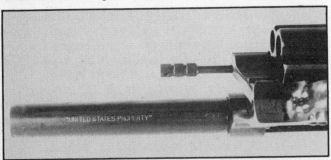

1909 Army Model wore this marking on the bottom of the barrel. There was a similar marking on the 1917s. The Navy and Marine Corps New Services did not sport this roll-marked legend. Some 1917s are WWII veterans.

The grips are hand-checkered walnut. The barrel markings are similar to the Army model without the "UNITED STATES PROPERTY" stamp. The butt marking is "U.S.M.C. No." followed by a service number that may or may not be the same as the last three digits of the serial number. Most were shipped to the USMC Depot in Philadelphia. They appear to have seen their primary use in the Caribbean and Central America. Total production was about 1300. Like the Army model, when the M1911 was issued, many M1909 USMCs were turned over to local counterparts in Cuba, Haiti, etc. Consequently, they are rare.

The Navy ordered their own version of the M1909. It was basically the same as the M1909 Army without the property marking on the barrel. The butts are marked "U.S.N. (anchor) .44 DA No." followed by a Navy service number. The last digits in the serial number correspond to the service number on the butt. Approximately 1100 M1909 USNs were produced and all were reportedly shipped to the Brooklyn Navy Yard. It appears that once these revolvers became part of a ship's weapon stores, they stayed aboard till the ship was decommissioned or overhauled. I know of one case where a ship first commissioned before WWI was still in service in WWII. It still had a few M1909 revolvers in its small arms locker. That shouldn't be too surprising, because it also had some Krag rifles. It would not surprise me to find some M1909 USNs languishing today in some Naval store house.

When WWI broke out in Europe, England and her Commonwealth needed a lot more handguns than could be supplied by the Webley company. Consequently, they placed large orders in the U.S. with Colt and S&W for revolvers chambered for the .455 Eley or Webley car-

Left: Two U.S. Army New Services. The 1917 is on the left and the 1909 is on the right. Most of the 1909 .45s went to the Philippines and never returned; they're not easy for collectors to find. Lanyard ring is standard.

The U.S. Military Model New Service revolvers. The top gun is a 1917, the middle one is the 1909 (either Army or Navy) and the lower revolver is the rare 1909 Marine Corps Model. For various reasons, the lower two guns are quite rare. The 1917 is easily the most common New Service; over 150,000 revolvers produced during WWI.

tridge. The New Service Colts supplied were basic Improved Models with 5½-inch barrels identical to commercial production of the period. Barrels are marked "New Service .455" and the finish is the bright commercial blue. These show up with a wide range of British and Canadian proof marks, broad arrow military stamps and other military markings. Total production of the military .455s is unknown but it is believed to be at least 50,000. There are some indications that it could be significantly higher.

When the .455 Colts were released as surplus and sold on the U.S. market, many were rechambered for the .45 Colt cartridge. Others were converted to take .45 ACP in half-moon clips. If you have a .455, I highly recommend *against* converting it to another caliber. For further details see section on Shooting the New Service.

When the U.S. entered WWI, we were grossly short of small arms to equip our forces. The nature of the trench warfare we became involved in made handguns more necessary than usual. We made efforts to issue every infantryman a handgun, increasing requirements many fold. While we tried to increase M1911 production, the fastest way to get a lot of handguns quickly was to get Colt and Smith & Wesson to convert their revolver lines. They were already going full bore producing .455s for the British. Army ordnance did not want to use a different cartridge than the .45 ACP because it would create supply problems. An engineer at S&W came to the rescue by inventing

the half-moon clip which held three rounds in a handy packet. This allowed quick loading of a pair of loaded clips and proper ejection. This system was adopted and the revolvers were put into production. Both the Colt and Smith & Wesson versions were called the Model 1917.

Except for the chambering, the M1917 Colt was fundamentally the same as the M1909 Army with the same markings, except 1917 is substituted for 1909 on the butt and the service number has no correlation with the serial number. Unlike the M1909, the M1917 barrel is tapered

Here's the little device that made the 1917s work. The half-moon clip was invented by Joe Wesson and used in both Colt and S&W revovlers. Three rounds were clipped together, then inserted into the cylinder. It worked well.

All of the military New Servies didn't go to American forces, many went to British Commonwealth troops. The top revolver is a Canadian .455. Revolver at the bottom is a British .455. The latter guns are usually found with an assortment of Broad Arrow and other marks. The .38 Special, center, is a Late Model Battle of Britain gun.

and has a pronounced shoulder at the frame junction. Also, instead of the bright blue of the M1909, the M1917 was a dull, coarsely polished blue. Some M1917s are encountered with a Parkerized finish. These were arsenal-refinished in the WWII period.

Early production M1917s had bored-through chambers. If rounds were inserted without the half-moon clips, they would slide right through the chambers. The Army decided that the chamber should be configured so that car-

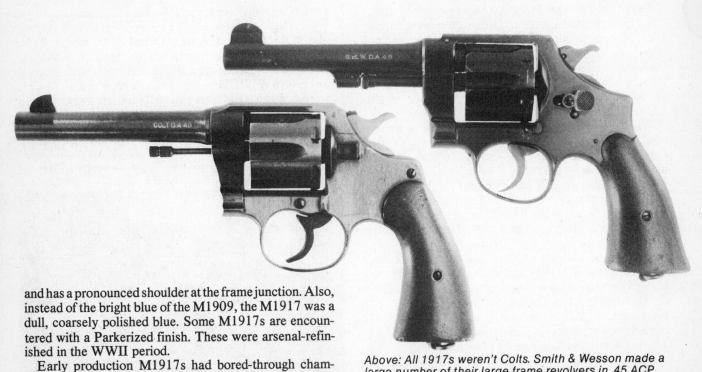

Above: All 1917s weren't Colts. Smith & Wesson made a large number of their large frame revolvers in .45 ACP to government order. Both guns had 5½-inch barrels and both used the half-moon clip. This photo shows the two guns in the same scale. They're about the same size.

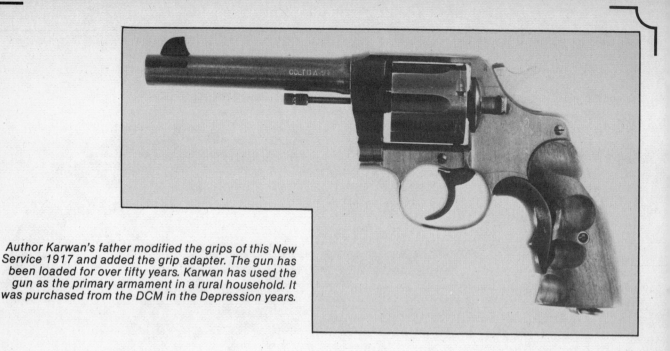

Author Karwan's father modified the grips of this New Service 1917 and added the grip adapter. The gun has been loaded for over fifty years. Karwan has used the gun as the primary armament in a rural household. It was purchased from the DCM in the Depression years.

tridges would headspace properly without the half-moon clips. Almost all M1917s with bored-through chambers had new cylinders fitted with the improved chamber and all subsequent production used it. M1917s with the bored-through chambers are quite uncommon. There is no doubt that the improved chamber also greatly improved the potential accuracy of the M1917, as the bullet has a properly fitting chamber throat to control the passage of the bullet down the cylinder and into the barrel throat.

The M1917 was produced in a larger quantity than any other New Service variation. Ordnance reports indicate 151,700 were produced by the end of 1918. However, production did not cease until several months into 1919. Since the highest butt number known is 154,800, that is probably the actual true total production with the discrepancy made up by deliveries made after the war was over or after 1918.

When WWI ended, the M1917 remained in Federal service. Thousands were transferred to the U.S. Post Office Department where they served as security guns for many years, finally sold off in the Sixties. Other M1917s were supplied to the U.S. Border Patrol where they served as the standard sidearm till 1938. This was a colorful and action-filled period in the Border Patrol's history and the M1917 saw a great deal of action along the Mexican border.

Between the wars the Director of Civilian Marksmanship (DCM) sold M1917 Colts for about $15. The old M1917 I cut my teeth on was purchased by my father from the DCM in the mid-Thirties. I asked him once why he bought a Colt M1917 and not a Smith & Wesson. He replied that the S&W cost something like $3 more and during the Depression $3 was a lot of money.

During WWII, existing stocks of M1917s were put back into service. Few saw service with frontline infantry, but they were widely used for rear echelon duties such as prison guards, MPs in non-combat zones, and the like. My uncle was issued an M1917 when he drew prisoner escort duty in WWII. Many personally owned M1917s were carried by troops that preferred revolvers to automatics.

The M1917 was the last of the military New Services except for the previously mentioned frames sent to Springfield Armory, a small shipment of 5½-inch barreled .45 Colts sent to Halifax for use by the Canadian navy in 1941, and several thousand that were sold to Cuba.

POLICE NEW SERVICES

New Services were used by a wide range of police agencies in the U.S. and abroad. Probably the most famous users of the New Service were the Canadian Mounties. Orders were placed over a long period from about 1904 till just before WWII. New Services in both .455 and .45 Colt were ordered at different times. Mountie New Service

Lots of New Services rode in the holsters of working cops. While the size of the gun made it hard to carry concealed, it was a natural for use in an external Sam Browne belt holster. This is a New York State Trooper's.

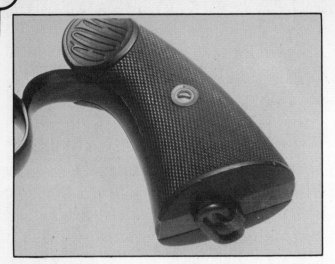

The lanyard ring, almost universal on the New Service, is a practical feature. An officer stands a good chance of retaining his revolver in a scuffle. The grips on this specimen are typical hard rubber in perfect condition.

Markings on the back of this Audley holster tell us the holster was made for 5½-inch New Service .45. The NYST stands for New York State Trooper. This agency used the New Service in .45 Colt caliber for many years.

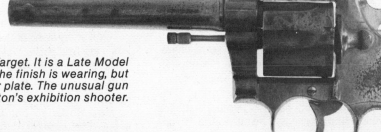

A special order New Service Target. It is a Late Model .44-40 with a six-inch barrel. The finish is wearing, but it is seldom-encountered silver plate. The unusual gun was made for Gus Peret, Remington's exhibition shooter.

examples occur in Old Model, Improved Model, and Late Model varieties. Early guns were stamped "N.W.M.P." for North West Mounted Police with subsequent purchases until 1920 marked "RNWMP" for Royal North West Mounted Police. After that the marking was "RCMP" for Royal Canadian Mounted Police. The very last purchases are simply butt-marked "MP" for Mounted Police. The New Service served with the Mounties gallantly for forty-nine years, not being replaced until 1954. Total number of New Services bought by the Mounties is estimated to be about 2000.

Another famous long-time user of the New Service was the New York State Troopers. They issued New Service .45 Colts with a 5½-inch barrel from about 1917 until well into the 1950s. Total New York State Trooper purchases run to about 1000. The back strap is typically stamped "NYST." Guns show up in both Improved and Late Model types.

Yet another famous user was the U.S. Border Patrol. They turned in their M1917 New Services for new four-inch-barreled .38 Special New Services in 1938. Supposedly the model and caliber choice was made by Charles Askins, Jr. If so, I cannot imagine why he would want a new Service in the wimpy .38 Special cartridge for a service gun, considering that .357, .45 ACP, .45 Colt and .44 Special were all available in the same gun.

The guns were roll-marked "U.S.I.B.P." for United States Immigration Border Patrol. These served into the mid-1950s. At last check, they were still in storage waiting

for some bureaucrat to decide to have them destroyed. I wonder how many dollars could be earned for the U.S. Treasury if they were to be sold off to collectors, instead.

Other police users are legion including the Connecticut State Police, the Kansas State Highway Patrol, the Boston Police Department, the Utah Highway Patrol, the Montana Highway Patrol, the San Antonio Police Department, the Richmond Police Department, among many others. The oddest police New Service I have ever encountered was a Shooting Master .38 that was marked "R.P.D. 2T" for the Richmond Police Department. Police purchases of the New Service always made up a large percentage of non-military New Service sales.

TARGET MODELS and SHOOTING MASTERS

Shortly after the New Service Target (NST) Model was introduced, it quickly became the foremost and prominent target revolver in the world. It was a natural evolution from the Colt SAA and Bisley flat-topped target models that preceded it. The quality of fit and finish in the NST was always superb. Revolvers intended for the U.S. market

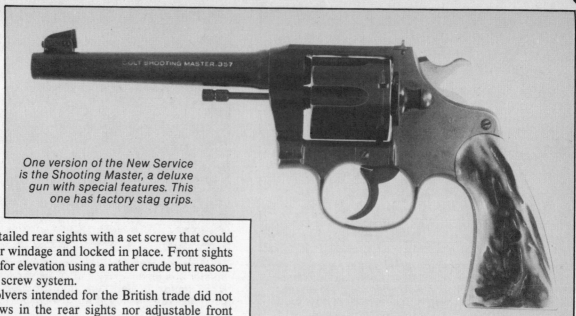

One version of the New Service is the Shooting Master, a deluxe gun with special features. This one has factory stag grips.

featured dovetailed rear sights with a set screw that could be adjusted for windage and locked in place. Front sights are adjustable for elevation using a rather crude but reasonably effective screw system.

Target revolvers intended for the British trade did not have set screws in the rear sights nor adjustable front sights. Elevation adjustments were accomplished by using different heights of removable blades. These differences on revolvers for the British trade were a result of the rules used by the British that did not allow readily adjustable sights.

Most NST revolvers for the British trade were chambered for the .455 Eley cartridge. They differ in another way from all other NST revolvers in that the .455 barrels of all the earlier production had English Metford rifling. This extremely efficient rifling system features parabolic-shaped grooves that have no sharp corners. The purported advantages are a tighter gas seal and easier cleaning. This system is good enough that it is currently undergoing a revival and shows up in modified form on H&K pistols and rifles as well as some Gale MacMillan target barrels.

Colt advertising of the time often stated that the NST shot the very first perfect revolver score, which is highly unlikey unless you limit such a claim to a specific match. Such

Three New Service Targets: An Early Model .455 on top, a Late Model .45 Colt in the middle and the Improved Model .44 Special at the bottom. Target Models were considered to be among the best revolvers of their day.

A Shooting Master .38 Special with round butt. Also note the uncheckered cylinder latch, a feature found only on Shooting Masters. The revolver butt is checkered both front and back.

Made in 1913, this New Service Target is an Improved Model. The caliber is .44 Russian. Note the checkering pattern on the grips. This is what collectors call the fleur-de-lis pattern. It is functional and attractive.

details are often notably absent. Regardless, NST revolvers will often shoot as well as the very best target revolvers made today.

Besides the evolutionary changes that the entire NS line underwent, the NST also had its own peculiar evolution. Unlike the service guns, the NST always featured checkered walnut grips. Early on, it was hand-checkered in a fleur-de-lis pattern, later with a Colt medallion, and finally it had machine-checkered walnut with a medallion. The front strap, back strap, and trigger were hand checkered. Though they were rarely fired in the double-action mode, the NSTs often have incredibly smooth and light double-action pulls. They rival the best of the Colt Pythons. Colt never offered a wider trigger or a wider hammer spur, though these features were often added by custom gunsmiths like King.

The sights started out with a U-notch rear and a bead front, but evolved in later production to the Patridge type of square front and square notch rear. Originally, the chamberings were only .44 Russian and .455 Eley. The former was soon replaced by the .44 Special cartridge and the latter dropped out of sight after WWI, although it was cataloged for some time later. The .45 Colt cartridge was added early in the Improved period and probably became the most popular chambering in the NST. Being a largely special order gun in the Post-WWI period, other noncataloged calibers such as .44-40 will sometimes be found, but they are rare. The standard barrel length was 7½ inches, until six-inch became an option towards the end. Total NST production is hard to pin down since they are serial numbered right with the rest of the New Services, but it was never large. A reasonable estimate would be 3,000 to 4,000, but it could be substantially less.

Late in the life of the NS, Colt introduced a new target version called the Shooting Master (SM). Originally it differed from the NST in that it was chambered for the super accurate .38 Special cartridge; it had a round butt much like the M1909 USMC, an uncheckered cylinder latch, a tapered six-inch barrel, and the barrel marking "SHOOTING MASTER." However, as more options were added, such as a square butt and chamberings in .45 Colt, .44 Special, .357 and a .45 ACP, the differences between the Shooting Master and New Service Target began to disappear. This is particularly so since the NST became available with a six-inch barrel and an optional round butt. It is entirely possible to have a Shooting Master and a New Service Target that are essentially identical except for barrel markings. Everything said about the quality of the NST goes equally for the Shooting Master. It would seem that the majority of production was in .38 Special with probably as many made in that chambering as all others combined. The .44 Special is a particularly rare chambering.

Because of their relatively fragile sights that are unsuit-

Left and below: Both sides of a rare gun. This is an original Fitz Special in .45 Colt. It was finished in plain blue when shipped. The plating and engraving were added on a later visit to the Hartford, Connecticut plant.

able for holster use, the NST and SM never got the following among outdoorsmen and police officers that the adjustable sighted S&Ws of the period did. However, they dominated the target field until Colt brought out its smaller framed Officer Model with a heavier barrel. The latter soon became the target shooter's favorite, though it was never any more accurate.

Below: Fitzgerald Specials were made up on a special order basis. The guns have short barrels, usually two inches long, plus bobbed hammers and short butts. The most noticeable feature of the guns is the cutaway on the trigger guard face. It was a fast-handling six-gun.

FITZ SPECIALS

No treatise on the New Service would be complete without mention of the Fitz Specials, a small group of special order guns made up to the specifications of Colt's colorful employee, J. Henry Fitzgerald. Fitz, as he was almost universally known, represented Colt at the National Matches. He was an armorer, put on shooting demonstrations and exhibitions for Colt, authored a book and a number of articles on handgun shooting, was a pioneer in forensic investigations and was Colt's most colorful, outspoken, and flamboyant promoter. Fitz developed a modified New Service for concealed carry that collectors call the Fitz Special.

Basically, they are New Service service guns with a two-inch barrel, a spurless hammer, and a cutaway trigger guard. Usually they were chambered for the .45 Colt cartridge, but .45 ACP and at least one .38 specimen is known. Some have full-sized grip frames without lanyard, but most seem to have grip frames that are slightly shortened and rounded. Many show personal attention or inscriptions from Fitz himself. Aside from the questionable desirability of the cutaway trigger guard, the Fitz Specials are superb powerful hideaway handguns, albeit large ones. Other Colt models sometimes also got the Fitz treatment as well. Total factory production of Fitz Specials probably does not exceed a couple dozen, though hundreds got the same treatment outside the factory. Collectors should be extremely careful in that regard.

SHOOTING THE NEW SERVICE

Present-day owners and collectors of the New Service Colts are missing a real treat if they do not occasionally take them out to shoot them. I do not recommend shooting mint condition, extremely rare, or highly engraved specimens, but for the rest a little careful shooting will do no harm nor will it lower their value.

I would not recommend shooting an original .450 Eley or .476 Eley New Service because they are so rare. However, ammunition for the rest of the New Service chamberings is readily available. In spite of the huge New Service cylinder, I recommend only factory ammunition or its handloaded equivalent be used. The two exceptions are that .38 Specials can be loaded to +P levels and .44

Specials can generally be loaded to slightly higher pressures with no harm. Revolvers chambered for the .44 Russian cartridge can be fired with handloads made from cut down .44 Special brass. New, Boxer primed .44 Russian ammunition can be obtained from Fiocchi of America.

The only factory ammunition available in .455 Eley is new production by Fiocchi of America. I recommend against converting .455 guns to .45 ACP or .45 Colts, as it is not necessary and it lowers the value of these old gems. Ammunition in .455 can be easily handloaded using cut down .45 Colt brass. Usually, the rims must be thinned slightly. For casual shooting, regular .45 ACP mid-range ammunition can be fired in unaltered .455 chambers because the internal chamber shoulder is in just about the right place to headspace the .45 ACP on its casemouth. Ejection must be one at a time with a rod or pencil, since the ejector star has no rim to push against and there is insufficient space between the cylinder and the breech face for half-moon clips.

A New Service in good trim will usually shoot right with the best of today's revolvers. Even the old M1917 military guns will often shoot as well or better than a modern Gold Cup .45 if one can overcome the crude sights. I have established this to my satisfaction many times with my old M1917.

The New Service grip, as issued, is not terribly comfortable for most hands. Most writers attribute this to its size, saying it is too large. My experiments indicate that is not the case at all. By the simple addition of a good grip adapter, such as the Tyler T-grip, the New Service can have a comfortable grip for even an average-sized hand or smaller. The addition of fatter grips will greatly improve the feel of the grip even for average sized hands.

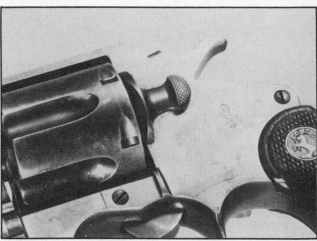

Right: The cylinder latch used on the Late Models is pleasingly rounded and checkered as shown. The last New Services manufactured, in the late 1930s, had this feature. Some of them handled the potent .357 magnum.

Left: An Improved Model has the flat, early type latch. It is a common feature of the early guns and works as well as the other type. The Rampant Colt marking is essentially the same on both guns. That never changes.

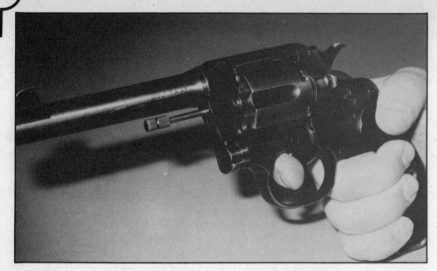

The Karwan family New Service booms often. Backyard shooting is permitted in rural Oregon and there are lots of .45 ACP cartridges around. This is one gun that Karwan will never trade off!

With a grip adapter, even 10-year-old Jake Karwan can handle the big 1917 with ease. This New Service still sees use, as do many others. They're strong guns and will handle most ammunition.

CONCLUSION

During WWII, the fixtures and tooling used to produce the New Service were accidentally destroyed. One report is that the New Service and Colt Single Action tooling was moved out of the factory to a back lot to make room for the massive machinery of war production. Left exposed to the elements for several years, the tooling was supposedly ruined. While popular demand eventually caused Colt to retool to produce the SAA in the Fifties, the Colt management did not feel there was significant demand for a large-framed double-action revolver.

Even with the introduction of the .44 magnum, Colt saw no need to bring back a new New Service. I distinctly remember my father talking to a Colt factory representative about such a thing a couple of years after the .44 magnum was introduced by S&W. The Colt representative said something to the effect that they felt that the .44 magnum cartridge would never catch on sufficiently to justify any need to bring back the New Service. Thirty years later, Colt still does not have a large-framed double-action revolver and none is in the foreseeable future. Very likely the New Service is the last in its class, but it is still the first in the hearts of its many admirers.

POSTSCRIPT

Many thanks to Marty Huber and the Colt factory, Richard Johnson, Gil Newton, and R.L. Wilson for the wealth of information supplied to me on the subject of New Services through correspondence or their articles and books on the subject — *Chuck Karwan*.

ABOUT THE AUTHOR

MY big buddy Chuck Karwan likes a great many guns, but he just plain loves the New Service Colt. When I gave him the chance to do justice to the grand old gun in print, he didn't hesitate. The result is the preceding long chapter, which Chuck laments is far too short. It is the first really serious treatment of the big Colt to have ever reached the popular firearms press.

Chuck is well-qualified to write on gun collecting matters; he's the Collector Editor of GUN WORLD Magazine and has been an avid collector since his teens. His interest never diminished through his years at West Point, where he nearly lived in the museum, to his Army service with the Green Berets, where he got to shoot everything. Chuck lives in rural Oregon at the present time and he still shoots a great deal. That he sometimes hits what he is shooting at is in no small way due to his first formal marksmanship training at the Camp Perry Small Arms Firing School — where he had a Marine instructor.

Karwan's work has appeared in a great many different periodicals and particularly in an assortment of Digest Books. It's a pleasure to have his meticulous research ad sharp writing in Handguns '89. — *WC*

CHAPTER 23

THE OUTDOORSMAN

*And
The Dawn
Of The
Magnum Era*

By today's standards, this is pretty sedate ammunition. It is an original box of .38-.44 ammo, dating to the early 1930s. The other side displays a dire warning against the use of the ammo in anything but S&W and Colt revolvers big enough to handle it. The Outdoorsman and the companion .38-.44 Heavy Duty were the first wheelguns made for high performance ammunition. Depression gunwriters (except Elmer) were slow to endorse it.

THE GREAT DEPRESSION gripped the nation with chilled fingers. Nearly everyone was dirt-poor and, when you're wondering where the next meal is coming from, you become downright conservative. It was not a time for any manufacturer to do anything but stay alive. New products went on the back burner until America could work its way through the crisis. Nowhere was this more true than in New England and in the firearms industry.

In those grim days — and even in the earlier so-called Roaring Twenties — the nation's gunmakers were conservative in the extreme. New models did not appear regularly at each year's SHOT show. There was no SHOT show and most years there were no new models. Colt was the dominant force in handguns, with Smith & Wesson a close second. It would be nearly twenty more years before Bill Ruger built his first handgun for commercial sale.

When the Depression provoked desperation, certain elements of society turned against the hated banks that held the paper on homes and farms. Forced withdrawals were sometimes made with the aid of the products of John T. Thompson's Auto-Ordnance Corporation. We entered a period of lawlessness like never before, so much so that the cop on the beat began to regard his revolver as more than a symbol of police authority. In the late Twenties, Colt astounded the gun world by announcing a high-velocity automatic pistol called the .38 Super. Some people began to regard the handgun in a new light.

Out West, a crazy cowboy was energetically experimenting with handgun loads that stretched wheelguns to the extreme. The *American Rifleman* even ran some of his articles. He was shooting handguns at extreme ranges with ammunition he loaded himself. Handloading had a long history in the republic, but most of the interest centered on the economics of less-expensive ammunition. Some people began to look on handguns in terms of their potential performance.

On target ranges throughout the land, shooters used handloaded ammunition assembled on Star and Potter loading machines. Some of them began to see the widely regarded .38 Special as something more than just a target cartridge. When the bullet-mould people began turning out semi-wadcutter designs to customer specs (that cowboy again!), a few hardy souls loaded them up to higher

No. 68701

OFFICE OF. SMITH & WESSON. REVOLVER Manufacturers

Springfield Mass ———— June 1, 19 87

Mr. Wiley Clapp, Technical Editor
GUN WORLD
P. O. Box HH
Capistrano Beach, CA 92624

Dear Mr. Clapp:

The revolver you inquired about in your recent letter is classified as a .38/44 Heavy Duty (fixed sight) or .38/44 Outdoorsman (adjustable sight) model.

The .38/44 Heavy Duty revolver was introduced on April 1, 1930 and designed on the .44 Hand Ejector Third Model frame. The gun was manufactured having a standard barrel length of 5" and weighed 40 ounces. However, during the course of its manufacture it was produced in 4" and 6" barrel lengths.

The Heavy Duty was manufactured continuously throughout the 1930's with the serial numbers being dispersed between serial number 35,037 and 62,350 of the N frame (.44 H.E. serial number series). The total production of the pre-World War II .38/44 Heavy Duty was 11,111 revolvers. At the end of Word War II, on June 18, 1946, this model was reintroduced at approximately serial number S62,940 of the .44 H.E. serial number series.

This gun differed from the prewar models in that it incorporated the new style rebound slide activated hammer block which had been introduced by Smith & Wesson during World War II.

In 1948, at approximately serial number S72,300, the factory incorporated the new style short action and the gun remained unchanged from that date until it was discontinued in 1966.

In 1957, when model numbers were assigned to various Smith & Wesson models, the .38/44 Heavy Duty became known as the Model 20. The total postwar production of this model was 20,604 revolvers.

SMITH & WESSON

- continued -

These pages display the new Smith & Wesson factory letter. It is available from the Smith & Wesson historian at a cost of twenty dollars. As you can see, a letter of this sort constitutes a short history lesson on a particular model. Letters...

Mr. Wiley Clapp
Capistrano Beach, California

Page Two
June 1, 1987

The sister model to the .38/44 Heavy Duty was a target sighted model called the
.38/44 Outdoorsman. It was introduced on November 21, 1931 and was standard
with a 6½" barrel in blue finish.

It was continued in production until 1941 when as its sister, it was temporarily
discontinued because of wartime production. The total prewar production for
this model was 4,761 revolvers. Shortly after the .38/44 Outdoorsman was reintroduced in 1946, the round barrel configuration was changed and a new barrel
with a rib and the newer micrometer sight was installed. The new short throw
hammer was added on September 26, 1950 and the gun was called the .38/44
Outdoorsman Model 1950 until 1957. When model numbers were assigned, this
revolver was given the designation of Model 23.

Production of the postwar long action version was 2,326 and 6,039 of the 1950
style were produced bringing the total postwar production to 8,365 revolvers.
The .38/44 Outdoorsman underwent the same changes as the Heavy Duty.

All guns produced after World War II can easily be identified by the use of the
S prefix which accompanies the serial number and signifies the incorporation
of the improved hammer block.

The .38/44 was designed to fire the .38 Special Super police loads. This
revolver prompted the idea of producing the .357 Magnum.

We have researched your Smith & Wesson .38/44 Outdoorsman revolver in company
records which indicate that your handgun, with serial number 44299, was shipped
from our factory on January 22, 1935 and delivered to Baker, Hamilton & Pacific,
located in San Francisco, California, one of our distributors at that time.

An additional check of factory records indicates further that your revolver,
serial numbered 44299, left the factory with six and a half inch barrel, Target,
blue finish and equipped with Call Gold Bead front sight.

We trust that the information furnished will be helpful as well as of interest.

Sincerely,

SMITH & WESSON

Roy G. Jinks
Historian

RGJ/dsg

*...are available on any Smith & Wesson, but the description should be complete. It
helps to send Historian Roy Jinks a clear photo. The resulting letter comes on a
reproduction of early company stationery and will include shipping data if available.*

This particular revolver is in choice condition. Labor costs were low in the depression years and careful hand fitting was an economically viable way for a maker to build a handgun. Days like those are never to return, so we're well advised to appreciate the quality of a gun that was really intended to be used by outdoorsmen.

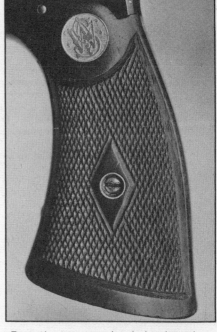

Even the two panels of checkered walnut that grace the butt of the Outdoorsman are beautifully done. Note the cleanly-executed pattern of checkering. The intertwined S&W logo in the medallion is as good as anything you're ever likely to see.

velocities. Some people started to ask for heavier guns for higher pressure loads.

In Gun Valley, the decision-makers at Smith & Wesson heard these things and pondered. Finally, without a great deal of fanfare, the old-line gunmaker announced a new model. It was called the *Outdoorsman* and was a superb revolver. The ammunition companies put up ammo for the Outdoorsman, printing dire warnings about use in other guns all over the box. They called the Outdoorsman's cartridge the .38-.44, but in reality it was simply a high-velocity .38 Special. Some people bought the guns and their ammunition

The revolvers, the Outdoorsman and its fixed-sight cousin called the .38-.44 *Heavy Duty,* were big, hefty brutes. Put up on what we now call the N-frame, they were hell for strong. They had to be, for this business of performance handgun cartridges was *terra incognita* in 1930 and '31. The Outdoorsman got a lot of extra touches. It had a silky-smooth action and adjustable target sights. The entire package was assembled with loving care, the likes of which we will not see again. Some people began to use them — hard.

When nobody lost their fingers and the name — with implications of hairy-chested masculinity — caught on, the decision-makers in Springfield heard. And when the nation began to pull out of the worst of the Depression, they introduced another new model. This time, there was a bit more fanfare. Colonel Wesson himself took the new

model afield and downed some hefty game animals with it. When the new model came out in 1935, the first one went to the nation's leading crime fighter, J. Edgar Hoover. It was pretty clear that S&W intended the new model for frontline service in the war against crime, as well as for field and forest. The new model sold like mad in the late Thirties; it came with an unprecedented *lifetime* guarantee.

Preceded by the Outdoorsman, the new gun wasn't really all that different from its elder brother. But it did shoot a different cartridge and it got a lot of attention. The new gun was the .357 magnum and, lordy, didn't it just start something?